Dr Cameron Murray is Australia's leading expert commentator on housing. He is an economist and co-author of *Rigged*, and he runs his own think-tank, Fresh Economic Thinking. He has been a tenant, a homeowner and a landlord, and he has worked in property development.

———

'If you're not sure you believe the official story of why house prices and rents are so high, read this.'

ROSS GITTINS, *The Sydney Morning Herald*

'The vast majority of what is written and said about Australian housing is either nonsense, property porn, clickbait or lies, all more-or-less to the benefit of interests vested in maintaining the status quo of ever-more expensive shelter with all the social damage that causes. Cameron Murray's *The Great Housing Hijack* is the exception that proves the rule—the only book you need to understand the giant con we have fallen for. Nobody escapes unscathed. Read it.'

MICHAEL PASCOE, *The New Daily*

'Cameron Murray unpicks Australia's housing market stitch by stitch and reveals the myths, falsehoods and vested interests that underpin the housing debate. His work uses extensive research to shine a light on an issue many in politics, academia and the media prefer to keep opaque. He challenges long-held opinions and brings a context that too often is missing from how we talk about housing.'

GREG JERICHO, *The Guardian*

THE GREAT HOUSING HIJACK

THE HOAXES AND MYTHS KEEPING PRICES HIGH FOR RENTERS AND BUYERS IN AUSTRALIA

CAMERON K. MURRAY

ALLEN&UNWIN
SYDNEY · MELBOURNE · AUCKLAND · LONDON

First published in 2024

Allen & Unwin
Cammeraygal Country
83 Alexander Street
Crows Nest NSW 2065
Australia
Phone: (61 2) 8425 0100
Email: info@allenandunwin.com
Web: www.allenandunwin.com

Allen & Unwin acknowledges the Traditional Owners of the Country on which we live and work. We pay our respects to all Aboriginal and Torres Strait Islander Elders, past and present.

 A catalogue record for this book is available from the National Library of Australia

ISBN 978 1 76147 085 1

Set in 11.5/18 pt Sabon LT Pro by Midland Typesetters, Australia
Printed and bound in Australia by the Opus Group

10 9 8 7 6 5 4 3 2 1

For Keith Murray

Contents

List of figures   ix

Property problems
1. Dwelling dreams   3
2. Property principles   20

Five housing market equilibria
3. Asset price equilibrium: Where prices come from   37
4. Rental equilibrium: Why incomes determine rents   57
5. Spatial equilibrium: Why location matters   67
6. Density equilibrium: How tall we build   76
7. Absorption rate equilibrium: What determines the rate of new housing development   84

Housing hijackers
8. Politics and politicians   99
9. Academics and policy wonks   113
10. Muddled media   124
11. YIMBY yammer   136

Distractions and distortions

12. Mismeasuring manors   149
13. Skipping the cycle   157
14. Proper planning   166
15. Immigration inspection   177
16. Vacant villages   185
17. Rental rules   195

Hoax housing policies

18. Supply superstitions   209
19. Zoning zealots   216
20. Financial fixes   224
21. Favoured first home buyers   243

Course corrections

22. Managing monopolies   253
23. Perfecting property   263
24. HouseMate   276
25. Future foresight   291

Glossary   295
Acknowledgements   299
Notes   301

List of figures

1 How moving sustains a spatial equilibrium in
   between two locations   71

2 Density equilibrium is where there is no net
   gain from going taller   79

3 Why monopoly property owners build housing
   in response to rising demand   91

4 Housing asset prices do not reflect 'affordability',
   whatever that means   152

5 The Speculative Index, 1983–2023   162

6 How planning limits interact with the density
   equilibrium   174

7 Direct policy programs can massively boost
   homeownership   273

Property problems

1 ◆ Dwelling dreams

'Third, and final, call . . .'

The gavel dropped. The auction was over.

A busy day at the auction hall had seen more than thirty landlords bid for the right to rent their property to the young Jones family.

The opening bid was $3000 per month. At that price, the prospective landlord bold enough to open the bidding stood no chance. At this auction, all the landlords who gathered feared missing out on the tenant.

Almost immediately, the landlord of a nearby property offered their similar home for $2200 per month. A neighbouring landlord quickly responded by offering their home at $1980 per month. Then a third landlord jumped in to bid $1730 to attract the Jones family to their home. After more than a dozen bids, the winning landlord offered their best price of $1270 per month for a three-bedroom cottage and won the auction to buy the Jones family as tenants with their lowest possible price.

Like all auctions, the winner was stretched to their financial limit. The winning landlord offered a price that barely covered their costs. But it was a risk they thought was worth taking.

All the properties at the auction had been inspected by the Joneses and were all high quality and at a location they desired. All the bidding landlords had agreed to the Jones family's offer of a three-year lease term with annual rental reviews set to market through a competitive bidding process. If the winning landlord bidder pulled out of the contract within that three-year period, they would be required to compensate the Joneses for the costs of relocation and any additional rent they would have to pay to live elsewhere.

The family knew that when the auction was over, they would have secured the home they wanted at the best price possible. The housing market worked. They were jubilant.

But then the Jones family awoke.

———

Cheap housing—whether renting or purchasing—is, unfortunately, just a dream for many young families. Whether it is the Great Australian Dream, the American Dream, the Canadian Dream or the British Dream, these deeply ingrained cultural aspirations are increasingly not matching reality. For some, it is a nightmare.

The average age of first home buyers has risen in Australia and in many other countries, including the United Kingdom and the United States. Publicly funded below-market rental homes have dried up, and homeownership rates are trending down in many nations. If you want stable and affordable housing, alongside broad and early homeownership, then these are not promising statistics.

How is it that at the richest point in human history we no longer achieve improvements in desirable housing outcomes, and are instead going backwards on many metrics? This is a question *The Great Housing Hijack* answers.

But, to begin to answer it, we need much more context, something all too rare when it comes to analysis of housing markets. In this case, we need to look further back in time. Unequal access to housing and declining homeownership might seem like a uniquely modern problem. Sometimes people today will attribute this outcome to too much greed or to housing being treated as an asset class instead of a necessity. Whatever it is, the problem is seen as new and therefore recent actions are to blame.

But the problem is age-old.

A problem for the ages

In his visit to Sydney in 1836 on HMS *Beagle*, biologist and father of evolutionary theory Charles Darwin immediately adopted the national pastime of commenting on the housing market. In his diary entry on his first day in Sydney, he wrote:

> the number of large houses just finished & others building is truly surprising; nevertheless every one complains of the high rents & difficulty in procuring a house . . . Sydney has a population of twenty-three thousand, & is as I have said rapidly increasing; it must contain much wealth; it appears a man of business can hardly fail to make a large fortune; I saw on all sides fine houses, one built by the profits from steam-vessels, another from building, & so on. An auctioneer who

was a convict, it is said intends to return home & will take with him 100,000 pounds. Another who is always driving about in his carriage, has an income so large that scarcely anybody ventures to guess at it, the least being assigned being fifteen thousand a year. But the two crowning facts are, first that the public revenue has increased 60,000 £ during this last year, & secondly that less than an acre of land within the town of Sydney sold for 8000 pounds sterling.[1]

Later in the nineteenth century, Friedrich Engels, who became a historical figure for his writing on class struggles and his work with Karl Marx on capitalism, wrote a series of articles in 1872 seeking an answer to 'The Housing Question' that puzzled those in the industrial cities of central Europe. He asserted:

The so-called housing shortage, which plays such a great role in the press nowadays, does not consist in the fact that the working class generally lives in bad, overcrowded and unhealthy dwellings. This shortage is not something peculiar to the present; it is not even one of the sufferings peculiar to the modern proletariat in contradistinction to all earlier oppressed classes. On the contrary, all oppressed classes in all periods suffered more or less uniformly from it. In order to make an end of this housing shortage there is only one means: to abolish altogether the exploitation and oppression of the working class by the ruling class. What is meant today by housing shortage is the peculiar intensification of the bad housing conditions of the workers as the result of the sudden rush of population to the big towns;

a colossal increase in rents, a still further aggravation of overcrowding in the individual houses, and, for some, the impossibility of finding a place to live in at all. And this housing shortage gets talked of so much only because it does not limit itself to the working class but has affected the petty bourgeoisie also.

Fast-forward to the early 20th century. In 1910, the New South Wales government commissioned University of Sydney academic Robert F. Irvine to investigate the problem of rising housing rents and learn from the policies other countries had adopted to remedy the problem. The report he produced in 1913 sought to answer these two questions.

1 How, in the congested areas of large cities and in certain industrial centres, to get rid of the results of unregulated housing—over-housing, overcrowding, high rentals for inferior accommodation, and all the evils that flow from them.

2 How society may best provide that each individual family unit, whether living in the city or country, may have a home that shall be self-contained, private, sanitary, open in every room to sunlight and fresh air, safe from fire and collapse, and yet at a rent consistent with income—a home that shall be artistic and hygienic, a home environment which shall be if not actually constructive, at least not destructive, of either body or character, and at a rent no higher than is paid for the slum tenements of to-day.[2]

Little changed after his report. In 1919, the Inter-State Commission conducted the Piddington Inquiry into housing rents and in 1939 the New South Wales government conducted yet another Rents Inquiry. When they met to discuss post–World War II housing policy in 1947, key Australian public officials noted the appalling housing conditions of the early twentieth century that prompted these inquiries.

> Cheap, mean houses were built all round and between the factories. With no legislative restrictions to set even modest standards of space and light, or even the humanitarian considerations of health and privacy, row upon row of workers' dwellings were jammed into every street. Land values rose with the high industrial potential, this was reflected in the rates and added rents until this spiral of values reached a stage when one family could not afford one terrace home. These were then subdivided to cram in more people, and so began the overcrowding that exists until this day.[3]

The age-old housing problem stretches back in time too. Archaeological records of property sales translated from ancient Mesopotamian stone tablets show similar price patterns to modern cities.[4]

There is not much new under the sun.

––––––

We only perceive the housing metrics in recent decades as being in a decline if we compare them with the rising metrics of the 'golden age' of economic expansion—the end of World War II until the mid-1970s. That age not only saw a great demographic change due to the baby boom, but it ended with a peak in many social indicators. That age, for example, saw the highest rate of public housing construction in Australia and the United Kingdom.

In 1955, for example, Prime Minister Robert Menzies was motivated to tackle the 'vital problem of home ownership' and boasted that his Liberal government had built more public housing than the previous Labor Party and would continue to do so. Because of heavy government interventions, rents in Australia fell 50 per cent in inflation-adjusted terms during the war and didn't return to their pre-war levels until the 1980s.[5]

In the early 1970s the amount of income spent on private housing rents was at its lowest point and homeownership in Australia was at its highest peak. There were similar increases in homeownership in the United States and United Kingdom, and this gave millions of households a lifetime of housing security by escaping the rental market.

Considered over a longer time frame, the housing market of the last four decades looks like a return to the normal operation of private property markets after an abnormal break in the mid-twentieth century. The rollicking free markets of the nineteenth century and the interwar period of the twentieth century saw extremely low homeownership, high rents, low-quality dwellings and violent boom-and-bust price cycles. In Australia, the rate of homeownership was under 40 per cent at the beginning of the twentieth century in metropolitan areas (though higher in rural areas), far from the peak of 71 per cent in the early 1970s, and far below its current 66 per cent rate. Those pre–golden age periods also saw rapid economic growth driven by new technologies, like electrification, but this growth and innovation never quite resulted in everybody having access to clean, comfortable and modern housing.

Back in 1879 one of the most influential books of the era in the English-speaking world was written by Philadelphia-born journalist Henry George. 'The association of poverty with progress is the great enigma of our times' he wrote in that book, *Progress and Poverty*. He concluded that the enigma was due to the ability of landlords and property owners to constantly extract from non-property-owning workers their rising wages, meaning that the 'prodigious increase in wealth-producing power' of the nineteenth century was a process that was economically linked to the impoverishment of the landless worker. Every gain made by wage earners resulted in further gains to landlords via higher rents.

George's observation—that private property markets by their nature tend towards concentration of ownership and rents that grow in line with workers' wages—is still relevant today. We see it in the steady declines in homeownership rates in many developed nations globally, the increasingly stark clustering of households by income and wealth at certain locations, and housing rents rising lockstep with incomes.

These patterns are not a radical and unique modern problem; they were the status quo in the free market economies of the nineteenth and early twentieth centuries when homeownership was an option only for the wealthy minority. Historically, housing markets were always divided between the haves and have-nots. What we are seeing since the 1980s is a return to the normal operation of housing markets after the post–World War II decades of heavy government intervention. Few acknowledge this; instead, they parrot slogans like 'let the market work'. This reflects historical illiteracy.

Cheap words, costly confusion

For most people, even for many so-called experts, the idea that the housing market is returning to normal is disguised by the obfuscating language we use. When we once called owners of rental housing *landlords*, indicating a degree of power to lord over tenants, we now call them *Mum and Dad investors*, implying instead that their financial interests are aligned with all families. But what about Mum and Dad tenants?

Once they were *property speculators*, now they are *housing developers*. Worse, the word *'affordable'* is a catch-all buzzword that allows everyone in the market to pretend to want the same thing—'affordable housing'—without ever articulating what that means. If instead we used the phrase 'cheap housing'—just like we do for cheap electricity, cheap food and cheap clothes—it would make clear that perhaps this is not what landlords and property speculators want.

Our corrupted language allows modern housing debates to appear informed, intellectual and pragmatic, all the while ignoring that there is a flipside to every housing story. The dream of the Jones family—of a world where landlords compete to lower rents for tenants—is a ghastly and undesirable world for landlords compared to the current situation.

To avoid the truth that 'affordable housing' means less money for landlords and speculators of housing development sites, the property owners as a group work hard to portray their interests as, strangely enough, identical to the interests of the renter. There is a relentless and well-funded propaganda machine that makes sure that no one realises that, if there is a successful change to make housing prices or rents cheaper, they will lose billions. These groups will never propose such policy changes. They have hijacked the housing debate.

In Australia about $60 billion per year is paid by tenants to the landlords of 3.4 million existing homes, which are worth about $2.5 trillion dollars. Wiping 20 per cent off the rent would mean landlords losing $12 billion per year in rent, and about half a trillion in asset value, if values fell in proportion to rents. Can anyone seriously think that this group of property owners wants 'affordable housing' if that means cheaper rents and lower property prices?

The symmetry of property markets and the high price of cheap housing

The reality is that, underneath this charade, every current home and every possible future housing development project is owned by someone—the landlord investor, the speculating land banker or the housing developer—and every economic gain for them is exactly equal to an extra cost for a new buyer or tenant. This 'owning' side of the market is driven by their desire for investment incentives so as to maximise their economic gains from the property they own; they are not interested in minimising the prices paid by renters and first home buyers. To give a sense of scale of these gains, the average Sydney home typically makes more income from rent and capital gains than the typical Sydney full-time worker earns.[6]

I call this core economic feature of the housing market the *symmetry of property markets*. For every tenant who gets a lower rent, there is a landlord who loses an equal and opposite amount of investment income. For every first home buyer who takes advantage of a price decline to buy into the market, there is a seller who has mistimed the market and sold at the market bottom.

The return to normal operation of private property markets after the mid-century deviation is a story of declining homeownership and declining public housing options. But the symmetry of property markets means it is also the story of rising private landlordism. The story of rising house prices is the story of higher costs for first home buyers, and of windfall gains to existing owners.

Most of us grasp this symmetry instinctively. We see the conflict. Landlords don't offer discounted rents when official interest rates go down just because they are saving some money on their mortgage. They try to increase rents if the market can bear it and they only reduce them if the market can't bear it.

The dream of cheap housing is also the dream of bad investment returns for landlords.

———

The symmetry of property markets does not mean there are no win–wins. When a property owner develops new housing for a buyer, that's a win for the buyer and developer. One of the most useful insights that economics offers is that voluntary trades are a win–win for both participants.

But once all the win–win trades are made, a market converges to a point that economists call a market equilibrium. This is the price and amount of housing where no one can be made better off through voluntary trading; therefore, from here, making someone better off means making someone else worse off.

A market equilibrium is a beautiful concept. But the property market equilibrium also creates a political and economic conflict around housing policy that cannot be ignored. If we want to change the market from its current equilibrium, someone must lose, economically, for someone else to win.

As it happens, I have been a renter, a landlord of multiple properties and a homeowner over the past two decades, experiencing both sides of the market firsthand, often at the same time. When wearing my landlord hat, I never desired for my leveraged housing asset to fall in value and my rental income to decline. But at the same time, wearing my renter hat and aspiring to own a home to live in, I wanted to save money on the rent and be able to buy a home in a desirable location with my income. I could feel the symmetry of property markets firsthand. If rents and prices increased, that was great as a landlord—I got more cashflow and higher asset values—but it also made renting more difficult, and the price to buy a place of my own further out of reach.

The games we play

Bizarrely, we treat this inherent economic conflict as a social taboo in polite circles. As a result of years of lobbying and propaganda, you would be forgiven for believing that landlords want nothing more than to offer tenants cheap rents and that speculative housing developers want nothing more than to flood the market to push down house prices.

But property owners have an incentive to keep housing expensive, not cheap. Housing is their asset after all.

Much of what we read in the media about housing is not factual or analytical. What we read are stories crafted by property insiders at expensive lunches with paid shills touting ever more audacious political slogans and marketing angles. Not only landlords and land speculators, but banks and real estate agents all have incentives to tell porkies about the property market that suit them, not you. Whether those stories contain a grain of truth is a secondary matter.

Every change to the market equilibrium—whether through tax settings, planning or tenancy rules, or financial regulations—has a loser for every winner. Every time a renter or non-property-owner wins, a property owner loses.

No doubt in Henry George's time in the late nineteenth century, vested interests were also prolific with their propaganda. But the problem now goes further. Today we have a hijacked housing debate. It is not just direct property interests but the media, housing researchers, political parties and governments, which all actively avoid the taboo of acknowledging the symmetry of property asset markets and hence avoid fact-based discussion and actual policy ideas that achieve cheaper housing. This taboo means that opposing economic interests can freely claim in the press that what is good for them is good for everyone, without being challenged, and ignoring the basic contradictions.

Just like the pharmaceutical companies don't want to cure disease, and the military hardware companies don't want to prevent war, these groups don't want cheap homes. But, unlike these industries, when it comes to property and housing, there is a Housing Cheer Squad that sings from the sidelines to sell political promises, academic analysis, media articles, advertising and culture-war signalling, all the while disguising the underlying economics.

For the media, ignoring the symmetry of property asset markets allows them to write scary headlines whichever way the housing market is moving. If rents fall, the headline 'Good for renters' would work, but most newspapers prefer 'Landlords fear low rents will reduce supply'. If house prices rise, it's doom and gloom for first home buyers, or an investment opportunity for landlords.

There's no attempt at internal consistency and, since any article about housing gets clicks, there is always an incentive to present the most recent data in its most extreme version. Consumers of online news will mostly get shown to them the most exciting data that relates to them—the suburbs where prices rose or fell the most, but less about average trends or other relevant economic context.

For example, during 2022 in the United States, widespread media reporting talked of a homeownership crisis. But, as economist Dean Baker from the Center for Economic and Policy Research repeatedly pointed out to journalists, homeownership had been rising since 2012, when it bottomed out after the financial crisis. If there was a crisis, it wasn't happening in 2022. But the idea that rising prices must be bad for aspiring buyers, even if the truth was that it was the existence of so many new first home buyers that was partly causing prices to rise, got more clicks.

No wonder most people have no idea what is happening in the housing market.

Whose crisis is it anyway?

What's wrong with housing today? I asked my X (formerly Twitter) followers—a well-informed bunch from academia, policy and the property industry—and here's what they told me.

◆ Too much density in the suburbs
◆ Not enough density in the suburbs
◆ Must tax property more
◆ Too many taxes on property
◆ Too many investor buyers
◆ Too few investors for the rental market
◆ Too many renters
◆ Not enough renters
◆ Need tiny homes
◆ Need better homes
◆ Need fast trains and transit infrastructure
◆ Too much infrastructure waste
◆ Mortgage interest rates are too low
◆ Interest rates are too high
◆ Banks are too restrictive with mortgage lending
◆ Banks are too loose with mortgage lending
◆ Too many vacant homes
◆ Not enough vacant homes
◆ Gentrification is ruining suburbs
◆ Gentrification is needed in the suburbs

Notice anything?

Contradictions at every turn. For every single problem identified, someone else thinks the equal and opposite issue is a problem.

We all think we've found out what's wrong with the property market. We can all agree it's not working the way we think it should. But no one can agree on what the housing system should be like or what changes would bring it closer to that ideal. Under the influence of the Housing Cheer Squad, all incentives are stacked in favour of the status quo, ensuring there are no major changes while appearing to want the opposite.

I fear that this kind of public debate about housing—one that features so many unique complaints with so many contradictory views—is one that property owners and those with vested interests in this sector are happy to have.

Even at the most basic level, it seems difficult to get broad agreement that lowering rents is a desirable outcome. When I again surveyed my X followers to ask if they prefer rents to rise or fall, 18 per cent of them said that it would be better if rents went up! That figure instantly made me recall that about 18 per cent of households in Australia are landlords.

The big picture of housing today

What most people lack in their housing analysis is both a long view and a coherent economic theory of property markets. *The Great Housing Hijack* will provide you with both, together with a policy prescription that works to make homes cheaper and just might navigate the hijacked housing debate.

I generally like to focus on the economic issues. I don't really care what shape or colour our dwellings are. Whether one building contains five, or 50, dwellings, or whether one dwelling comprises five buildings. I won't bore you with questions of design, the curse of modernism or sustainability, unless these have significant economic effects on the rent, price, quantity and quality of housing.

In this book I dispel many common misconceptions about the economics of housing. We all think we know about housing. After all, we've lived in homes all our lives and many readers would have bought and sold dwellings numerous times. But a coherent understanding of the housing market as a complete economic system, and how the Housing Cheer Squad distracts more than informs, is what matters if we are to enact housing policy changes to keep up with the dream of the Joneses.

2 ◆ Property principles

It is quite true that land monopoly is not the only monopoly which exists, but it is by far the greatest of monopolies—it is a perpetual monopoly, and it is the mother of all other forms of monopoly.

—Winston Churchill identified the property monopoly
as a main economic driver in a speech delivered at
King's Theatre, Edinburgh, on 17 July 1909[1]

The symmetry of property asset markets is fundamentally about property rights to spaces: who needs them, who has them and at what price they are willing to sell them. Property rights are what turn physical spaces into places where you can build housing. Property rights turn a location into a financial asset. Without property rights over a small part of the Earth, there would be no legal basis to exclude others.

You might think that before you build a house at a location what you own is 'land'. But land is a bad description of what is left after you remove the house. After all, you can dig out all the soil and rocks to astonishing depths, as happens during high-rise construction, and you still own the property rights to that big empty void left behind. Property titles, or certificates, are what you own. These define the space you have rights to. In New South Wales, property titles once stated that they were 'limited to a depth of fifty feet [15.24 m] below the surface'. You aren't buying soil, or land. You are buying space.

'Land' is just the name we give to a property right that applies to an invisible three-dimensional box somewhere on planet Earth. Inside these imaginary boxes you can put a home, caravan, factory or farm, knowing you have the right to keep out others from it. It is this system of property, or real estate, that carves up the Earth with property rights and drives the economics of housing.

If you want to understand the housing market, where the prices come from and how policy changes interact with the incentives of property owners, buyers and renters, you need to understand the economics of a system of invisible imaginary boxes drawn around the planet, inside which we build homes. It is this system that generates the conditions where renters compete for homes rather than landlords competing for tenants. In this chapter, we unpick the legal and philosophical basis of property as a system and explain why the property monopoly sits at the heart of all the economically important housing questions.

Real estate, real problems

Wherever a property, or real estate, system is created, problematic outcomes arise. Even online virtual worlds are not immune. Ultima, one of the oldest massive multiplayer online games, has had a housing crisis since 1999. Demand for property in the game *Final Fantasy XIV* saw people queuing in real life at sales events to outbid other players with real cash money for in-game virtual housing. As game designer Lars Doucet explains:

Digital real estate is not actually a new phenomenon, and history consistently shows that when 'digital land' sufficiently resembles the economic properties of physical land, we see digital land speculation, digital housing crises, and even full-blown digital recessions. That means a period of exciting growth suddenly grinds to a halt once scalpers corner precious digital property and keep it out of the hands of those who actually want to play the damn game or perform valuable and productive activities for the community.[2]

Virtual housing markets in computer game worlds in the 21st century show that the outcomes of housing markets left to their own devices look a lot like the nineteenth-century housing markets of the real world—subject to boom-and-bust cycles, with low homeownership and rents rising to absorb gains in worker wages.

———

One of the best ways to think about property is to first think about what it is not. I borrow from lawyer and policy analyst Matt Bruenig the idea of the 'grab world'. Fittingly, Bruenig just grabbed this idea from another guy, philosopher Roderick Long.[3] The grab world is a thought experiment about a world without property. In the grab world you cannot initiate force on the body of another human; but, other than that, any object that exists in the world is yours to grab. Nothing is the property of anyone. Absolute freedom.

In the grab world, each house can be occupied by the first person to be there. A house can be built wherever you want to build it, by anyone who can grab materials from wherever they find them.

Your clothes? When you're not wearing them, they are free for anyone to grab and wear. Want to burn down a building, push a car over a cliff to see what happens? No problem. No one has any claim to these objects in the grab world. Go for it.

Since anyone can occupy any dwelling they want in the grab world, all our housing woes would be solved. There would be no one there to collect the rent, so there would also be no need to buy a home to avoid paying future rents.

You might be thinking that the grab world sounds like a world not just without property, but without law, without rules, without order. And you would be right. Property is, at its core, the law. Property is not about physical objects but a social order. These days, with intellectual property, we also divide up the world of ideas, sounds and images with similar laws. Property is what the rules collectively created by human beings say is property.

Many libertarian thinkers wrongly treat property as a natural law, like gravity, that we humans merely discovered. But if property rights are a natural law that human beings are subject to, how is it that there have been many societies throughout human history that have not had the concept of property? Do natural laws pick and choose which human groups they apply to? Gravity doesn't.

Indigenous Australians and many other cultures, for example, were renowned for not having a concept of property. The idea that individuals could own and trade spaces of the Earth made little sense to them.[4] Columbia Law School professor

Katharina Pistor explained that for the Mayans in Belize, for example, 'the notion of individualized private property was an alien concept'.[5] They had other non-property rules to sustain their social order.

I often imagine the conversations of European explorers, like James Cook, sitting around the campfire, telling a local Indigenous leader that there are invisible imaginary lines all around them that define property. That, according to a natural law, after trading with them some gold, silver, axes or blankets, it becomes okay to violently attack anyone who comes inside these boxes.

Because the legal rights that any community grants to property owners are always incompletely articulated, property is often conceptualised as a bundle of rights. Property contains in that bundle explicit rights created by laws, such as to exclude others, to charge rent, to trade ownership, and to erect certain types of buildings. It excludes those explicitly not allowed by laws within that space, like murder and slavery. Plus, it includes undefined residual rights, which are all the actions you might like to do with your property space that aren't excluded nor explicitly defined by law. Property is the name we give to this bundle of explicit and implicit rights.

Property is not real

Consider for a moment the invention of intellectual property (IP). This system of laws, which deals with patents, copyrights and similar concepts, was created to replicate real estate in the world of ideas. Brands, inventions and artistic works such as books, music and film, became property.

24

Because of these laws, I can possess a thing, like a musical recording or a book, but not *own* the sounds or words in it, because the song's composer or the book's author, or whoever, is the copyright holder and *owns* the intellectual property.

The Beatles famously sold the intellectual property rights to their song collections in 1969; these were eventually acquired by Michael Jackson in 1985 when he bought a catalogue of music publishing rights to more than 4000 songs written by other people for US$47.5 million.[6] In a 2001 radio interview with Howard Stern, while contemplating buying back the property rights to the songs, The Beatles' main songwriter Paul McCartney said: 'The trouble is I wrote those songs for nothing and buying them back at these phenomenal sums, I just can't do it.' Finally, in 2017, McCartney initiated legal action to regain ownership of the property rights to his own songs, citing the 56-year copyright period that applied in the United States when the songs were written.

Because the idea of property, or real estate, is so entrenched in our society, it is hard for us to see how arbitrary those rights are. But the parallels with property rights in other areas, like intellectual property, are useful. There is a heated policy debate, for example, about the fair use (i.e. free use) of intellectual property and the expiry period of intellectual property rights of all sorts, whether inventions, books, films, software or songs. Similar debates have historically happened with real estate too, which is why, when the Australian Capital Territory was established after Australia's federation in 1901, all property rights created there explicitly included a 99-year expiry date.

The fair use provisions for copyrighted works, which allow usage without permission or charge, can also apply to real property. In many nations, people can walk across privately owned property, so long as they do not disturb the activities of the owner. The 'freedom to roam' is like a real estate version of 'fair use' provisions of intellectual property rights. But in some countries, these actions would instead be defined by property law as trespass.

Changing the rules of intellectual property is the most powerful way to change the price of access to songs, books, films and other creative works. But changing the rules of property when it comes to housing, especially about how to access and use these rights, is not part of the modern debate about how to make housing cheaper.

Property is an ownership share of the nation's business

We all have read articles in the financial press about whether property or shares are the best investment. But what if I told you that property is just another type of shareholding in the monopoly national business of allocating space?

We know this is the case because property titles and share certificates in companies are interchangeable ways to carve up ownership of locations. Before the invention of strata title, where property titles to space can be subdivided vertically into strata, or layers, individual apartments were owned as shares in the company that owned the whole building. This type of apartment ownership structure was introduced in New South Wales in 1961 and is known as 'company title'. Each apartment owner has a share certificate, not a property title, that comes with the contractual right to exclusively occupy their apartment in the building.[7] These company shares can be bought and sold, just like any other property or share.

We can take this logic further and see what insights it brings.

What if all spaces were owned by one company? Not just the space containing one building, but all the spaces across a country, whether for agriculture, industrial, commercial or residential activities, and whether they contained a building now or might in the future. One person could own that company and it would clearly be a monopoly. But, just as with other monopolies, this company ownership could be split up into smaller pieces.

One way to divide company ownership is to sell part-ownership shares as a fixed percentage of the company. Such percentage ownership portions are what we call stocks, or shares, in financial markets. Another way is to sell ownership shares as a fixed location portion of the company. This is how company titles work and is perhaps more easily recognisable as a franchise model of part ownership. Indeed, land ownership was historically called 'enfranchisement', freeing owners from obligations to a (land)lord. Nowadays franchising is a way of dividing ownership within larger organisations, such as fast-food chains, by defining rights linked to locations.

Although the logistics would be insurmountable, it is technically possible for property owners to collectively decide to incorporate a company that owns all their property and convert their part location-ownership share to a part percentage-ownership share in the new company. Company towns like Cadbury estate, at Claremont in Tasmania, or Starbase in Texas, where SpaceX operates, are places where property is owned by the company and the shareholders of those companies thus own a percentage share of property there.

Just as a company can raise cash by selling ownership shares to the public (what's called an initial public offering, or IPO) or through private equity sales, a nation can too. Throughout the 1800s, Australian colonies auctioned off property rights to private owners to raise public revenue to invest in the growing nation. In China today, local governments operate in much the same way.

A start-up company sometimes pays workers with company equity; similarly, nations can pay workers in property. In Australia, former convicts were given property titles on the condition they farmed the land and increased national production. James Ruse was famously granted Lot 1 on the New South Wales land registry in 1791 on the condition that he farmed the land to produce food for the new colony. Similar land grants were given to returned soldiers after the two world wars of the twentieth century on the condition that they commenced farming on that land.

This logic—of property being a part-ownership share in a location monopoly—has implications for how we understand the market forces generated by the property system. Property owners are not competitors. They are co-owners. After all, you can't compete in the provision of space without first buying space from a current owner. A competitive property system would allow others to claim the right to your location. When intellectual property rights expire, books, music and films become cheap and competitive, as they are no longer protected by the intellectual property monopoly. Others can use that property freely.

The monopoly nature of the property system was acknowledged historically, such as by the young Winston Churchill in the quote that began this chapter. It was even thought that 'property is just another name for monopoly'.[8] In fact, the famous board game Monopoly was originally called the Landlord's Game and was invented by American activist Lizzie Magie in 1902 as 'a practical demonstration of the present system of land-grabbing with all its usual outcomes and consequences'.[9] Despite many players and part-owners competing, the system of in-game property always generates a monopoly outcome of concentrated ownership, unequal access to property and higher prices over time.

In the original version of the game, you won by becoming the richest player; the current version is won by sending all the other players bankrupt, knocking them off, starting with the poorest player first. Like in real estate, in the board game Monopoly, any policy, or rule, change that makes non-property-owning players better off comes at a cost to property-owning players. The symmetry of property is replicated because a property system is replicated.

In board games, online games and throughout history, property markets have a tendency, like all monopolies, towards concentrated ownership and high rental and asset prices. Today, this core economic feature is widely ignored. Instead, it is commonly assumed that if real property markets are left to their own devices they will tend towards fair and equal outcomes and broad ownership. This confusion only persists because the housing debate is hijacked.

How a monopoly becomes hidden

Imagine that I claimed intellectual property rights over the idea of food. Everyone who wanted to get food had to buy the right to use that idea from me before they ate.

As the owner of the property rights to the idea of food, it would be my choice how much food was produced. The existence of these property rights would regulate the pace of food production; dietary intake would be far below what would otherwise occur. I would extract the maximum value from my monopoly through the choices I would make about selling or leasing my rights, which would dictate the rate of food production.

Imagine now that, as a smart operator, I start selling percentage shares in this intellectual property monopoly so I could diversify my investments. Because the intellectual property right to food is extremely valuable, in very little time I would split up ownership among thousands of new shareholders.

This intellectual property monopoly is a raging success, and everyone needs to lease or buy this idea from me. But the management of my intellectual property business grows administratively cumbersome. So I bring the shareholders together and we agree that more localised management would help solve our administrative problems.

Inspired by other business models, we vote to change the way our ownership is split—from fixed percentage shares to location shares, where each shareholder now has a franchise covering an exclusive geographic area. This way, each owner can better tailor the way they sell access to the intellectual property in response to local market conditions.

We now have a system of intellectual property businesses with many different owners, all tied together by the existence of intellectual property rights over food. Although people who want to eat can deal with any franchise they like, by choosing to eat at a different location, the system of location franchises is still a monopoly, just like when these franchisees were previously percentage shareholders.

While the material production of food becomes more efficient over time, due to technological improvements and improved breeding of crops and animals, the price of food does not. All the extra value is captured by the franchisees of the food monopoly.

Because of the rising market price of food, some people begin arguing that removing regulations about food quality standards is the only way to make the price of food come down. In fact, the food intellectual property franchisees have argued for this themselves, because they know that, since food still provides the same value to consumers, they can extract more of the value for themselves when food costs less to produce.

Over time, the food monopoly becomes an accepted part of life. Franchisees start running for politics and telling stories about changes they promise to make to get the price of food down, even though this clearly conflicts with their own personal financial incentives.

As time passes, people forget that the intellectual property system is a monopoly and pretend that, because there are thousands of franchisees, it is in fact a competitive market and that franchisees can be tricked into pushing the price of food down, rather than up.

They argue furiously about it on social media.

There's power in understanding that property is not a natural law

Every powerful group since the dawn of humanity has used the idea of natural law, or natural order, to justify its social and economic advantages. But the grab-world thought experiment shows the obvious fallacy in perceiving property rights as a natural order. As a society, we devote enormous efforts to documenting and protecting the collectively imagined property rights that we have created. Many of the most well-preserved written archaeological records are of property ownership and property transactions, as the elites of those times required such records to justify their possession of property and power. But we need to understand that property is not natural and that we can radically change the way we create, use and access property. This is the key to understanding how to improve housing outcomes, even if it means battling powerful interests.

To drive home this point, imagine if today's property titles office, which records who owns which part of the property system, burnt to the ground one night—our records of who owns which property, and who owns which dwellings on that property, were destroyed. Imagine too that smoke from this fire caused a strange collective amnesia about what was recorded at the titles office.

We would wake up residing in the same homes as the day before. Suddenly, every renter would immediately stop paying rent. Everyone would be housed as they were the day before, but now at almost no cost. The $60 billion that Australian renters currently pay to landlords would be reduced to zero. Each household would, rather quickly I suspect, revert to claiming ownership of property rights to the home they occupy. In doing so, they would begin paying for the upkeep and any taxes associated with ownership. The problem of cheap rental housing would be solved by reinventing the property monopoly with new owners.

If the bank records were also caught up in this fire, every mortgaged homeowner would stop paying for their mortgage. Every household would live rent and mortgage free. The flip side is that landlords would lose their property assets and rental incomes, while the bank shareholders who owned these mortgages would lose the value of those assets.

I'm not saying that arson is the solution to expensive housing. I'm saying that the property system is not a physical thing, but a record of our collective imagination. I'm saying that this system creates a monopoly outcome, even though it creates many voluntary transactions (as described in absurd detail in the following chapters), just as it does in board games and virtual worlds where the system is replicated. And I'm saying that this insight into who owns a share of the property system is the insight needed to understand how to change housing outcomes for the better.

Calls for more competition in housing supply demonstrate a flawed understanding of property. Sure, there is competition for homebuilding, but not for invisible boxes to put these homes in. We can see how calls for more competition don't make sense in the example of an intellectual monopoly on the idea of food; but we can't see it in real estate.

The existence of property and its monopoly is not necessarily a problem either. It is the bedrock of capitalism and provides necessary order and investment incentives. A fire destroying records of who owns real property would not destroy the idea of exclusive property in our minds, so society would not devolve into the grab world. It would merely be a new way to reallocate property ownership so as to give everyone a share in the property business without first paying the market price.

Take it as given that a property system should exist. But, by understanding the economic features of this system when it comes to providing housing, we can look at ways to modify and improve it. The possibilities are broader than we might think. In the 1950s and 1960s, when Australia was much poorer in economic terms than today, we were able to get desirable housing outcomes. We changed the property rules around who gets those rights, how they get them and what they pay, and we got different results.

Property owners have always had an incentive to hijack the debate and steer it away from fundamental questions about property rights and their allocation. Like every elite class in history before them, they justify their power as the natural order, and claim that changes will backfire. But unlike many previous historical periods, most citizens, journalists, analysts and policy-makers have been taken in by their stories. A Housing Cheer Squad, whose main business is selling their own stories, is steering us further from a coherent understanding of how the economics of property markets determine housing outcomes, and how we can change these outcomes.

Five housing
market equilibria

3 ◆ Asset price equilibrium: Where prices come from

'When I use a word,' Humpty Dumpty said in rather
a scornful tone, 'it means just what I choose it to
mean—neither more nor less.'
    'The question is,' said Alice, 'whether you can
make words mean so many different things.'

—Lewis Carroll, in *Through the Looking-Glass*,
could have been describing the word games that
hijack the analysis of housing markets and policy

In August 2022 an Australian news headline stated that 'Falling prices won't fix housing affordability.'[1]

Huh?

People were furiously complaining that rising prices made housing more expensive and unaffordable (whatever that means). Now, apparently the opposite was true. If house price falls don't help affordability, maybe price rises don't hinder affordability either. What on earth was going on?

I have already explained how 'affordability' is a nonsense word. But you would think people know what they mean when they say 'the price of housing'. Here's a lesson for you. Most people don't. And most don't care what they mean.

It is not useful to splash around terms like 'price', 'cost', 'rent', 'demand' and 'supply' with no regard to an underlying view of the economics at play. Clear statements need clear definitions. Here's one such statement: 'I paid a price of $500,000 for this housing property asset, and the total cost to me each month for my mortgage interest, outgoings and upkeep is about $3000. The rent of the same home would have been $2000 per month.'

This statement contains three concepts relating to the cost of housing. They are distinctly different, but specific.

- *Rent* is the consumer price of occupying a house for a period.
- *Price* is the sale price of a housing property asset.
- *Cost* is how much you spend on housing during a period.

Each of these words now means something.

In addition to being precise about what words mean at an individual level, we need a precise language to describe the economic processes and outcomes at a property-system level. The price you paid to buy your housing property asset didn't come from nowhere—it was part of a system-wide outcome that depends on the actions of others, or what economists call a market equilibrium.

The idea of an economic equilibrium is extremely useful and powerful. In finance it is also known as a 'no arbitrage condition'. For example, if it is possible to make a different choice, or trade, and be better off, that's what people will do, until no one is left who is clearly better off by making a different choice.

Understanding the equilibrium outcomes of a property system is the key to understanding housing markets.

What is an equilibrium?

A classic way of helping to understand the concept of a market equilibrium is to consider the situation of choosing from multiple queues at a set of supermarket checkouts.

If there are two cashiers and the queue for the first cashier is ten people long, while the queue at the second cashier is two people long, then it makes sense to choose to line up at the short queue, not the long one.

In fact, there is a time saving to be made by anyone from fourth to tenth in the first queue shifting to the second queue. The situation of a two-person queue next to a ten-person queue is not an equilibrium, since there are voluntary choices that people can make to improve their outcome. As each person shifts to the second queue, it increases in length. At the same time, the first queue shortens, thus reducing the time saving to the next person who switches. Ultimately, when there are six people in each queue, there are no gains from switching and this becomes an equilibrium.

The interaction of many people's choices to create an economic equilibrium is also the reason that changing lanes in a traffic jam doesn't seem to help get you moving faster. If one lane starts moving, some people switch lanes, slowing that lane and freeing up the other lane. Because of the choices of just a few people who switch lanes, a traffic jam will sustain an equilibrium where both lanes move at the same speed on average.

Back at our supermarket checkout, the queue-length equilibrium can also be accompanied by an equilibrium set of prices for positions in those queues. Someone from the back of a queue could pay someone at the front to swap. The amount they would have to pay would be a negotiation that would make them both better off. Once all the voluntary priced position swaps have taken place, that pricing outcome is an equilibrium. It might be the case where trading to the first position is priced at $2, and the price of switching up to the second position is $1, and so on. This whole set of prices is an equilibrium.

Any involuntary change from this equilibrium outcome means creating winners and losers. There are no changes any individual can make to be better off. A new regulation—which changed the price of a position in the queue or forced a position swap—would create a loser and a winner. For example, taking someone from the back of a queue to the front would give them a gain at a cost to the others in the queue.

Economic pressures generate an equilibrium in checkout queues and traffic jams just as they do in property markets. Once a property monopoly has been created, the economic incentives of property owners and residents interact in predictable ways.

There are, in fact, five related housing market equilibria in the property system:

1 housing asset prices
2 rental prices
3 the spatial variation in rents and asset prices
4 the density of new housing at a location
5 the rate of new housing development across a market, known as the absorption rate.

These different equilibria determine different aspects of the housing market.

The five chapters in this section describe the economics of these equilibria. Unlike most housing analysis, which pushes financially interested policy agendas and backfills a theory for why they are 'a good thing', we will first ensure we have a coherent theory of housing markets arising out of the property monopoly, and then use that theory to inform policy options for cheaper housing.

Why asset prices are not the economic price of housing

The sale price of a housing property asset is not the 'economic price' of housing in any meaningful sense. We wouldn't say that the price of BHP shares represents the 'economic price' of iron ore, copper or coal. BHP shares are an asset representing ownership rights to an entity that mines and sells these minerals.

Prices, in the economic sense, are the relative cost of consuming newly produced goods and services in a certain time period. The economic price of housing is therefore the rental price, which represents the market price of being housed for a certain period relative to the prices of new goods and services you must forgo to consume housing instead.

The rental price is what goes into consumption price indexes. It is used in national accounts (gross domestic product, or GDP) as part of the measurement of new housing service production. It is what standard economic theory says is the price of housing. For clarity from here on, I will call this price the rent, or rental price, to differentiate it from the concept of housing asset price or sale price. I will also use the term 'construction cost', to mean the cost of building a home, and 'development cost', to mean the cost of construction plus other costs required to get a home built, like engineering and architectural expenses, government fees and charges, and marketing and sales costs.

The sale price of a house represents the value of getting your name on a property title. It is a type of financial product, as we explored earlier. Its value comes not just from providing housing today, but from the fact that the property right lasts indefinitely and provides an ongoing profit stream from housing services.[2] That profit stream is the value of not having to rent a home for an owner-occupier, or the net rental income for a landlord. It also includes the value that comes from the flexibility to renovate or modify the dwelling, change uses, rent to other occupants, re-develop or undertake any other legal action within the property rights bundle that can generate future cashflows.

Why is it important that the sale price of a housing asset is not its economic price? Because sale prices of housing assets can rise while the economic price of occupying housing falls, or vice versa. The economic price of housing, the rent, translates into an asset sale price via other factors to generate an asset price equilibrium.

Maybe you have heard that those factors are 'fundamentals', like supply and demand. Sounds plausible. But let me translate: 'I don't know what factors determine price, but it must be some-thing to do with buyers and sellers who are the ones who agree on prices.'

Economist Richard Denniss, in his book *Econobabble*, explains this way the appropriate response when someone starts using supply-and-demand language: 'Walk away when they start talking in generalities about "supply and demand" or "market forces". Blaming "the law of demand" for an economic outcome is like blaming the law of gravity for a plane crash—it's proof that the speaker has no idea what they are talking about or no intention of explaining their thinking to you.'

Deals between sellers, aka supply, and buyers, aka demand, set prices in all markets. But this provides as much insight as saying the person who wrote the price on the contract set the price! It doesn't explain why that price was chosen.

A deeper understanding requires asking why sellers of housing hold out for a particular price and why buyers are willing to pay it. The first part of the answer requires knowing why any asset has a value, and the second part of the answer requires knowing about the equilibrium in asset markets.

Why property assets have value

Like other asset markets, the value of owning property assets comes from their ability to generate future incomes. Since that income is rent, a good way to think about property asset prices is that they are the answer to the question of 'How much is it worth to avoid paying rent to live in this home for the infinite future as a lump sum payment today?' The answer must also consider that property owners pay costs that are not paid by tenants, such as property taxes, maintenance and building insurance. Hence, the asset price reflects the lump sum value of the *net* cost saving of no longer renting, which is also what a landlord buyer would receive as *net* income.

When an income flow is converted into an asset price, it is 'capitalised' into that price. The capitalisation rate (cap rate), also known as the yield, is the first year's income flow divided by the asset price paid. An asset that earns $10,000 of net income next year, and sells at a $125,000 asset price, has an 8 per cent yield.

The yield is also a type of price. If you put a dollar in the bank, the yield is the interest you earn as a percentage of that dollar. If you put a dollar into buying a housing property asset, the yield similarly is the percentage you are earning from this investment.

In fact, in commercial and industrial property markets, when you ask real estate insiders what a property sold for, they will often quote the yield (capitalisation rate) rather than the price, because that is the best way to compare returns with other assets. They will say things like: 'That property sold with a 7 per cent yield, but this one sold with a 6 per cent yield because it has a blue-chip tenant and better prospects for redevelopment.' It is common for the word 'price' to not even appear once in commercial property market analysis.[3] Just like we ask the rate of interest on your money in the bank, or the rate of return from your superannuation account, the important question is not the asset price of property, but its yield.

The science behind capitalisation is imprecise, as no one can predict what these future net income flows will be, or whether rents will rise or fall. In general, assets that are seen as riskier will require a higher yield than assets that are perceived as less risky, as the likelihood that those returns persist in a stable manner is lower.

Unlike money in the bank, assets like company shares and property also earn returns from changes in the asset's value over time. These changes in value are known as capital gains, or losses if the value falls, which occur due to changes in the market's assessment of the value of future net income flows. If you expect capital gains of 3 per cent each year, this is a return in addition to the net income received. If you paid, for example, $125,000 for the property to get an 8 per cent yield from net rent, but also got a 3 per cent capital gain each year, your total rate of return, or total yield, would be 11 per cent.

Equilibrium forces in asset markets

Just as understanding the equilibrium in a checkout queue means understanding the switching choices available, understanding property asset prices means understanding the switching choices among assets that buyers and sellers in property asset markets can make. Money spent on housing assets could instead be spent on other financial assets to generate a return. The ability to swap housing assets for other assets in financial markets is the economic force that generates the housing asset market equilibrium.

Current property owners have a choice of selling or not selling. They have what is known in economics as a reservation price, though you can think of it like an auction 'reserve price'. This is the value current property asset owners place on their property. The supply of property for sale reflects the demand from current owners for holding property instead of other assets.[4] This is visible during home auctions when sellers place bids on their own home to compete with other buyers.

The price at which housing property assets trade is the point where a seller thinks they are better off swapping the property asset for cash to invest their money elsewhere, and a buyer thinks the reverse. They make a bet against each other about which asset is better to have today. It is a little like the two people at the back of each checkout queue swapping because they each think they will be better off after the trade.

This trading logic seems intuitive, but it also contains a puzzle. If an asset has a yield that makes it worth buying, then it is also probably worth keeping for its current owner. This applies as much to property assets as to company shares or bonds. So why are assets traded at all?

The answer has two parts. First, buyers and sellers have different alternative investment options and priorities. This is truer in housing than other asset markets. A housing asset inherited by multiple children, for example, might be less useful to them than cash to use for other investments or spending priorities. As real estate insiders often quip, the 'three Ds' of real estate are death, divorce and 'de' bank. A nicer way of putting this is lifecycle factors, relocations and financial constraints mean that there is always a reason that some property owners have better alternative investments and wish to sell.

Second, people's expectations of the future differ. Some people shift lanes in a traffic jam because they expect to be better off. Since an important part of capitalising rent or income into an asset price is the expectation of future capital gains, differing views about the future generate trading. If a seller and a buyer have even slightly different expectations, then both can be better off from the trade. Just as only a few people need to switch places in a checkout queue because of different expectations, only a few property asset trades need to take place to sustain the asset price equilibrium. In fact, fewer than 5 per cent of Australian homes are traded each year.[5]

People's differing expectations of capital gains not only help to explain why asset trading occurs at all, they help explain why property market price cycles can seem so irrational. High capital gains expectations can be held by some buyers, allowing them to justify prices that reflect a lower capitalisation rate of the net rent. During a boom, it can appear sensible to pay a higher price, expecting prices and rents to continue to rise. If a capital gain of 4 per cent is expected on a property with a $10,000 net rental income and you are seeking an 8 per cent total return, then you can capitalise the net rent at 4 per cent and purchase it at a price of $250,000 ($10,000 net income divided by 4 per cent is $250,000). That is 25 per cent higher than the $200,000 price when only 3 per cent capital gains are expected and an 8 per cent total return is required, meaning the net rental yield must be 5 per cent ($10,000 net income divided by 5 per cent is $200,000). If the expectation of 4 per cent capital gains is correct, then the higher price is worth paying. If not, the price will seem irrational in retrospect.

During a price crash, expectations usually reverse. If there have been recent capital losses, and prices are expected to keep falling, you don't catch the falling knife. That same housing asset, with expectations of a 1 per cent capital loss per year, would be priced at only $111,000 ($10,000 net income divided by 9 per cent). That is 56 per cent lower than the price when there are expectations of 4 per cent capital gain, yet both prices give an 8 per cent total yield on a rental income of $10,000 per year.

As we will see later, booms always end because the market runs out of buyers with both the expectation of further gains and the money to spend on housing. The shift back into other assets after a property boom means that, over the long term, the rates of return of different asset classes, like commercial property and corporate shares, are almost identical.[6] They must be, or there would consistently be trades available to swap assets and make more money!

Rent money to be your own landlord or rent housing from a landlord

Another way to think about the housing asset price equilibrium is that there are two ways to occupy a home—you either rent from a landlord or you rent money from a bank to become your own landlord. This is why the interest rate on mortgages is a key ingredient in the capitalisation rate of housing assets and hence their price.

Even if you have the money in cash to buy a home, you can still think of renting this money from yourself at a cost of the return on other investments. Since everyone needs to occupy a home to live in, these are the investment alternatives you have in life that determine whether buying or renting makes more financial sense.

Let us dig down into this equivalence by trying to answer the question 'How much should I pay to buy the house I am renting and be equally well-off?' To do this, we look at the relationship between the cost of renting and the cost of owning.

Let us flesh out the example of a house with the following characteristics.

◆ Rent is $15,000 per year.
◆ Owner's maintenance costs and taxes are $5000 per year (tenant does not pay).
◆ Mortgage interest rates are 5 per cent.
◆ Expectations of growth are zero.

If you paid $200,000 for this dwelling and rented (borrowed) that full $200,000 in the form of a mortgage to become your own landlord, you would be equally financially well-off as renting. The interest on the mortgage at 5 per cent is $10,000, and the other ownership costs are $5000, meaning the total annual cost of renting (borrowing) money to acquire and occupy the home is $15,000, which is the same as physically renting it.

You might notice that I have only considered the interest cost of the mortgage, not the total repayment. That's because paying the principal on the house is not an economic cost. It is an asset investment: its value stays on your balance sheet as home equity, and you can get it back when you sell it. Tenants pay rent and don't get any assets, just the occupancy, so the appropriate comparison is renting the money from the bank, not buying the housing asset. Although our home buyer is probably making $12,900 mortgage repayments per year, or $2900 more than the interest alone, this includes the purchase of $2900 of housing equity each year.

Since interest rates change the yield on alternative financial investments, they are extremely important in determining the price of housing. When mortgage interest rates are 5 per cent, you can borrow twice as much for the same interest cost compared to when the mortgage rate is 10 per cent. If you can afford a $10,000 per year interest repayment, you can borrow $200,000 compared to only $100,000 at the higher interest rate.

————

Such is the power of the interest rate on the equilibrium asset price that in May 2020, when the panic about Covid-19 was high and Australian banks were stress-testing their mortgage books against a potential 30 per cent reduction in housing asset prices, I argued in a podcast interview that prices were more likely to rise 20 per cent than fall 20 per cent over the next eighteen months.

The simple truth was that prices had fallen substantially from 2017 to 2019, especially in Sydney. Incomes had risen and interest rates had fallen. Mortgage interest rates had dropped roughly from 5 per cent to 4 per cent between 2016 and 2019, which should have increased housing asset prices 20 per cent, everything else being equal. But this adjustment had not yet happened, as property markets adjust slowly, unlike, say, share markets. Mortgage interest rates then fell further after the cash rate was dropped to near zero, so a mortgage rate of 2 per cent became easy to get. Concerns about unemployment leading to falling housing asset prices made little sense, as the historical record showed no relationship between unemployment and house price growth.

Rents did fall 20 per cent at this time in many suburbs of our capital cities. If all else was constant, this should have meant a 20 per cent reduction in price. But because the mortgage interest rate had halved, you could now borrow double the amount with the same interest cost. There was a negative impact of 20 per cent from the rental effect and a positive impact of 100 per cent from the interest rates; even with substantial changes in growth expectations, this indicated to me that housing prices should rise.

And that's what happened. Housing asset prices increased at a record pace for the next eighteen months before interest rates were tightened again. The crazy part about this was that many social media comments on that podcast were rude and panicky, and my favourite went along the lines of 'Where did Cameron get his economics degree? The back of a cornflakes packet?' Yet all I did, in order to correctly predict rising prices, was to apply the basic logic of the asset price equilibrium.

The asset price of vacant property

Prior to building a home, property rights to spaces with no buildings on them have an asset price too. Many people wrongly assume that 'land' prices determine house prices. After all, to create a new home you need to first buy land and then add a building to it, so it makes intuitive sense that the price of homes is the sum of the cost of land and the cost of developing buildings.

But this gets the causal story backwards.

It is true that the price of land and the price of building a home usually add up to the asset price of a home because this is the equilibrium outcome.

To show the equilibrium process that generates the price of undeveloped property, consider the case where the price of land is $300,000 per developable lot, and the cost of developing a home is $300,000, but the price of a home is $500,000. No one will buy the land at the $300,000 price. Why would they? If they did, they would be paying $600,000 to buy land and build a home that would be worth $500,000. The price of the vacant property must adjust back to $200,000 so that the cost of buying an existing home, or building a new one, is the same.

The opposite adjustment would happen if a plot of land was priced at $100,000 and the cost of building a home was $300,000, while the price of existing substitute homes was $500,000. This situation can't be sustained either. Why would the landowner sell for $100,000 when they could take two assets—the $100,000 of land and $300,000 of cash to build a home—and combine them to create an asset worth $500,000, pocketing the $100,000 difference? In finance, the ability to buy an asset at one price and immediately sell at a higher price in another market is called arbitrage. In this case, the housing asset is bought for $400,000 by buying land at $100,000 and constructing a home for $300,000, and it can be immediately sold for $500,000. Property sellers don't generally give up these opportunities when they are also available to them before they sell, so the price of undeveloped property converges to a point where there is no gain from the development arbitrage.

Building a home is an asset allocation decision that converts an undeveloped land asset, together with a cash asset, into a developed dwelling asset. Like all asset markets, arbitrage opportunities in the housing market ensure that equilibrium pricing is sustained, and that point is where the price of undeveloped property (or land without a dwelling) is the residual of dwelling value, minus the cost of developing that dwelling and a margin for the perceived risk of that arbitrage. If that wasn't true, there would be asset swaps of cash and land in the market that could generate risk-free gains. The causality runs from the price of dwellings to the price of land via the cost of development.

There is also a substantial margin for risk in property arbitrages because the asset swap of cash and undeveloped land for new housing assets is far from risk-free or instantaneous, unlike arbitrage opportunities that occur in electronically traded financial markets. For large sites and projects, these risks are significant and hence additional buffers are included to account for risk, which further reduces the value of undeveloped property. Property asset markets are no different from other asset markets in how risk is incorporated into pricing.

Furthermore, the asset pricing equilibrium concept explains why owners of undeveloped land are the most patient owners— they don't want cash in a hurry but prefer the long-term nature and risk profile of owning undeveloped land. After all, these owners can sell for cash at any time, and every buyer will be one that prefers to own undeveloped land rather than owning cash.

Feasibility and property value

We say that a site is *feasible* for development into housing if the residual land value, or housing price minus development cost, is higher than the value of the undeveloped land considering only the capitalised net incomes from its current use.

For example, if a property is being used for an industrial warehouse, and the net income flow is $100,000 per year, a capitalisation rate of 5 per cent gives the property an asset price of $2 million. If a residential apartment tower with 100 apartments worth $600,000 each can be developed at a cost of $30 million, which includes a risk buffer, then the residual value for that use is roughly $30 million. On this site, an apartment tower is feasible because the value of the property when used for development is higher than the value if only its current use is allowed.

Because property owners have the right to choose what to build, within legal limits that define property rights, such as planning regulations, they can test many alternative projects against each other to see which has the highest residual value after accounting for the relative risk of each option. The choice of a housing development project design that maximises the residual property asset values is known by the term 'highest and best use' by property valuers, who are routinely faced with the task of assessing the value of undeveloped property.

A feasible new housing project is therefore one where the asset value of homes in that project, minus development cost, which includes a margin for assessed risk, is higher than the asset value of the property if its current use was the only possible use forever. The highest-and-best use is, out of many potentially feasible projects, the one that generates the highest residual land value, and is hence the one that determines the value of an undeveloped property in an asset price equilibrium.

Property asset prices are a big deal

It is common to hear that Australians are some of the richest people on the planet. One calculation in 2021 put Australia's mean wealth per adult at US$550,000.[7] Such calculations are simple additions of the total value of our traded assets, like property and business shareholdings, divided by the number of adults (or residents) in a country.

Australian residential property was worth about $10 trillion in 2023, of which only about $3 trillion reflected the construction cost to replace all the existing homes. Commercial property was worth $1.3 trillion, with about half the value being the cost of the buildings, and rural land was worth about $0.5 trillion.[8] By comparison, listed company shareholdings were worth about $3 trillion.

Australian wealth is mostly the value of the property monopoly, and most of it is used for housing.

But we should remember where the price of housing assets comes from. The equilibrium value is a financial representation of the liability of a renter, or the price they are willing to pay to rent money rather than rent housing. The value of the 33 per cent of the housing stock owned by landlords (private and public) exactly matches the rental liability of the more than three million renting households.

This is the symmetry of property asset markets writ large.

We see the same symmetry if we try to subtract the mortgage liabilities from the measure of wealth. A home buyer's mortgage liability is an asset to the owner of the bank; it is reflected in the value of the bank. These cancel out exactly, just like the value of property should. For some reason we ignore the unpriced liability of renting.

In Germany, for example, where housing assets are on average much cheaper than in Australia, measuring wealth by adding up property values gets you a rather low number. The same calculation that gives US$550,000 per adult in Australia gives US$257,000 in Germany, or slightly less than half. This is not because German homes are in poor shape or for any other physical reason. It is because their asset price equilibrium is different.

It is true that the buildings we construct in the imaginary property cubes have a productive value that is very real. These buildings make us wealthier by expanding our productive capabilities. But the point is that we must understand property asset pricing across the market as a whole is predominantly affected by financial features, like interest rates and market expectations, rather than physical features.

———

The asset pricing equilibrium is a core ingredient for understanding housing markets. It helps predict future prices and provides many useful policy insights. For example, a policy change that increases taxes for property owners will be fiercely fought because a tax is a negative cashflow, which reduces both net income and asset value. Understanding the asset equilibrium matters because we often pretend that policy can break this equilibrium without prohibiting the voluntary asset trades that create it. Housing asset prices can't just fall independently. If they did, asset trades would happen to bring those prices back to an equilibrium. This equilibrium concept also shows that when housing prices change while rents stay flat, this must be caused by interest rates and the expectations of asset traders, not by any physical properties of the housing or the size of the housing stock.

But it is still the case that a main ingredient in housing asset prices is rent. So where do housing rents come from?

4 ◆ Rental equilibrium: Why incomes determine rents

This rule of thumb for rent dictates spending no more than 30% of your income on housing each month. The reasoning behind it is that by capping your rent payment at 30% of your monthly income, you'll still have plenty of money left to cover other living expenses and to work toward your financial goals.

—Folk wisdom on rents as stated by
United States commentator Rebecca Lake[1]

One of the puzzles in housing markets is that rents rise very consistently with incomes, with only a little variation due to macroeconomic cycles. In Australia, the average rent-to-disposable-income ratio for renter households in the private market in 1993, rounded to the nearest single percentage point, was 20 per cent. In 2023, it was 20 per cent.[2]

Despite all the consternation about housing affordability in the intervening three decades, the market has been doing what private property markets always do.

Regardless of which rent-to-income metric is used, and there are many variations, they are almost always nearly perfectly stable over long periods of time. Flat lines on a chart. Data from England shows that market rents were 24 per cent of net household incomes in 2013, with nearly the exact same ratio in 2020 (and if anything, a slight decline).[3] In the United States, the Bureau of Labor Statistics consumer spending survey shows that renter households have spent a stable 22 per cent of after-tax income on rent since 1986.[4]

Looking for historical rent-to-income ratios in Australia leads us to a 1912 New South Wales parliamentary inquiry into rising rents. It concluded that a sudden supply shortage was to blame, which would sound familiar to most readers. But the best historical data, which is by no means as reliable as today's large surveys, shows a surprisingly stable rent-to-income ratio for a male worker from 1911 to 1941 in a tight range of 26–30 per cent despite the tumultuous economic times of that era (note that this ratio is higher because it measures only a single worker's income, not a household's income).[5]

It is rare to hear that the rental outcomes we have today are the normal outcomes of private property markets responding to household income growth, and that this is the same trend we have seen for centuries. Just like in 1912, we are drawn to the emotional logic of supply shortages when we see queues at rental inspections. But queuing is a symptom of rental price adjustment, not a cause.

———

Landlords are acutely aware of an equilibrium relationship between incomes and rents; they are always looking to invest in areas with high-income growth. But there is a huge incentive for many groups in the Housing Cheer Squad to ignore this boring fact and dress up the most recent rental price changes as a crisis, then to pick and choose the location that is seeing the highest rent growth and call that place the 'epicentre of the crisis'.

Politicians, for example, need to appear to be acting tough. Academics need to appear to be doing important work. The media needs to get clicks and sell advertising. Collectively these groups misrepresent how the rental market is priced, which is a problem if you are in the business of crafting policy to lower the rental price.

A common trap that many people fall into is to observe that in the 1970s and 1980s, some metrics show a lower rental share of income; they therefore reason that policy changes since that time must have caused higher rents. While the metrics are true, the reasoning is not.

Analysis of the rental market in the United Kingdom, for example, found that the share of income spent on rents for low-income households was around 12 per cent of income in 1979, but 28 per cent in 2019. Yet the market rental price was consistently around 28 per cent of income the whole time. According to that research, the reason so many households were paying below the market rent in 1979 was a combination of 'cash payments, social housing and rent controls' that had 'the effect of lowering the net amount of rent tenants pay out of their own pockets'.[6] In fact, researchers of long-term housing trends often set to one side the post–World War II period, up to the 1970s, as an abnormal period of rent controls and public housing.

This fits one of the main arguments of *The Great Housing Hijack*: that our housing concerns in recent decades are a return to normal property market outcomes.[7] The astonishing fact that, in private property markets, rent-to-income ratios have been flat for decades, if not centuries, is because of rental equilibrium.

The rental equilibrium and how it is sustained

Why don't housing rents fall as a share of income over time? The prices of clothes, furniture, electronics and other household items, typically fall relative to income. Why are homes different?

The trick to answering this is to think about what happens to consumption choices when the price of those other household goods falls: households respond by buying more of them. Economists call this the 'law of demand'. Lower prices induce more purchases, so the share of income spent on each type of product doesn't fall as fast as the price of each product.

In fact, for many products, households consume so many more of the goods when prices fall that, regardless of the item's price, households spend roughly the same share of their income on that type of product.

Here's an example. Imagine that clothes cost $100 per item and a particular household with an income of $100,000 spends $3000 per year on clothes—they buy 30 items, spending 3 per cent of their income. The price drops to $75 per item. Because of the lower price, this household buys more clothes. They now buy 40 items, spending the same $3000 per year, or 3 per cent of their income.

We have now jumped from thinking on a per-item basis to a per-category-of-expenditure basis. This is the trick to understanding the equilibrium forces that ensure that rental prices track incomes. A dwelling is a single item, but housing is also a category of expenditure for the household that occupies it.

If housing rents fall, households consume more housing, just like they do for all goods and services. The difference is that a dwelling is not just a building, but a location as well. Each home has both a 'dwelling quantity' element, in terms of its size, and a 'location quantity' element. A household can consume more housing in these ways:

1 Moving to a bigger home
2 Reducing the number of people in a household
3 Renovating and improving their homes
4 Moving to a better location, or
5 Some combination of all the above.

Consuming more dwelling quantity happens in 1 to 3, while increasing location quantity happens in 4 and possibly 5.

The trade-off that generates the rental equilibrium is the relative benefit to a household from spending an extra dollar of income on more housing or spending it on more non-housing goods and services. Which queue will you spend this extra dollar on?

On average, housing rents track renter incomes as a nation gets wealthier, staying around 20 per cent of income in Australia. In economic lingo, this means that housing is a 'normal good'. An 'inferior good', on the other hand, is one where households spend a smaller share of their income on it as incomes grow, like no-name brands of food or clothes. A 'luxury good' is where a higher share of income is spent on it as incomes rise, like international travel.

The 'normal' rental equilibrium means that regardless of what happens to the stock of housing or the composition of physical housing types (apartments, detached houses, or other types), we reorganise households into these dwellings and spend roughly the same 20 per cent share of income on housing. Since an equilibrium is a market outcome, not an individual income, it is still the case that high-income renter households spend less than this share on rent, while low-income renters typically spend more than 30 per cent of their income on rent.

Because of this equilibrium, incomes of renter households constrain how much households will spend on rents. But they constrain on the downside too. To show this, imagine a scenario where a temporary government decree is passed that rents can only be 10 per cent of the income of the current tenant for the next year. All current tenants are required to declare their income and landlords are required to write a new lease for a year at 10 per cent of those declared incomes with those current tenants.

Do rents stay at 10 per cent of incomes after the year is up?

Tenants will quickly realise they can move to a bigger, better-located dwelling after their one-year lease, possibly for less than what they paid before the decree. They will try to do that. In the second year, tenants who try to relocate into bigger and better homes will end up outbidding each other, putting pressure on rents to rise back up towards where they were before. This pressure on rental prices will continue until tenants find that there is no longer a net benefit to them from giving up other goods and services for more or better housing.

It is because of collective preferences that renter households spend 20 per cent of their income on rental housing, not 5 per cent, or 10 per cent. We want more and better housing, but also more and better other goods and services, and there is a trade-off that must be made. Of course, some households choose differently, spending more on housing and less on other stuff, and vice versa, but on average this results in a stable rent-to-income ratio across the market.

Lessons from the rental equilibrium

That rents are tied to incomes, due to an economic equilibrium driven by our collective willingness to give up other goods for more housing, is an important insight that helps resolve a few myths and stories that dominate housing debates.

First, there is a popular idea that increasing welfare payments to low-income households gets 'eaten up' by higher rents, and hence is of little value. Sure, a low-income household might spend more than 20 per cent of their income on rent, maybe 35 per cent. But if you give them an extra dollar, they won't spend 100 per cent of that extra dollar on rent. At most they will spend 35 cents on more rent, sustaining the same rent-to-income ratio. Because the share of income spent on rent generally falls as relative incomes rise at any point in time, they are likely to spend a much smaller share of the extra dollar on rent than 35 cents, perhaps only 10 cents. Yes, a fraction of that money will go on rent, but most of the money will be spent on other goods and services.

Higher incomes always make households better off. If it were true that higher welfare payments got completely eaten up by higher rents, it would be true for all types of income, including higher wages, which would apparently achieve nothing because landlords would get those gains, dollar for dollar.

Second, the story of rents being determined by incomes helps explain the phenomenon of gentrification. This is the process whereby a cheap location, originally occupied by low-income renter households, changes because of the influx of richer households and redevelopment. These new higher income households bid up rents, forcing out existing low-income residents.

Because rents are determined by incomes, a relocation of high-income households will change which areas have higher rents. Often this occurs when well-located urban areas are 'revitalised' by public investments; but during the 2020 and 2021 Covid-era, this also happened in lifestyle regions and small towns. High-income households still spent up to their equilibrium share of income on housing, but the best locations they could afford changed because of new macroeconomic conditions and the ability to work remotely. This change in location preferences increased market rents and prices in these newly desirable areas and decreased rents for households left behind in inner-city Sydney and Melbourne areas, which saw record rental declines.

The reality that renters are stuck in bidding wars, in which incomes are the firepower, presents a genuine social issue. The inequality of incomes across the economy generally, not just in gentrifying areas, makes renting more difficult for lower income households. Since we allocate who gets to live where by price, those with higher incomes and wealth always have the advantage.

A third insight concerns rent regulations that limit rental price increases. Just because the tenants who benefit from these rules pay less rent doesn't mean the market price goes away or gets reduced. If rent regulations create a gap between what sitting tenants pay and the market price, like they have in the past, it creates an arbitrage opportunity for tenants to sublet. This is not necessarily undesirable. Subletting is a common commercial property arrangement. But regulations must be designed and enforced in a way that recognises the economic forces that generate the rental market equilibrium.

For example, in 2022 the New South Wales government followed other states in banning rental auctions. Rental properties henceforth had to be advertised at a fixed price, rather than advertised with a price range with tenants making offers.[8] But rental equilibrium doesn't change because a different type of auction is used to set the price.

If a landlord starts with a low rental price and tenants bid against each other until only one tenant will pay the final price, that's technically called an English auction. This is used in housing sales, but now banned for rentals. But if a landlord advertises a high rental price and lowers it until they get a tenant, that's called a Dutch auction. Either way, the rent is the same. At best, this ban saves tenants time when they shop for housing. Instead of having to make many losing bids for many homes before striking an agreement, they can shop for rentals knowing that, if they offer the advertised price or close to it, they are likely to get a rental contract.

Fourth, the fact that rents are roughly a fixed share of household income means that rents are not a good metric of the quality or sufficiency of the housing stock. In the late 1940s, rents paid were a lower share of household income because of rent controls in private and public rental options. But housing was poor quality, small and crowded. Now, rents are the usual 20 per cent of household net incomes, but houses are the biggest and best they have ever been, with the fewest people per dwelling.

Lastly, the fact that rents rise with incomes over time is a reason that homeownership has such large long-term benefits and why high homeownership rates were a policy goal for much of the twentieth century. Homeownership allows households to avoid ongoing rental price competition throughout their life, whether from gentrification or simply rising incomes in general. This is especially valuable in retirement, when household incomes typically go backwards compared to others in the rental market.

5 ◆ Spatial equilibrium: Why location matters

Savvy homebuyers could save themselves hundreds of thousands of dollars by looking just a few minutes up the road, with neighbouring suburbs often offering the same lifestyle for less.

. . . Expanding their search to bridesmaid suburbs could have the added benefit of allowing buyers to get into the market while they could still afford to, without compromising on their lifestyle.

> —Real estate investors know that nearby suburbs can't sustain a large price gap for long—Alanah Frost, 'The Melbourne "bridesmaid" suburbs where you save the most', 18 June 2021, <realestate.com.au>

In 2005, rents were rising in my hometown of Brisbane. To avoid this cost to my meagre 23-year-old's budget I considered buying a cheap boat and living in it on the Brisbane River. I went to inspect a few of the cheapest liveable boats I could find to investigate the cost of this option. If it worked, it would get me an inner-city location at a fraction of the cost, but with the trade-off of less comfort. Instead, I took the alternative, which was to shift one extra suburb away from the city and the locations I needed to regularly visit; I moved to a bridesmaid suburb, adding a little cost and time to my daily routine, but saving on rent.

I wasn't the only one thinking this way. Jonathan Srirangana-than was elected as my local councillor in 2016. Before being elected he had lived in a share house; but he took the opposite decision to me and moved into a houseboat after being elected.[1] For him, the added inconvenience of living on a boat was worth the cost saving, compared with renting a house nearby.

Why am I telling you this?

Because although I didn't know it then, the actions by both Jonathan and me are among the many mechanisms by which housing markets adjust towards a spatial equilibrium. This is the third housing market equilibrium and, in my view, provides the most powerful insights into housing markets. If you have ever moved house, you will appreciate its logic.

Where we live and work

Spatial equilibrium is the idea that moving equalises quality of life. Put a different way, all locations are substitutes at the right price. If this wasn't the case, people would be better off by voluntarily moving. In the lingo, there would be a spatial, or locational, arbitrage opportunity and people would move to take advantage of it.

Spatial equilibrium adds a crucial spatial (or locational) dimension to the other housing market equilibria. Rents and asset prices vary enormously across locations, for example, as does the density of housing and the rate of new housing development. It is not just the level of rent on average, but the rental gradient between locations that is an equilibrium market outcome. Recall the checkout queue analogy. The spatial equilibrium is the difference in price that someone at the front of the checkout queue would charge for giving up their spot compared to those further back in the queue. The rental equilibrium reflects only the average level of those prices.

Usually, a central location in major cities is the most attractive from a transport accessibility perspective. Here, there is the shortest distance to everywhere else in the city. This location is like the person at the front of the checkout queue, who has the shortest waiting time.

This is why larger employers prefer central city locations. The town centre usually has the biggest commutable catchment of workers. If a business chose to locate on the northern outskirts of a city, people living in the south would not work there because the commute would be twice as far for them, compared to the business being in the centre of the city.

It is not just work commute times that make the city centre more accessible. Travel times are shorter to social events, schools, sporting events, museums, nightlife, grocery and specialty stores and more. These activities cluster in the centre because it is most accessible to their customers, and people cluster close by because they desire accessibility to these activities, resulting in a higher value for these locations. In economic lingo, this clustering leading to increased value is called the 'agglomeration effect'.

As well as accessibility benefits, local amenity is a major determinant of the desirability of a location. Suburbs with few services, crumbling local infrastructure, bad schools and few recreation options, are less desirable and hence less valuable. As my good mate and planning professor Peter Phibbs would say, 'If you want to make rents cheaper, set a few cars on fire in the street. That should do it.' The joke gets at a core insight from spatial equilibrium—any policy change that makes housing rents in a city cheaper in the long run only does so by making it a worse place to live.

How is a spatial equilibrium sustained?

Consider identical houses on identical size lots but House A is in a desirable inner Sydney suburb and House B is on the far outskirts of the city in a new estate. Any difference in rent must only be due to the different location. That difference is a spatial equilibrium that will reflect exactly the value in the rental market from moving from one location to the other.

To show how this equilibrium rental gradient is sustained by the ability of households to relocate, imagine that the Lee family is paying $350 per week to rent House B, but would pay an extra $350, or $700 in total, to live in House A. The solid black line in Figure 1 shows their personal rental gradient, or what they would pay to live in each property based on their own desires for the relative accessibility and amenity of each location.

The Jones family lives in House A and is paying $600 per week and would move to House B if they could save $200 a week, or pay $400 to rent House B. Their rental gradient is the dashed line.

There is a gain to be made from these two families swapping homes because the Lees value House A more and the Joneses value House B more. When they do that, there are no further gains to be made from relocating. The resulting gradient between

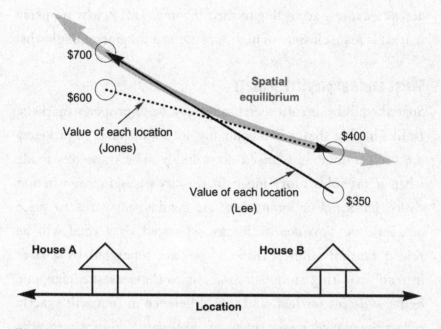

Figure 1 ◆ How moving sustains a spatial equilibrium in between two locations

the two rental prices, shown in the grey curve, reflects the spatial equilibrium. The rental equilibrium is just the average height of that curve.

Spatial equilibrium is what limits further relocations to high-amenity locations. Rental prices adjust so that extra rent paid to move to these locations is worth exactly the benefits of moving to that location for the next mover in the market.

A result of spatial equilibrium is also that households sort into different locations according to how much they value the benefits of each location. But where does that assessment of value come from? Households with higher incomes can pay more for better locations because, in order to pay the higher rent, they need to make fewer sacrifices in their consumption of other goods. So spatial equilibrium also distributes households across locations according to their income. This is why property markets create clusters of high-income and low-income suburbs.

Secret sauce of property markets

Spatial equilibrium is a secret sauce unique to property markets. Unlike buying shares in a company, location shares in property are each unique and priced accordingly. The trade-offs made when households move mean that a city's geography, whether rivers, harbours or mountains, are flexibly navigated by price adjustments. Two nearby homes separated by a road will be priced similarly. But if these homes are separated by a river instead, requiring an hour round trip to the nearest bridge, one home will rent for less, and that difference in rent will exactly reflect the market's assessment of extra value on moving to the more accessible side of the river. Building a new nearby bridge that made each home as accessible as the other would result in the rent of these homes converging, as it removes most of the spatial trade-off between the two homes. Relative rents adjust for geography automatically.

Regardless of the geographical compositions of homes in a region, households will spend the same share of their budget on rent. Some households will spend more than that to locate in a place and a type of dwelling that saves them travel costs and provides better local amenity. Others will spend less, devoting more time and money on travel costs. Some might even choose to live on a houseboat once all location and rental prices trade-offs have been considered.

It doesn't matter for the rental equilibrium that some cities like the Gold Coast or Chicago are skinny and long, or that

Sydney has a harbour in the middle, or that Adelaide is on a flat plain. Location choices adapt so that the relative advantage of each location, however that arises, is reflected in the difference in rents between locations and even between cities. After all, people relocate between cities, and the pattern of domestic emigration from Sydney over the past decades suggests that some people are still relocating and that this force will sustain the inter-city spatial equilibrium in rents.

Covid-19 lockdowns created a major change in how households valued different locations. The travel time and accessibility benefits of living close to the capital city centres fell away due to people working from home. Because of the lower value attached to these locations, relative to others, the logic of spatial equilibrium dictated that people would even relocate from capital cities to cheaper towns that offered other lifestyle amenities. So people did. In Melbourne, for example, 80,000 people left the urban area in the 2020–21 period. That process resulted in a rapid re-pricing of rents, which fell in the cities and grew rapidly in smaller towns, especially those that offered a coastal lifestyle.

Lessons from spatial equilibrium

Spatial equilibrium can be obvious and intuitive. But, as we will see, ensuring your analysis of housing markets is strictly consistent with spatial equilibrium is rare in public debates about housing.

For example, when analysing the effect of planning regulations on the rent and price of housing, spatial equilibrium is almost always ignored. We must apparently build 'where people want to live'.[2] But spatial equilibrium tells us that people will live anywhere, because all locations are substitutes at the right price. Sure, higher value areas have lower travel times and better amenity; the value of this location benefit is exactly equal to the additional rent compared to other areas.

Property investors know that, even if there are sudden rental or price increases in high-status desirable suburbs, a steeper rent and price gradient is unlikely to be sustained. That's why 'brides-maid suburbs', adjacent to the premium suburbs, are often a good investment; they are likely to follow the rent and price trends of the premium suburbs upwards to sustain the spatial equilibrium.

Investors also know that a spatial equilibrium usually isn't one smooth curve from the centre of the city; it involves many 'humps' of local premium locations where activities cluster. A city itself is a clustering of activities and services, and within a city there are clusters too. Large new development projects, whether they are mixed-use urban projects or master-planned housing estates, are often now designed with a cluster of different uses and services so as to generate their own local amenity premium.

Many traditional economists have taken spatial equilibrium to its logical conclusion by arguing that city governments should invest in public infrastructure in a way that maximises total housing rents paid in the city. After all, this means they are investing in a way that maximises the amenity and accessibility of the city relative to other places. In fact, most economic research still uses higher rents or prices as a way to measure the value of local infrastructure and amenity. Again, this reflects the symmetry of property markets, whereby the benefit of a location goes to the owner of property rights at that location but is a cost to those moving to that location.

Importantly, combining the rental and spatial equilibrium concepts implies that aliens could suddenly and immediately construct a million extra homes in Australia, or about 10 per cent more that at present, and within a few years rental prices would still be on average 20 per cent of household income. Spatial equilibrium dictates that people will move and relocate to these homes when it is advantageous, and rental equilibrium would ensure that the level of rent paid on average converges to the usual 20 per cent.

It might seem hard to believe, but a naturally occurring experiment that took place in Melbourne from 2020 to 2022 bears this out. Hundreds of thousands of people left the city, causing a massive increase in the stock of dwellings compared to the population.[3] This surprise departure of people was the equivalent of dumping 6.7 per cent extra homes into the city, or about 2.8 years of the normal rate of new housing supply.

Rents fell only temporarily, and by 2023 they were up 10 per cent and rising at the fastest rate in history. The effect on rents of a sudden increase in the stock of homes relative to people was real, but temporary. The rental and spatial equilibria are also real; they help us understand how households adjust.

6 ◆ Density equilibrium: How tall we build

Increasing density might be the answer to housing costs, research shows

—A *Sydney Morning Herald* headline reflecting
a common view about density and housing,
article by Tawar Razaghi, 26 July 2022

In 2023 the Victorian Civil and Administrative Tribunal (VCAT) heard a matter concerning Wyndham City Council's refusal to approve a housing subdivision by the Peet development company because it was not dense enough.[1] The proposal, on the outskirts of Melbourne near a proposed new rail station, was a new housing project that included only detached homes, with no townhouses or apartments. This conflicted with the council's town plan that had zoned for higher density housing. Yet the property owner didn't want to build more homes there.

How could this be?

Many people in the Housing Cheer Squad claim that a lack of density is the main cause of high rents and prices, and that regulations inhibit the creation of denser housing, which property owners desperately want to build.

So why didn't Peet want to increase density on its project, and why is the idea of a density equilibrium so important for understanding the housing market?

———

It is surprisingly common in our hijacked housing debate to confuse density, which is the number of dwellings per area, with the rate of new housing supply, known as the absorption rate, which is the rate of new homes of any density at all locations in a region per period of time. Sometimes I call the absorption rate the 'time density' to differentiate it from the 'location density'. A major housing subdivision with a 'location density' of 50 homes per hectare can radically vary its 'time density' by building homes at a rate of five dwellings per year, or twenty dwellings a year.

This fourth housing market equilibrium is about density, meaning dwellings per unit of land. The fifth equilibrium in the next chapter is about the absorption rate. Property owners create both equilibria and, in the process, maximise their economic gains.

To understand the density equilibrium, we need to revisit the asset pricing equilibrium for undeveloped property. Recall that the value of a property reflects the value of future cashflows. For undeveloped property there are often many feasible projects that could be built, with the one project that generates the highest risk-adjusted residual value being the *highest and best use* at that time. The density equilibrium is the density of the *highest and best use* new housing project when there are no other legal constraints on density, such as planning or zoning regulations.

The reason that building taller isn't always better is that per dwelling construction costs and risks rise as density increases, meaning there are diseconomies to building at higher density. These rising costs must be weighed against the additional revenue created from more housing on a site. The critical question for property owners who want to build housing is whether the increase in dwelling sales revenue from a denser housing project is higher than the added cost of that extra density, or what is known as the marginal cost. If the economic gain from more density exceeds the added cost, then there is an opportunity to make more money by increasing density. If the gain doesn't exceed the cost, then a lower density project makes more money.

A simple density equilibrium example

Figure 2 shows three feasible building densities on a property: low, medium and high. For simplicity, all three have the same dwelling type.

Construction costs and risks rise with density. For the low-density option—containing just four dwellings—the development cost, which includes construction, fees, design and management, commissions and a margin for the risk of that project, is $2 million. Revenue from four dwellings is $4 million. So the risk-adjusted residual value for the property owner from building this density option is $2 million.

Add another three dwellings for the medium-density project, and revenue goes up to $7 million. Total development costs rises by $2 million to $4 million. The risk-adjusted residual value of this medium density project is $3 million.

The high-density option has ten dwellings. But the construction cost rises substantially because of such things as an extra basement carpark level and another elevator. The risk goes up, because it takes longer to sell more dwellings and prices could change, while construction costs over the longer build time could escalate more.

Here, there is an extra $3 million in revenue compared to the medium-density option, for a total of $10 million. There is also an extra $3.5 million in costs and risk to go taller, producing a $7.5 million total development cost. The risk-adjusted residual value is $2.5 million.

The density equilibrium in this case is the medium-density option as it has the highest risk-adjusted residual value that the property owner can get. All three options might be feasible, but only one density maximises the property value today.

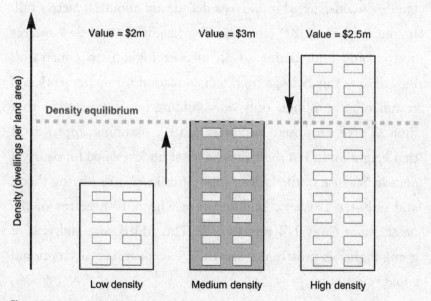

Figure 2 ◆ Density equilibrium is where there is no net gain from going taller

Back when I worked for a major residential developer, one of my jobs was to plug different numbers into our feasibility spreadsheets to test whether a 20-storey tower gave a better return than a 15-storey one, or a 40-storey one. There is only one shot to get the density right when you develop a site.

The density equilibrium is widely forgotten in contemporary housing debates, whereas town-planning regulations that limit density are a hot topic. But town-planning regulations often try to achieve more density and fail, just as we saw in the Peet case at the start of this chapter. The reason is that the density equilibrium in many locations is far lower than the town-planning density limit.

In Beenleigh, south of Brisbane, for example, town planners have tried to get more density by allowing buildings up to 90 metres tall. But Beenleigh is a cheap location. The tallest new buildings constructed in the past decade are about 20 metres tall. In the Brisbane CBD, the building height limit is 274 metres and is only limited due to an airport flight path constraint. But, despite this being a high-value location for apartments and commercial buildings, only one building is constructed to that limit. Three proposed buildings have a planning approval at that height limit, but their sites have sat undeveloped for nearly a decade because of the lack of interest in leasing or buying them, and only ten Brisbane buildings are within 100 metres of the height limit (over 174 metres tall). The added cost and risk of going higher is mostly not worth it, except in very exceptional situations.

Lessons from density equilibrium

First, the density equilibrium explains why over time new housing estates have been building bigger homes on smaller blocks of land—this increases density. They could produce larger blocks of land, but that would leave open an arbitrage opportunity to reconfigure, say, a dozen large lots into 16 smaller lots that are 75 per cent as large, and make more money across a project with a fixed total land area. The decline of large housing lots in major new subdivisions is not occurring because people don't value them; it is simply that not enough people value them sufficiently to make it a better option for property owners over smaller lots and bigger houses.

Second, density equilibrium explains why high-value areas have tall buildings and low-value areas don't, even where there are no regulations that prohibit tall buildings. It is why record-breaking tall buildings are almost always built during the peak of a property asset price boom, when extremely high sales prices can justify the extra costs of building taller. And it is why the world's tallest buildings are now mostly not built for economic reasons, but as political statements; the value of the extra height at these extremes rarely justifies its cost.

Third, density equilibrium happens only at a moment in time when new housing is developed. Immediately afterwards, if market prices or development costs change, these buildings will be the 'wrong' density for the rest of their economic lives until they are again redeveloped, many decades or centuries into the future. Almost all existing dwellings in every city in the world are the 'wrong' density, since they were all built under previous market conditions. This means that the actual density of a city is relatively unimportant in assessing aggregate housing market trends like rent and price—the rental and spatial equilibria allow households to adjust to fit in all the legacy buildings at the 'wrong' density.

Related to this, density equilibrium explains why 'missing middle' housing—townhouse, terraces and small apartments—can be rare even when there are no regulations prohibiting them. This is easy to understand when we imagine a scenario where there is a sudden boom in rents and prices that occurs immediately after the completion of a new 20-storey building. That building would have been designed to reflect the pre-boom density equilibrium. Even if apartment prices rapidly increased by 50 per cent in the year after completion, so that a 40-storey building became the new density equilibrium, that 20-storey building won't be knocked down and replaced. The additional cost of buying a new 20-storey building, only to demolish it to build a 40-storey building, makes the site unfeasible for incremental redevelopment.

Our previous hypothetical example shows this clearly. The medium-density project in Figure 2 provides the highest residual value of $3 million. This is what a developer could pay for the site to build that project. But if there is already a low-density building on the site, which may have been built in the past when that was density equilibrium, the medium-density building would be unfeasible because to buy an existing low-density building costs $4 million, or $1 million more than what a site is worth to develop into a medium-density building.

The same happens with detached houses. Paying the extra cost to buy one large house on a site, only to knock it down and build two or three smaller homes, often makes these projects financially unfeasible. Only the most degraded houses on the biggest lots are usually feasible for redevelopment into smaller 'missing middle' housing.

Fourth, regulations that limit density below the equilibrium at a location at a particular point in time will reduce the asset value of the property. In our hypothetical (Figure 2), if only the low-density project was allowed because of planning or zoning rules, then the property would be worth $2 million. But removing that limit would make the property worth $3 million, because now the medium-density project is possible. So there is an enormous incentive for property owners in areas where planning regulations are below the equilibrium density to lobby for these rules to be changed.

Strangely, we seem comfortable regulating maximum housing densities in planning regulations—with height limits and floor area ratios and other stipulations—but never minimum density. For all the political push to increase density for affordability, there is no movement promoting minimum-density planning laws. In Figure 2, a planning regulation limiting density to the low-density scenario would cost the property owner $1 million in residual value, but a minimum density regulation that forced development to be at the high-density scenario or denser would reduce the property value by only half a million. As we will see later, there are political reasons for this.

Lastly, we often confuse regulations that limit density at a location below the equilibrium with a regulation that limits how quickly new housing is built across all feasible locations. Just as it is true that not all locations need to be developed into housing at once, not every project needs to be at its density equilibrium. As we will see now, the absorption rate equilibrium is at play.

7 ✦ Absorption rate equilibrium: What determines the rate of new housing development

You are a housing developer with a large plot of land on the fringes of a major city with no planning constraints. How quickly should you sell these lots to supply them to the housing market?

Housing academics do not have a good answer to this question. Housing developers have rules of thumb. Yet despite the uncertainty about what factors determine the rate of new housing supply, radical policy changes are being considered in many cities, states and countries around the world to entice faster housing supply from private landowners.

The words above are how I began an academic paper in 2020. It was astonishing to me that, for over a century, economists didn't have a useful model for the rate of new housing supply.

Property owners seek out the optimal housing density to maximise their return, but they also seek out the optimal rate per period of time to develop. This is why large housing projects are broken down into smaller ones and 'staged' as a sequence rather than built much faster in parallel. It reduces risk and allows sales to occur incrementally to meet changing market demand, increasing the overall return from a project.

Housing analysts who argue that we need to *let the market rip* to increase the number of homes always overlook the absorption rate equilibrium. Property owners will not flood the market with new homes just because the rules allow it. They haven't done that for hundreds of years or more, even before there were planning regulations. To develop new housing gradually is a normal part of the property monopoly.

This equilibrium rate of new housing development is known as the 'absorption rate'. Out of the queue of feasible sites across all locations, the absorption rate is how quickly those sites are picked off for development so as to maximise total economic returns. There is an equilibrium because, even when it is profitable to build, it can be more profitable not to build. Property with feasible housing development rises in value over time even when undeveloped, and oversupplying housing means selling at a discount, so most feasible development opportunities are left undeveloped. The absorption rate is where the gain from selling faster equals the gain from delaying and developing more slowly. In the analogy of the supermarket queue, you can move the next new home from the queue of dwellings for sale today to the queue of dwellings for sale tomorrow (or next month, or next year).

When I worked for the publicly listed property developer FKP in 2004, I was told by one of the managers there that in the 2002 boom they misjudged the pricing for off-the-plan sales at a

Sunshine Coast apartment project because the market had moved so quickly. Market prices had risen more than 30 per cent in a year.

There was a queue of people at the sales office on opening day, and by mid-morning dozens of sales were made. The listed prices, which had been set a few months earlier, now seemed cheap to buyers. Continuing to sell quickly at these older prices and undercutting rivals was not the optimal thing to do. It was a giveaway to buyers, who could turn around and resell their purchase to the next buyer at a higher price if they wanted to.

In response, the company closed the sales office early and put all the prices up. Instead of the project selling out in a day, it took years to sell the remaining apartments in that building at higher prices. But selling slower was the approach that maximised the overall return from the project.

The relationship between selling new homes and building new homes

In Australia, new housing is almost exclusively developed with a build-to-order model so as to minimise risk. New homes are sold before they are built, whether that is off-the-plan apartment sales or land and construction packages.

Like in every market, selling faster requires lower prices or, as economists would say, 'demand slopes down'. This is why businesses discount prices to clear old inventory faster. Property developers can observe how fast they can sell at different price points and discover what is the best rate-of-sale and price combination. It is possible to determine whether the sales rate last month was too high or too low by seeing what is possible next month and the following one, as selling too fast one month will mean slower sales and lower prices the next month, and again the following month, and selling too slowly means more sales next month.[1]

Since buyers only enter the market at a given rate, it makes sense for developers to match that rate. You adjust sales rates and prices over time to capture the most gains, and this rate is the absorption rate equilibrium.

A useful analogy might be how quickly you choose to eat. Sure, with your budget and the stocks of food in your fridge you could eat faster. But you match your intake of food to your appetite as it grows. In any meal you could eat more, but you have a 'downward sloping demand' for food per period of time, which means you stop eating now and save food for later on, when your appetite has recovered. The same with developing property. You don't eat tomorrow's lunch today.

This happens for each housing project and across the whole market. If your local rival starts selling and building a new project, it is often better to wait until their project has finished to start yours. As property industry consultant Brian Haratsis told the *Australian Financial Review* in 2023: 'If you understand your competitors and that they have not got much land left, you'll reduce your supply and wait for them to finish and jack your price up.'[2]

The same principle also applies to build-to-rent housing. Buyers of that housing are just a different type of home buyer; they happen to be large investors instead of small investors or owner-occupiers. They will be responsive to local rental market conditions; when rents fall, it pays to slow down new supply so that future rental returns are not depressed.

A hypothetical

Consider the hypothetical case of a new apartment project, consisting of five buildings. One way to approach this project is to develop it all in one go: to set the prices and start selling today. If sales slow down at the current price, then decrease the price to boost sales. After all, inventory backlogs are cleared with massive price discounts for most other goods.

But that approach doesn't make a lot of sense here. What's the rush? You only have one shot at this project. It's not like bananas, where you need to sell all this season's harvest before the next season arrives and so you discount prices to clear that inventory.

Another approach is to break the project into five stages with one building in each. Sell one building at a rate per period where there is no gain from selling faster and pushing prices down, or from selling more slowly and pushing prices up. Keep the other four as an undeveloped land bank—an asset on your balance sheet like any other—and only start them after the first building is successfully sold.

Another option is to stage the project, but to sell off the remaining four stages to other developers so that the new apartments can be built in parallel by many developers rather than in sequence by one developer. This is akin to the first option, of a single developer selling and building all five buildings at once; it produces less overall return. But, as Brian Haratsis explained in the above quote, these five different developers will quickly work out the collectively optimal approach.

Despite such admissions from the industry, it is still popular for the Housing Cheer Squad to argue that, when many different property owners have sites and where development is feasible, we get more parallel development and less sequenced development because competition creates an incentive for each developer to undercut on price so they can sell and build faster than the other guy.

To see why this doesn't actually happen, let's return to our example of five apartment buildings. If the original owner of the five feasible apartment buildings thought the way to maximise their economic return was to sequence these five buildings, then any buyer of those four other properties would also understand they are buying into a market where their optimal approach is to wait their turn. If they chose not to, they would make a lower economic return.

Why are any homes built if waiting pays?

The property system is a monopoly, in which ownership is carved up by locations, and this produces a built-in speed limit on the rate of new housing supply by owners of real property; this is known as the absorption rate equilibrium. When I explain this, some people wonder why owners of the property monopoly supply any new housing at all. If there are gains from waiting to develop, why doesn't every property owner wait and make even easier money in the future? Why build any new homes?

The answer comes from the economic theory of monopolies. Yes, monopolists put prices up when there is more demand for their products, but they also are very responsive to market conditions. When demand rises, monopolists produce and sell more products in a way that maximises their total return by increasing both price and the rate of production together.

A couple of economic diagrams show this. If that's not for you, skip ahead to the next section. On the left side of Figure 3 we see the usual downward-sloping grey demand curve, which shows that, at a lower rent, the market of renters will consume more or better dwellings (remember the rental equilibrium). If that demand rises to the higher line, property owners will respond. Yes, they could keep the same number of homes and put the rent up from point A to point B. With the same five homes in this simplified example, property owners get $6000 per month instead of $5000 by doing that. But building more homes and renting them at a price between A and B generates a larger economic gain. In the left graph, where there are many renters or buyers at each price—in a 'thick' market like a big city—they will build two extra homes and rent seven homes at $1100 each to get $7700 in total revenue. In the right graph, where there are few renters or buyers at each price—in a 'thin' market, like a small town—they will build only one extra home and rent six homes at that same $1100 price, to get $6600 total revenue. In both cases, building more homes increased total revenue compared to building no new homes, as happens in all monopoly markets.

The absorption rate is about how many new homes are built over this time period, while demand is shifting. In the 'thick' left market in Figure 3, the absorption rate equilibrium is two dwellings per period; in the right 'thin' market, it is one dwelling per period. No other rate of new housing development makes more economic gains than this.

Recall that I said earlier that supply is just demand from current property owners. The slopes of the arrows showing the

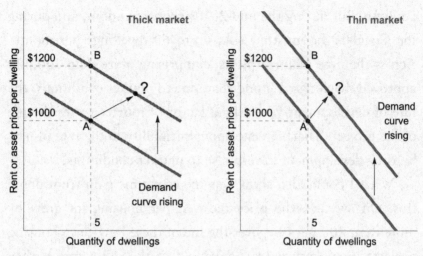

Figure 3 ◆ Why monopoly property owners build housing in response to rising demand

new quantity of dwellings and price in Figure 3 are what economists would call supply curves, and they exactly mirror the slope of the demand curves in each market. Supply *is* demand.

The monopoly property market is why construction trends track broader economic and asset price cycles closely. Demand for buying homes not only raises prices, but also increases the output of new homes as well. The reverse occurred after the 2008 financial crisis when new homes in Spain, for example, were being demolished rather than completed and sold. This was a huge waste of resources. The massive decline in demand meant that the equilibrium absorption rate was temporarily negative.

Responsive absorption rates in action

In a research paper in 2022 I looked at the rate of sales at nine major Australian master-planned housing projects containing more than 3000 approved (or planned) dwellings.[3] In slow months, these property owners would sell and build five dwellings a month. But during the mid-2010s property boom, and during the Covid-19 boom, they sold up to 60 dwellings per month. Across the nine major projects, comprising more than 100,000 approved dwellings, I found that, due to market conditions, the rate of development varied by a factor of fourteen over the life of the project. That's an enormous variability in the rate of new housing development in response to market conditions.

What I could also show was the economic gain from doing this. On average, the price received per housing lot grew by more than 200 per cent over the life of these long-term housing projects. For every extra home sold at the initial price, they gave up selling one more home later at a higher price. Cleverly, these projects did not undercut their future gains by selling too quickly early on.

Property development businesses know there is a limit to how fast they should build housing, and this rate can change suddenly. To ensure they can respond to sudden market changes, developers often accumulate a buffer stock of undeveloped property; known as their land bank, they hold this for many years. There is nothing strange about this. If they didn't own undeveloped land, other people or businesses would. It merely allows these businesses to make gains on the value of this property while also optimising their rate of development under changing market conditions.

Absorption rates as a policy problem

In January 2017, Sir Oliver Letwin, a Conservative member of the United Kingdom parliament, was provided with the terms of reference for an independent review to 'explain the significant gap between housing completions and the amount of land allocated or permissioned in areas of high housing demand, and make recommendations for closing it'.[4] As in Australia, it was just the last in a long line of public reviews and inquiries in the United Kingdom into housing supply and price, like the 2004 Barker review, the 2008 Lyons review, and more. The Housing Cheer Squad is global.

Surprisingly, on this occasion the findings were spot on. Letwin, during his initial six-month review, found that on average it took nearly 16 years to complete a large housing development after planning consent had been granted, or more simply '[t]he absorption rate . . . was agreed to be the primary constraint on build out rates'. What was puzzling was the political incentive to ignore this reality once it was identified. Instead of Letwin arguing that the private property market generates an equilibrium that limits the rate of new homebuilding, he tried to say that building a variety of dwellings of different sizes and quality would enable more types of sub-markets to be tapped into and hence sidestep this limit.[5]

If this is true, why wouldn't housing developers already do this? Are they stupid? I don't think they are.

In most housing projects, there are a variety of options. Most apartment buildings have studio and one-bedroom options, two-bedroom and three-bedroom apartments, and often more bedrooms in the penthouse. Some new buildings are targeted to the top end of the market, and some are smaller and offer more modest entry-level dwellings. If developers could produce a different mix of dwellings and make more money, they would.

Like most major housing developers, the one I once worked for had a deliberate strategy of 'diversifying development activities by geography, product mix and project size'.[6] Doing exactly what developers already do is what Letwin argued was the solution to developers doing exactly what they already do.

We should also recall that different sub-markets are parts of the one housing market because of rental and spatial equilibrium. A buyer could buy a three-bedroom apartment or a two-bedroom apartment, but whoever ends up residing in one is not residing in the other. At the right price, all dwelling types and locations are substitutes. Just like it doesn't make sense to say 'housing developers should be able to sell more green-coloured apartments as well as blue ones' it doesn't make sense to say 'developers are building dwellings in the wrong shape, but if they changed their shape they would trick buyers into buying homes faster at the same price'. Yet that's the argument.

I don't see widespread acknowledgement of the absorption rate equilibrium yet in Australia, but no doubt, when it becomes too hard to ignore, we will see a similar reaction: try to ignore the fundamental economic logic and instead divert our attention to things like tax breaks for property owners, or other planning tricks to remove dwelling design standards or density regulations. When the absorption rate equilibrium is too hard to ignore, why not use it as a new excuse for the same tax breaks and deregulation you were already lobbying for?

The five equilibria and the hijacked housing debate

One reason it is hard to pin down the housing debate is because the five property market equilibria are not stable over time and interact with each other. When the world changes, the property market adjusts.

We accept that these equilibrium outcomes evolve over time and are a normal part of everyday life when it comes to housing. Like the planets in our solar system move their positions over time, but are kept in an equilibrium by gravitational forces, housing market outcomes move over time but are kept in an equilibrium by economic forces.

For example, when incomes rise, they usually do so unevenly. This means higher rents, but also spatial reallocations and higher asset prices. It might be that rising interest rates are leading to falling asset prices, as they were in 2022. But then falling asset prices mean a lower density equilibrium, so very tall buildings that are no longer the density equilibrium choice get postponed or redesigned. Across the market, the declining demand for home-buying will push down the absorption rate equilibrium. In Chapter 13, the predictability of the cycles that arise in this system of five housing market equilibria is explored further.

The beauty of these market outcomes is that, as a society, we can collectively believe that they are natural, like the property monopoly itself. It is politically stabilising not to rehash debates about the validity of the property system and its market outcomes during every electoral cycle.

The housing debate has been hijacked because property owners are a powerful group who want policy changes that advantage them and disadvantage others; they want to avoid changes that disadvantage themselves and benefit others. Cheaper rents mean lower incomes for landlords. A tax on owning housing assets means a lower asset price equilibrium. The public budget wins, but property owners lose. The regulation of rental prices means tenants win, but landlords lose. Higher home-ownership means fewer landlords and tenants.

So the idea of these equilibria as a natural outcome has powerful backers. Additionally, there has emerged a social taboo about acknowledging this symmetry in debates about housing policy and that leads to very strange outcomes. The most active participants in housing debates have an incentive to avoid the unavoidable economics of the five market equilibria and the symmetry of property markets.

Housing hijackers

8 ◆ Politics and politicians

[Rising prices] makes for happy voters.

—Ross Cameron, parliamentary secretary
to the Minister for Family and Community Services,
dropping truth bombs about the politics of housing[1]

A political sweet spot is to sell policies that pretend to solve the problem of expensive housing but avoid the political costs of creating winners and losers due to the symmetry of property markets. But when the rubber hits the policy road, you can guess which side of the property market symmetry ends up winning.

As for all the groups discussed in the next chapters, there are specific political and social incentives for politicians to hijack the housing policy debate, rather than steer it straight.

Most voters are homeowners

First, is the electoral incentive. Of Australia's nearly eleven million households, 66 per cent own their own home (with or without a mortgage). Around 18 per cent of Australian households are landlords or own a second home. Both these overlapping sets of property owners skew toward higher income and older households. Contrast this with the 31 per cent renting in the private market, and the 1 per cent of households (about 100,000 households) who are first-time buyers each year. The electoral calculus falls heavily on the side of satisfying the majority, who benefit from higher housing rents and prices, rather than the minority who benefit from lower rents and prices. Ross Cameron's comment about how to make voters happy was spot-on.

Think about it. Australia's housing stock is worth roughly $10 trillion. Not billion. Trillion. That's $1 million per household on average. It's the largest asset class in the economy by far.

A policy that reduced home prices by 30 per cent would wipe $3 trillion of value from household balance sheets, hitting hardest the households with the highest income and the most political influence.

And for what? Just so some politically unimportant people might buy their first home a few years earlier. But if prices start falling, these first home buyers might not even want to buy at all. There is no political upside.

In 2016 the Australian Labor Party (ALP), led by Bill Shorten, went to the federal election promising to moderately wind back some of the tax benefits available to landlords in the form of negative gearing. Negative gearing is a hot topic in Australia. In short, it allows investment property accounting losses, where the costs—like interest, maintenance, insurances and depreciation allowances—exceed rental income to be deducted from other income before any tax is paid.

This minor policy change would have only affected the roughly half of all landlords who negatively gear—that's 8 per cent of households. But the policy proposal caused a media uproar and was arguably among the key policies that lost the ALP that election.

While the pure numbers fall on the side of property owners, electoral considerations can still mean that signalling concern for renters can be politically useful, even if you are doing nothing meaningful for them. Tell property owners you won't cut their returns and tell renters the opposite, ignoring the symmetry of property markets.

One way to fake this signal is with an 'inquiry'—a political decoy to win votes from gullible renters without losing votes from property owners. Australian governments at all levels have had dozens of these. In 2022 I gave expert testimony to the Falinski Inquiry into Housing Affordability and Supply. It replicated many previous inquiries and reports on the topic over decades, including the 2003 Prime Ministerial Taskforce on Home Ownership, the 2004 Productivity Commission's First Home Ownership Report, the 2008 Senate Select Committee report on Housing Affordability, various National Housing Supply Council reports from 2008 to 2013, the 2012 Housing Supply and Affordability Reform, the 2014 Senate Inquiry into Affordable Housing, the 2015 Parliamentary Inquiry into Home Ownership—to name just a few.

Dozens, if not hundreds, of reports from think tanks have assessed Australia's housing system over recent decades. Combined, it is hundreds of thousands of work hours and millions of dollars in salaries and fees. For what? To create a fake political signal.

Other nations, like the United Kingdom and Canada, are similarly prone to the 'housing inquiry' fake political signal.

As was Australia in the early twentieth century. There was a 1912 inquiry into rising rents, a 1919 Inter-State Commission inquiry into housing rents, a 1937 slum inquiry in Victoria and a 1939 New South Wales inquiry. And no doubt more.[2]

Politicians are homeowners and landlords

But there are more than electoral incentives at play. The second main incentive comes from personal finances, as politicians and their families and friends are almost all housing asset owners.

Analysis of the financial disclosures of federal politicians in 2022 found that 205 of the 226 federal politicians, or 91 per cent of them, owned 421 dwellings between them. That's a touch over two per pollie on average and most of them—some 60 per cent of them—own two or more homes.[3] That is down from the 525 residential properties, or 2.3 per pollie on average, back in 2017 when the Liberal–National coalition had the majority. Even the Labor Party's federal Housing Minister in 2023, Julie Collins, from Tasmania, declared ownership of three homes in her register of interests.[4]

If the homes owned by federal politicians were valued today at $1 million per dwelling on average, which is a touch above the national 2023 average of $900,000, that's nearly half a billion between them.

There are another 660 elected politicians in our state and territory houses of parliament. Across the 537 local councils there are also around 5600 elected councillors. Altogether, that's roughly 6500 politicians in Australia across all levels, and they are predominantly homeowners and landlords.

If Australia's elected politicians all owned two properties on average, as do federal politicians, with an average dwelling value of $1 million, that's $13 billion in property assets. Making private housing rents and prices 30 per cent cheaper, for example, would wipe off nearly $4 billion in asset value directly from the balance sheets of Australia's elected politicians, as well as massively reducing their investment incomes as landlords. One could also add the property portfolios of families and friends into the mix of personal financial considerations.

What are the chances of 6500 people across various committees, parliaments and councils enacting new laws to wipe billions in value from their own balance sheets? Implausible.

Personal financial incentives extend also to revolving-door financial interests. Former Liberal Party Prime Minister Scott Morrison's first job after graduating from university was in policy research for the property developer lobby group, the Property Council of Australia.[5] Jason Falinski, who chaired that 2022 inquiry into housing affordability, lost the next election and was soon the chairman of a short-term rental management company that helps remote landlords run Airbnb.[6]

A neat example of how a revolving door and a political fake signal can be combined was the creation of a National Housing Supply and Affordability Council, which as the name suggests, signals an intent to make housing cheaper. Susan Lloyd-Hurwitz, the CEO of Mirvac and previously the president of the Property Council of Australia lobby group, was appointed in December 2022 to chair the council and began immediately after she stepped down as Mirvac CEO in March 2023.[7] Mirvac makes its money from property investment, residential development and by being a build-to-rent landlord. Regardless of how socially minded Lloyd-Hurwitz is, are we to believe that she is comfortable wiping billions in value from the company she led for ten years?

The revolving door is wide open when it comes to earning an income from the property industry before or after politics. This is why there is little difference between the major political parties on housing. Both parties face the same electoral and personal financial incentives. Changing housing policy for the benefit of renters and first home buyers is going to require one hell of a political crisis to overcome these incentives.

Our macroeconomy is linked to the five property market equilibria

The last political incentive is macroeconomic. For three decades Australia and its peer nations have used the housing market as a macroeconomic stabilisation tool. We call this property price regulation 'monetary policy' so that it doesn't sound like the housing asset price control that it is. When economic trouble looms, we lower interest rates to boost house prices and generate flow-on effects to other property market equilibria, like the absorption rate.

The Reserve Bank of Australia (RBA) explains how controlling the price of money affects housing in three mains ways. First, 'lower interest rates support asset prices (such as housing and equities) by encouraging demand for assets. One reason for this is because the present discounted value of future income is higher when interest rates are lower.' This is a restatement of the asset price equilibrium.

Second, 'higher asset prices also increase the equity (collateral) of an asset that is available for banks to lend against. This can make it easier for households and businesses to borrow.'

Third, 'an increase in asset prices increases people's wealth. This can lead to higher consumption and housing investment as households generally spend some share of any increase in their wealth.'[8]

This is no secret. It's in the economic textbooks too.

On the flip side, monetary policy can be a built-in restraint; during boom times interest rates are increased to push back against inflation. Higher interest rates eventually bring down house prices, reducing the absorption rate in the process and leading to lower construction, lower household spending and in the process lower inflation. For two years from early 2022, central banks globally increased interest rates, which pushed down housing prices, at least for a time. This came at enormous political cost, with talkback radio filled with mortgaged homeowners complaining.

We saw during the Covid-19 panic of 2020 that, when major economic disruption occurs, economic policies are swiftly directed at rescuing the housing market. Not only were interest rates reduced to their lowest on record; mortgage holidays, superannuation withdrawals, and housing construction and renovation stimulus were promptly enacted. This is why housing prices around the world boomed. We have designed our macroeconomic stabilisation policy as an insurance system for the housing market.

But, speaking broadly, it is true that falling house prices are a macroeconomic risk. This is why the former RBA Assistant Governor Luci Ellis said at Australia's 2022 Housing Supply

Inquiry that 'there are no examples internationally of large falls in nominal housing prices that have occurred other than through a significant reduction in capacity to pay, such as a recession and high unemployment'.

Take note. There are no examples, anywhere in the world, where cheaper prices have been engineered politically. Price declines only happen as an undesirable side effect of declining macroeconomic conditions. This is the final political incentive that cannot be ignored.

Political reality in action

What real choices does even the most community-minded politician have? The political sweet spot is to ensure returns to property owners stay high—through price growth and market rental returns—while pretending to want the exact opposite. Sure, they might intervene in the spatial and density layout of a city but, even then, this often happens in a way that is favourable to well-networked property owners over everyone else. Any politician who acts contrary to these incentives will simply be replaced, either by their party or by the electorate.

It can all get a little weird. My former local councillor in Brisbane, Jonathan Sriranganathan, whom you met earlier because he chose to spatially optimise and live on a houseboat, provided the following transcript of a council meeting on 1 September 2021. It shows his attempts to get the lord mayor, Adrian Schrinner, to put on the record his view about whether he wants higher or lower house prices.

Here it is. Word for word. It could be a script for a political satire, but I promise it is completely real:

Councillor SRIRANGANATHAN: Thanks, Chair. My question is to the Mayor, and it's similar to a question I asked about a year ago, but I wanted to know if the answer had changed at all.

Lord Mayor, there has been a lot of commentary and debate and a little bit of mud-slinging around homelessness and housing affordability policies, but at the end of the day, I think a fundamental and underlying question is, how can we make housing cheaper for people who need it, and whether we want housing in the private sector to get cheaper?

So, I want to be clear that I'm not talking about public housing here. I'm talking specifically about private housing. Would you, Lord Mayor, like to see house prices increase or roughly stay the same or fall and get cheaper? Do you want housing in this city to get cheaper?

Chair: LORD MAYOR.

LORD MAYOR: Thank you for the question, Councillor SRI. Well, when it comes to the issue of affordability, we know that it's not the house price alone which makes something affordable or not, it's people's ability to actually get into the properties based on factors such as the availability of supply. The houses may or may not be affordable, but if there's nothing available, you won't be able to get into it. It also depends on incomes and how incomes have changed over time. It depends on a whole range of things. So, the house price alone is not the only factor when it comes to affordability.

So, I have talked previously on this issue, as Councillor SRI has, and it's important to remember that, for many people in Brisbane who currently either own a home or have a mortgage, their house is their number one investment. It's their biggest investment that they'll ever make in their life. So, when Councillor SRI or someone like Councillor SRI in the Greens suggests that houses should get cheaper, what they are saying is that they are quite happy—

Councillor SRIRANGANATHAN: Point of order, Chair.

Chair: Point of order to you, Councillor SRIRANGANATHAN.

Councillor SRIRANGANATHAN: Thanks.

Chair: My apologies for that, earlier.

Councillor SRIRANGANATHAN: You're all right. Just, the question was pretty straightforward. Does the Mayor want to see house prices get cheaper? I'm wondering if the Mayor can give a direct answer to the question.

Chair: The point of order is about relevance, LORD MAYOR, to the question.

LORD MAYOR: So, as I was very clearly explaining, this is not a question that comes onto the issue of house prices only, but we must bear in mind that this is what we're talking about for many people in Brisbane, their number one investment.

It is the biggest thing they'll ever own, the most important thing they'll ever own, and I wouldn't wish on anyone that someone's investment would decrease in value. I wouldn't wish that on anyone. Now, we know that investments do rise and fall, and whether it is a house or whether it is some kind of other investment, that they are subject to ups and downs, they are subject to market forces, but I wouldn't wish onto anyone that their investment—

Councillor SRIRANGANATHAN: Point of order, Chair.

Chair: Point of order, Councillor SRIRANGANATHAN.

LORD MAYOR:—would decline in value.

Councillor SRIRANGANATHAN: He's really dancing around the question here. Does he want house prices to increase or stay the same or get cheaper? It's a very simple question.

Chair: I believe the LORD—

Councillor SRIRANGANATHAN: What does he want as the Mayor of the city?

Chair: I believe the LORD MAYOR is being relevant to the question.

LORD MAYOR: I'm simply pointing out that house prices alone do not equal housing affordability—

Councillor interjecting.

LORD MAYOR:—Councillor SRI wants to simplify this as some kind of binary choice between one option or another or another, and I have heard him in the past rail against binary choices. Have you not, Councillor MURPHY?

Councillor interjecting.

LORD MAYOR: He doesn't like binary choices because things are complicated. Things are complicated and this is a complicated issue. I was simply pointing out that I would not like Brisbane residents to see their major investment or asset decline in value because I wouldn't wish that on anyone. I wouldn't wish that on anyone, but we know that one of the ingredients in housing affordability is housing supply.

Councillor interjecting.

LORD MAYOR: That's where we have an important role to support housing supply and growth in—

Councillor SRIRANGANATHAN: Point of order, Chair.

Chair: Point of order to you, Councillor SRIRANGANATHAN.

Councillor SRIRANGANATHAN: This is a wonderful essay, but I deliberately asked a very specific question, and the Mayor can talk about supply if he wants, but at the end of the day, the point of increasing supply is, I presume, to make housing cheaper.

So, I want a direct answer to the question, does the Mayor want housing to get cheaper?

Chair: Councillor, the nub of the question is about housing affordability. The LORD MAYOR is answering that question.

LORD MAYOR: So, to answer the question, to answer the question very simply, I want to see housing affordability improve, not reduce. I want to see housing affordability improve, not decrease, but by the same token, house prices are not the only factor in housing affordability.

So, don't try and simplify it into that simple thing about whether I want to see house prices decrease or not. I don't want to see people's major investment decrease in value. I don't want to, but I do want to see housing affordability increase and improve. The way that we can have a role in doing that is by making sure that there is appropriate supply for a growing city. I think that's a very reasonable response.

Councillor interjecting.

LORD MAYOR: It may not be a response that impresses an anarchist. It may not be a response that impresses the Greens, but we know that they offer fake solutions to very complex problems— even Terri Butler made that point just recently. They offer fake solutions, simple, easy to digest things where—guess what, everyone—everything can be free.

Everything can be free. We'll build millions of houses across the country. We don't know who will pay for it, but it's all free. This is a utopia that doesn't exist.

Councillor SRIRANGANATHAN: Point of order, Chair.

LORD MAYOR: This is—

Chair: Point of order to you, Councillor SRIRANGANATHAN.

Councillor SRIRANGANATHAN: Look, I've been so patient. I've heard the Mayor's long and detailed preamble explanation, but I want him on the record very clearly saying whether he wants houses to get cheaper or not. If he's not—if he's too scared to say that clearly, he should just say that, but does he want house prices to stay the same or get cheaper?

Chair: Thank you, Councillor. You're now debating your point of order and—

Councillor interjecting.

Chair:—LORD MAYOR, you have a few seconds to respond.

LORD MAYOR: I have answered this question, and he may—

Councillor interjecting.

LORD MAYOR:—he may not like the answer, but I've answered the question in very much detail and with accuracy, and so—

Chair: Thank you, LORD MAYOR. Your time has expired. Further questions?[9]

In 2022, after housing asset prices in Australia leapt 30 per cent in the previous year, I spoke on the phone with a prominent politician about a policy idea to copy Singapore's public homeownership system (more on this idea in Chapter 24). Their response was to ask 'Where is the market failure?' They thought that the rising asset prices at the time were good, since it was the intended effect of monetary policy, and that rental markets were functioning as normal, rising with incomes. I asked: 'Are you not interested in improving on the market outcome, like we did with schooling and hospitals, with a public system available to all?'

The short answer was no. If it involved government action to change the market outcome, then it was a no-go. I couldn't have been more disappointed when I hung up the phone. I realised that no one really wants Australians to have cheap housing; I was being tricked by fake signals.

I should have known. In 2016 I spoke with a ministerial staffer in the Australian Capital Territory (ACT) about housing policy. I had recently learned that the ACT government owned all the undeveloped land in the city and was selling new housing lots at market prices to raise revenue, but then running a parallel subsidised 'land rent scheme'. I asked why they created a convoluted scheme rather than just sell the housing lots at the price they thought was fair to residents who don't already own homes.

I'll paraphrase their response: 'We don't want to devalue people's homes.'

It was a remarkably frank comment that I never deeply accepted until that phone call years later. But it is the key to why the housing debate has been hijacked and the reason I felt the need to write this book.

The ACT example also shows how the symmetry of property markets is a political ball-and-chain, stopping change. New home buyers there get upset when the public land developer makes a lot of money from development projects, as they feel they are being ripped off by high prices. But existing homeowners also don't want the government to sell new homes cheaply and reduce the market value of their own home.

Bringing a housing policy debate back on course means being much more honest about these political incentives. But it remains a puzzle why academics and policy wonks are so averse to pointing it out, and why journalists often prefer not to cover this conflict.

9 ✦ Academics and policy wonks

Thousands of work-hours and millions of dollars worth of salaries and consultants' fees have been spent on these reports and absolutely nothing has come from them.

—Leith van Onselen, Chief Economist at MacroBusiness, makes the point more reports and research doesn't make housing cheaper[1]

It is not hard to understand why politicians prefer not to crush the value of their property investments and the value of homes in their electorates.

We are all grown-ups, and we understand political trade-offs.

But surely the researchers, the frank and fearless public servants, and the various not-for-profit housing agencies and homelessness organisations have been pushing back against this politics, facing up to the symmetry of property markets and putting forward real solutions, not fake ones, so that all Australians can be housed cheaply and comfortably?

We can only hope.

Policy wonks of all stripes succumb to the incentive to ticket-clip. It is no surprise that property owners tell stories, even lies, to ensure that policy change works in their favour. But the transformation of these stories into acceptable political discourse is a process that needs to be investigated.

The hijacking of housing research comes from two incentives. First is the direct influence of property owners, their own researchers and funding of research organisations. Second, it has become the business of these groups—academics, housing and homelessness organisations, think tanks and public servants—to sell housing problems and their analyses of it, not solutions.

It was funny and obvious when a Goldman Sachs analyst in 2018 asked a fundamental question about the future of the biotech sector: 'Is curing patients a sustainable business model?'[2] This problem plagues the health and medical sectors of the economy because cheap and effective cures are less profitable than slow, ineffective and expensive treatments. It's all about creating demand for your product, not destroying demand.

So it is with housing. The business opportunities it creates are the consultancies, the board positions at not-for-profits, the academic jobs with the status that comes from travelling the world to talk about your unique insight into why the housing market has some new and previously unforeseen problem. Solving housing puts you out of a job.

The worst part of it all is that, when real effective change is proposed, those who are meant to be the adults in the room often end up pushing back hardest. It's just like when a pharmaceutical company pushes hard against a new competitor with a cheap and more effective treatment that will destroy the incumbent's business. But it is far less obvious to outsiders.

_____

In 2017 I co-wrote a book about grey corruption and political favouritism in Australia called *Rigged: How networks of powerful mates rip off everyday Australians*. About six months after it was first published, I received a phone call that went something like this.

'Hi, is this Cameron Murray?'

'Yes it is.'

'You don't know me. My name is Kate.'[3]

'Hi Kate, what can I do for you?'

'I've read your book and I think I have another interesting case study for you. I've been working at a homeless charity for the past year. When I first started, it really seemed like everyone was working hard to make a difference. The CEO does the annual sleep-out to raise awareness of the homelessness crisis. We give people food and wash their clothes. But what I've noticed is that, when real solutions are proposed, with real money attached, the leaders of the organisation start finding holes in these programs and eventually do not support them. It's like they don't want to solve homelessness because it will mean the organisation might no longer be needed and they will lose their high-status job.

'This realisation has really shaken me. After reading your book, I figured you would be someone who would understand what I'm saying. It is so disheartening to realise that the whole organisation is mostly about appearing to care rather than achieving results for homeless people.'

I didn't really know how to respond. I did my best. The conversation shook me.

Here we were, facing the blunt reality that the product of the homelessness industry is the research activity, the conferences, the glossy strategy documents and the job status that comes along with it. The product is not solving homelessness, because without it the industry would cease to exist.

Property owners and their research funding

Academia should be insulated to some degree from these incentives. But it's not. Consider the case of the Ralph & Goldy Lewis Center for Regional Policy Studies at University of California Los Angeles (UCLA). It produces reams of research about what policies might improve housing market outcomes, influencing Australian researchers and others around the world.

The research produced by this group always puzzled me.

While digging into its research in more depth, I discovered that it is funded by a major property developer. It all fell into place. This group is an example of powerful economic interests covertly influencing academic and policy debate.

The Lewis Group of companies founded the centre in 1989. In 2019 the Lewis Center launched its 'Randall Lewis Housing Initiative', named after Randall Lewis, the senior executive vice president for marketing for the Lewis Group of Companies, one of the biggest housing developers in the United States. The Lewis Group reports having a land bank of more than 50,000 detached homes and 16,500 apartments, meaning that, on property it already owns, the group can build 66,500 new dwellings any time it wants. The Lewis Group's land bank is more extensive than the holdings of most of Australia's large publicly listed property developers like Lendlease, Stockland, Mirvac and Peet.

In a 2014 article, Randall Lewis explained how his company takes the financially sensible approach (for them) of land-banking and adjusting rates of new housing development to meet the absorption rate equilibrium. Out of the group's 16,500 feasible new apartments, it plans to only build 500 per year over the next decade, which is just 3 per cent per year.[4]

There is no way that a property owner with a balance sheet in the billions has a financial interest in policies that bring down the value of property assets, or that increase property-related taxes, or that force him or her to develop faster than the absorption equilibrium. The Lewis Group is also a landlord with 11,000 units, so it won't support policies that reduce rents to benefit tenants.

Like property lobbyists in Australia, research from UCLA's Lewis Center is focused on deregulating town planning—what I call the supply myth, and discuss in Chapter 18. Having a research group housed at a university gives credibility to the Lewis Group's research; coincidentally, its research is always beneficial for its property-owner funders.

Soft political influence

I am not claiming that all academic research is manipulated by property industry funding and donations. Influence can be softer and political incentives can seep into the wonk realm in other ways.

For example, the Australian Housing and Urban Research Institute (AHURI) is a federally funded agency that each year provides millions in grant money to academics to conduct housing research. To apply, academics must spend a huge amount of time crafting a research proposal that fits with the agency's Research Agenda for that year. Where exactly does this agenda come from? It comes from meeting with key political stakeholders across government and the property industry—the very groups with an incentive not to make homes cheaper. In many cases academics are inadvertently dedicating their time to politically suitable research topics because of the financial incentives.

This is a good career move. You get the money, which helps with your academic status. You get the citations, because in future years the same topics come up again. But the system can't change anything. There is nothing radical here. It is research as the handmaiden of political convenience.

———

Influence creeps in via government agencies and their own research. The National Housing Supply Council (NHSC), for example, was an Australian agency created at the peak of the 2000s housing price boom. Its agenda was to establish why there weren't enough houses being built and to promote research on that question. The agency, like so many others, had no actual power to acquire property, build houses or spend money. What it did was promote fear about a lack of supply and support a research community focused on this question, which fitted nicely the interests of property owners, who would happily accept zoning and planning decisions that added value to their property rights.

At the time the NHSC was established, the market was at its peak. For a decade afterwards, rents and prices were flat or falling across most cities, and the research council was abandoned in 2013. In fact, all its forecasts of impending supply shortages were wrong. Looking back at their ten-year forecasts, dating from 2008, we can now see that the lived reality was that new housing was built at a pace that exceeded even the NHSC's highest forecast need, while new demand from extra people didn't even reach their medium-level forecast. Yet in 2023, this type of organisation was being rehashed in the form of the National Housing Supply and Affordability Council.

Research traps

One of the traps for housing research is to take seriously the fake stories peddled by property lobbyists and politicians. Rather than push back directly, the research game is about finding ever-more-niche concerns that have little to do with the fundamental questions of the rent and price of homes. This is unhelpful. Add to this the fact that rewards flow from academic publications and citations, impressing other researchers can become a focus. Quirky new insights and analysis can descend into obscurantism. As an example, here are a few lines from a widely regarded recent academic paper on the value of urban areas.[5] See if you can decipher it.

> The urban process encompasses vast structures and practices engaged in creating, extracting, and accumulating value in and from the urban landscape. But what is value and how does it attain its coercive power over urban life? The unreflective deployment of axiomatic assumptions regarding the source and substance of value constitutes a form of

magical thinking conjuring something out of nothing and transforming an immaterial abstraction into a material force that is real in its consequences. Unpacking the concept of value reveals a contentious debate regarding the ontological status of value as a driver of the urban process. Alternative formulations posit value as intrinsic or extrinsic, objective or subjective, residing in the world or constructed in the mind, driven by universal law or spatially and temporally contingent. Transcending all such dualisms, a transactional approach drawn from Deweyan pragmatism understands value as a co-constitutive interrelation among a valuing subject, an object of valuation, and the enveloping context in which valuation occurs. The delineation of value's ontology is fraught with political consequences for reproducing or altering the urban status quo. The move toward desired outcomes begins with articulating the foundational assumptions that underlie the value practices propelling the urban process in specific situations. Pluralizing value assumptions focuses the problem on the political question concerning whose value(s) prevail in a given situation. This redefinition shifts the focus from ameliorating current practices of extracting value to politically contesting the value commitments at work in the world.

Sometimes the abstract world of academia takes leave from reality. Perhaps there is an insight here. But in terms of concrete economics of housing, you would learn little from reading even thousands of such articles.

New housing interest groups

Recent decades have seen the rise of community housing providers, which are a privatised version of public housing that rely on subsidies to offer below-market rental housing, usually at a minimum of 20 per cent below market rent. Community housing providers build and own a stock of housing. But they rely on a stream of public subsidies to offer below-market-price rentals to tenants. They have an incentive to support 'affordable' non-market housing policies that benefit them, rather than compete with them or make their organisations redundant, and hence they too have fostered a research agenda. Despite the often good work they do, community housing providers are also property owners who face a financial risk of ruin if property rents and prices fall substantially.

Because of these interests, it is difficult now to avoid the new language of 'social and affordable' housing, a catch-all term designed to encompass both community housing providers and traditional public housing that charges rent based on residents' incomes. This further muddies policy debate and analysis. Even after a decade in this field, it is still not clear to me what these terms mean and how to compare these various kinds of assistance. Is one year of a single dwelling, renting to a tenant at 20 per cent below the market rent, equal to one 'social housing dwelling'? Sometimes one affordable home means one dwelling at 20 per cent below local market rent for one year. At other times it is one dwelling at 25 per cent of income for ten years. Outsiders have little chance of understanding what will be delivered by various housing subsidies when it comes to dwelling counts, and there is little incentive to talk straight about it.

Just as outsourcing a retirement income system to the super-annuation sector creates an industry that soaks up over $30 billion in fees per year and has a huge incentive to influence academics and policy researchers to find ways to support it, community housing providers have an incentive to foster research that suits their business model, even if there are cheaper alternatives.

———

In 2019 I spoke at an event about housing hosted by the local Greens political party. At the time I had started looking in more detail at different non-market housing systems from around the world. I told the audience: 'We know we can solve our housing problems because Singapore is a real country. Why aren't we copying something that we have seen work elsewhere?'

At lunch, a lady walked up to me and said 'I'm from Singapore. It's funny that you mentioned housing there. I'm a social worker dealing with homelessness. I had to come to Australia because we don't have homeless people in Singapore. It is so weird the way you do things here.'

Amazing. Although I have paraphrased her words here, this is not an exaggeration.

In 2022, National University of Singapore Professor Chua Beng Huat spoke on a podcast hosted by the UCLA research group mentioned earlier. His response to the question 'Is there a homeless population in Singapore?' shocked the interviewers: 'No. Homelessness is not a problem because the government gives them homes at very low cost.'[6]

You could almost hear a pin drop. It was so radical for this research group—one that had spent years thinking of every conceivable policy tweak—to face the reality that a nation solved homelessness by giving people homes and requiring people reside in them. But that's too simple, and there would be few rewards from writing an academic paper titled 'People without homes would have homes if they were given homes'.

10 ◆ Muddled media

If we eliminated all the BS and stuck to the facts, most of the so-called property experts would be out of a job.

—One of my X/Twitter followers (StreetNewsAU) accurately summarising how the media reports housing market analysis, 5 June 2023[1]

The incentives faced by journalists and the media are different from those for academics, think tanks and public agencies. Like academics, these journalists need clicks—in their case, on their websites rather than through citations of their academic papers. They need talking heads and quotes that grab your attention.

Building up a coherent picture of how the world operates plays no part in their incentive structure. It's 'he said, she said'. Outrage. Click. Read, or watch, this ad.

There are the usual suspects who capitalise on the interest in property and housing investment as a cultural obsession. Some are useful when they report new data. Most are terrible and rely on stories from very unrepresentative households at the extremes, whether it's the struggling renter or the investor with ten properties. Or the classic 'I scrimped and saved and bought a house young so you can too', where you wait until the last paragraph to find out that this young couple's parents mostly paid for it. My favourite 2023 headline was 'Meet the 37-year-old who bought a $20.5 million house with no mortgage'.[2] You want to know who this is, and to find out you must click. It's genius.

Another fun one is when the media finds a nurse or truck driver to be the face of the landlord lobby, when the most common profession for landlords is medical specialist. Sure, 10 per cent of truck drivers are landlords but more than 40 per cent of anaesthetists are landlords; I've never seen an anaesthetist on the television talking about housing. The top five professions most likely to be landlords are all medical specialists. Surgeons, anaesthetists, dentists, psychiatrists. You get the picture.[3]

Sure, there are working-class landlords. But does anyone really think that older professionals being the tenants of young nurses and truck driver investors is a representative picture of reality? The proportion of people who are landlords rises in line with income. Landlordism is a proxy for income.

These media distortions are fine as far as they go. We live in a country where housing is not just a place where you live, but a cultural status symbol and a financial investment as well. The media is mostly putting up a mirror to our broader culture.

For example, in 2022 the editor of Queensland's biggest newspaper wrote a warning: 'The state government should shudder at the prospect of finding itself at war with both property developers and property investors—particularly in a housing crisis.'[4] It seems outrageous for a newspaper to take a political stance like this. But if we are honest, they are mostly reflecting the views and values of their readers.

In addition to mirroring the broader views on housing and property, there are specific incentives in the media that allow housing debates to be easily hijacked. First is the incentive to cover extreme situations without context, whether rents or prices are rising or falling. Second are the incentives of advertisers, of which the property industry is a large part. And third, there are plain old incentives to take the easy route and publish media releases of property lobbyists with little effort at balance or calling out the obvious financial conflicts behind their policy positions.

A case of missing context

An experience I had in October 2021 showed exactly how facts, evidence and context lose out because the media has incentives to tell attention-grabbing stories that mirror the fears and hopes of their audience. Australian housing asset prices were booming, just as they were doing globally due to the low interest rate monetary policy that was enacted during the 2020–2022 Covid years. Australia had recorded a 24 per cent average home price increase in the previous twelve months, with prices in regional areas rising much more. Eighteen months earlier, Australian banks had predicted price declines of 20 per cent to 30 per cent. It was a boom I had been nearly alone in predicting. The way reality completely blindsided many experts made this boom an intriguing one.

Australia's premier investigative news program, *Four Corners*, produced a feature on the housing market in November 2021 entitled 'Going, going, gone'. Veteran journalist Stephen Long contacted me for the program. In our first phone conversation I told him that mortgage data was showing that first home buying was at record highs. According to mortgage lending data, there were more than 171,000 first home buyers in the 2020–21 financial year, compared to 92,000 per year over the five-year 2015–19 period. We had just seen an astronomical 86 per cent jump in first home buying.

Unfortunately, the story was meant to be about home-ownership getting further out of reach. Rapidly rising prices might intuitively lead you to this conclusion, but the data was showing the exact opposite. It was first home buyer demand itself that was partly causing the rising prices. After all, renting money from a bank to become a homeowner had become cheaper than renting a home from a landlord for the first time in decades.

In fact, for three years there had been a decline in investor borrowing, allowing me to predict that landlords were on balance selling to first home buyers, increasing the overall home-ownership rate. A national census in August 2021 confirmed that the homeownership rate has bounced a touch from 65.4 per cent to 66.0 per cent since 2016. In other words, the number of Australian households that had become homeowners was now 60,000 more than if the rate had stayed flat.

I spoke on camera to *Four Corners* for nearly an hour, discussing the details of the market, the big trends in the data, the macroeconomic context and outlining various policy options if we wanted a different housing outcome.

In the end, the program told the story its producers had wanted to tell from the start about the challenges facing first home buyers. While the program was airing, I tweeted about how I hoped the program would provide some context and policy discussion: 'I really hope we don't get to the end of this

4Corners episode without noting that rapidly growing housing asset prices are 1. global, and 2. the intended effect of low interest rate monetary policy.' Alas, the show predominantly featured flashy real estate agents driving their convertible sports cars through Australia's most expensive suburbs.

To my surprise, I received a long text message from the journalist Stephen Long, who thought my tweet had been 'incredibly harsh' and that 'it's easy for academics who don't have the duration constraints someone working in my medium faces to criticise'.

My response concluded as follows: 'The way I see it, the story was about rising home prices and first home buying. It was quite a surprise to see so much precious time showing real estate agents in the country's most expensive suburbs, or second home buyers in Noosa, etc. For example, Earlwood prices are double the national average. The suburb has also only recovered its recent price decline to be back where it was in 2017. There were 171,000 first home buyers last year, a record high (compared to 99,000 in 2019). Where did they buy and why now? Yet there were 5 real estate agents and 2 buyers agents all making the same point the prices are rising.'[5]

Long explained that the production brief overrode his preference for more context and depth. Judging by the range of knowledgeable housing analysts that he interviewed, the program could have easily been crafted this way. Instead, it included an astonishing seven real estate agents all conveying the idea that prices were at record highs, and that first home buyers were missing out, neither of which was true, but neither of which was expressly stated. The important context that first home buying was at record highs didn't make the cut, nor did the fact that buying was cheaper than renting in most Australian suburbs.

An honest alternative version of the program could have conveyed that prices were still at 2017 levels, mortgages were historically cheap because of monetary policy, which itself is designed to increase property prices, and there were record numbers of first home buyers across the country, reversing previous declines in homeownership among younger households. In fact, the data shows that homeownership by households aged 24–45 caught up to the homeownership levels of earlier generations at those ages during this exact period.

Every single example in this program presented a shocking fact, but without the context that made it much less shocking. I want to dissect them here because it really shows the incentives within the media to avoid context and pick the most extreme examples to attract attention, even in serious news programs. It's what the audience wants.

The first example was from Earlwood, in Sydney, where it was announced that the median value for a detached home had gone from $1.1 million to $1.8 million since 2019. But it is also true that from 2017 to 2019, housing prices fell nearly 30 per cent in Earlwood. According to SQM Research data[6], houses in Earlwood in late 2022 had only just regained their 2017 levels. Without that context, the sudden price growth looks shocking. With the context of recent declines, and lower mortgage interest rates for all new buyers, there isn't really a story.

To really drive the point home, mortgage interest rates in 2016 were about 5.5 per cent, but just 2.5 per cent for new borrowers in 2021. The cost of renting money to buy that Earlwood house had dropped 55 per cent in five years! No wonder there were buyers swarming houses—not just there, but in suburbs like Earlwood in cities around the globe.[7]

The next segment focused on a 29-year-old single nurse caring for a disabled mother living in social housing—one of the least likely households to ever become a home buyer. To me, the bigger issue here was that for some reason the social housing dwelling they occupied was perceived as insecure and unsatisfactory.

Then we went to Coorparoo, a suburb in Brisbane. Prices in Coorparoo in 2019 were the same as they were in 2009—a decade of no nominal growth. The sharp jump during 2021 might seem quite large, but again, a longer-term context matters.

Then it was on to Melbourne, where '19% price growth in the past year' flashed up on the screen, and we visited an online auction to show how hot the market was. When I looked up the sales history of the property being auctioned, which sold for an astonishing $1.79 million, I discovered that the last sale had been in 2013 at a $1.4 million price—so it had only increased in value by 3 per cent per year over eight years. Again, with a slightly longer context, the story looks very different. The ferocious bidding was the main hook for the audience, but this is just what coming out of a slump and into a boom looks like.

Then off to Bondi, one of the most expensive suburbs in the country, with a median house price above $3 million at this time. Here the people being interviewed were 'Looking for an average house and spending up to $3 million'.

Sure, the house was average. But the location was not. This was three times the Sydney average, and four to five times above the average of other capital cities. Presenting these places and these people as representative of the housing market is like presenting a household with an annual income of $350,000 to $1 million and saying 'Look at the troubles these average Aussies are having buying a home.'

Momentarily, we got some context in this *Four Corners* program: a newspaper from August 1963 with the headline 'Why can't young couples buy homes?' Back then, the problem of home-buying was the difficulty in getting a mortgage, because of high deposit requirements of around 30 per cent of the purchase price. Yet nothing further was made of this.

Then we had a 28-year-old looking for a one-bedroom unit in inner Sydney. The program claimed, 'she's still going to have to borrow so much'. Yet in the footage shown, she scrolled her online search results for one-bedroom units in Ultimo and a price of $209,000 flashed across the screen. A reasonable price by any standard. With mortgage interest rates of less than 3 per cent, even if she borrowed 100 per cent of the price, that would have been about $6000 per year in interest, or about $120 per week, which was far lower than the cost of renting. Even at an interest rate of 5 per cent, it is $10,000 of interest every year. Include the body corporate fees and insurances and it is hard to see how that is more expensive than renting the same apartment.

Oh, and one-bedroom units in Ultimo were cheaper in 2022 than they were in 2010, which is context that would have changed the story dramatically.

In the next scene is a buyer scrolling advertised apartments in Ashfield, postcode 2131. You'll never guess. Apartment prices in Ashfield were the same in 2021 as they were in 2015.

Then lastly, off to Noosa, the most expensive and unrepresentative part of Queensland's Sunshine Coast, where a middle-aged executive couple downsizing from Sydney found a house no problem and said 'It's been really great, really good financially. We managed to reduce our mortgage significantly by taking the sale price from our house in Sydney and converting that up here, where your money goes a long way.'

Cut.

Property advertising and media incentives

In Australia, an estimated $1.5 billion per year is spent on real estate advertising, which is about a third of all media advertising revenue.[8] In the United States, real estate media advertising is about US$27 billion.

There is also property-related advertising, such as from hardware chain Bunnings and other businesses that rely on our real estate obsession. The reality television show, *The Block*, is simply an extension of this. Contestants undertake house renovations using their free labour and discounted materials from sponsors and advertisers. The winning contestant makes a 'profit' by selling for more than their costs. It mixes advertising with the drama and extremes of housing that the media, and its viewers, find irresistible.

For advertisers, it really doesn't matter whether the housing market is a boom or bust, as long as people who are interested in property click and read. This means that building up a coherent picture of reality from media reporting is near impossible.

In 2022, for example, there were pages of news articles with headlines like 'Rude rental shock for Irish expat living in Sydney'.[9] It baffles me how an Irishwoman's day-to-day efforts to find a rental home becomes a news story. But when I clicked, I saw advertisements for home solar, appliances, new cars and financial advice. When renters who have been actively searching for housing clicked that article, they were likely shown even more targeted property advertisements.

To show how little it matters which direction the housing wind is blowing, in 2016 there were headlines such as 'Good news for everyone locked out of the housing market: Rents are going down' and in 2018 it was 'Rents are falling: Fiona's new home is bigger, better and cheaper'.[10]

In 2019 there was a headline having it both ways: 'The Sydney suburbs where rents are rising and falling the most'.[11] Here's the first paragraph: 'Sydney tenants are haggling over rents or leaving for newer properties as the city's building boom continues to reduce rents with suburbs recording declines of up to 25 per cent in the past year, new figures show.'

Then, just a few years later it was 'Expert says there's no end in sight for Australia's rental crisis'.[12] But the relevant context here is that, for the average Sydney renter, they were at the time paying a lower rent in mid-2022 than they were in 2017 and prices listed in rental advertisements had grown just 12 per cent in five years. It was like those previous headlines were forgotten. Not once will you even learn that to recover from a 25 per cent decline, prices need to rise 33 per cent. Context ruins the story and that means fewer clicks.

Lobbyists make media easy

As we have seen, property owners have an economic motive to ensure that public debates are conducted on their terms. They know that one way to get their views amplified by the media is with a prized 'exclusive' story.

For example, a minor change to rental laws was enacted in Queensland in 2023 that limited the number of times rents could be increased each year, from twice to once. The landlord lobby planted 'exclusive' stories about renters being kicked out of their homes even prior to the law taking effect to demonstrate how it had backfired. A minor policy change was transformed into a news story about how rental protections are actually bad for renters, not good for them.[13]

It seems there is no way to stop media outfits providing this lazy gift of free publicity to vested interests. The story that if you tax a landlord they will sell and that will create a housing shortage and higher rents is obviously wrong. But it was part of the lobbying at Australia's first inquiry into rents in 1911 and it remains a story well ventilated today in the press. Yet not one journalist seems to be able to ask these lobbyists who these landlords will sell to? Selling a home is swapping a name on a property title. It's not demolishing a house. But pushing back means another outlet will run the story and, as we know, stories about property get clicks.

The trick to more accurate and contextual media coverage means using these same incentives. Renter interest groups can drop exclusive stories that make extreme claims and ignore context if it helps get clicks. Sure, these stories may not be accurate either. But the current hijacked housing coverage won't change by itself. One emerging group is playing this media game well. The YIMBYs.

11 ◆ YIMBY yammer

*Everyone has been or will be a NIMBY at least once in
their lifetime over some planning/development issue.*

—An insight on the emotional reality of local
development politics from Associate Professor
Paul Maginn on X/Twitter, 6 June 2022

A bizarre cultural shift changed Australia's housing policy debate
in the early 2020s. It came as a cultural import from California,
exported via social media, and comes with American over-the-
top religious fervour for a cause.

That cause is YIMBYism.

In response to the traditional 'not in my backyard' NIMBYs—
local groups that form to oppose rapid densification and change
in their neighbourhoods—a new type of political campaign was
created. Taking a simple supply-and-demand story of housing
rents and prices to its logical conclusion, the 'yes in my backyard'
YIMBY position is that local political opposition to certain
types of new housing is the primary cause of 'unaffordable' rents
and prices.

Of course, the reality is that YIMBYs also want new housing
on property owned by others; they only differ from NIMBYs

in their preference for its location—nearby, or a little further from them—and its density. They are known to smugly explain how their 'one neat trick' sidesteps the symmetry of property markets and that, if we remove regulations, property owners will voluntarily build homes faster, ignoring the absorption rate equilibrium.

As a cultural force, the YIMBY business is selling status signals. Even when zoning and planning regulations change, it is never enough. While it is great that more people are taking an interest in planning regulations and how cities evolve, the cultural shift is a little puzzling and I think reflects how off-course the hijacked housing policy debate has gone.

A new cultural dimension to the housing debate

A 2017 article in *The Guardian* called San Francisco YIMBYs 'angry millennials': 'Fierce is a leader of one of a series of new groups that have sprouted up in cities from Seattle to Sydney, Austin to Oxford, lobbying not against development but for it. They say their lives are threatened by housing shortages and skyrocketing rental prices. Calling themselves yimbys, they are standing up to say "Yes, in my back yard" to any kind of new housing development.'[1]

The clearest evidence that YIMBY is a cultural movement without a solid grounding in the economics of housing is that it focuses exclusively on expensive suburbs, often those with cultural cachet where young people once congregated—near universities and hipster cafes—and which are now being priced more highly because of their attractiveness to older, wealthier, households. As a movement, it has entirely skipped over working-class suburbs.

Since new housing should affect rents and prices, regardless of where it is built, it is strange that the YIMBY movement is so focused on certain high-status suburbs. Perhaps there is a class of people who can no longer afford the lifestyle and location they hoped for. They prefer the easy story that the fault lies with planning regulations rather than with the collective decisions of property owners and with overall income and wealth inequality.

I see this new YIMBY cultural dimension to housing debates as an unfortunate distraction for several reasons.

First, it has no good evidence in its favour. I don't disagree that planning rules can be simplified and that, over time, higher densities are desirable in key areas of our cities, simply on the grounds of efficient urban design. But, as we have seen with the five property market equilibria that arise in any monopoly property system, YIMBYs misdiagnose the problem. The problems of high housing rents and prices existed for centuries before planning and zoning; in fact, the reason modern planning regulations exist is because of the squalor of private unregulated housing.

Don't forget there were more bigger and better dwellings per capita in 2023 than at any time in human history. There are the fewest people, living in the largest dwellings in the history of humankind. Yet YIMBYs don't see this as a great success. When Sydney had record apartment construction in the mid-2010s, with rents falling for three years prior to the 2020 Covid-19 shock, YIMBYs would not credit the planning system for this, despite blaming the planning system in 2023 for a small decline in new homebuilding.

Second, some of the objectives of the YIMBY movement—such as infill housing, more public transit options, and densification around transit—are desirable from an urban efficiency perspective but they require careful planning and regulatory intervention.

Some years back I worked in the Queensland state government, assessing and approving the calculations councils were required to make to estimate the infrastructure costs of their forecast growth. I learned here that there are efficiency gains from incremental infill—splitting one large housing lot into two, adding granny flats, and the like—since they effectively required no new public infrastructure investment to accommodate them. The roads, sewers, parks and other services that already were built could accommodate small additions in use without much detriment to others.

It was the major densification changes that required costly upgrades of public infrastructure in already built-up areas. This is why these major densification projects were typically planned for former industrial sites and other places where these major works could be done more cheaply—an efficient and successful strategy many cities have adopted.

In both these cases, ensuring private housing investment and public works are built in tandem to support each other requires a degree of planning and coordination. That's what the planning system is primarily for, in my view. To my mind, these are important urban design and city growth issues. Simply shouting YIMBY isn't going to help coordinate new public works with market-driven new housing. What the YIMBYs desire from an urban design perspective requires planning regulations.

Third, the rise of the YIMBY culture frames housing rents and prices as primarily being about planning and zoning regulation, not about the property monopoly and the five equilibria.

It relies on the false assumption that property owners have an interest in lower prices, not higher prices.

Think about it this way. If one individual owned all the property in a suburb, they would be a local monopolist. Would YIMBYs see this monopoly behaviour and think 'You know what? We should give this monopolist some more property rights to build higher density for free'? I think not. Just like giving the DeBeers diamond monopoly a tax break won't make them sell diamonds more cheaply, up-zoning owners in the property monopoly won't either.

Fourth, the YIMBY movement is rife with many contradictory views. A fundamental premise of the movement is that there are too few homes for the number of people. But, almost without fail, YIMBYs also support open borders policies to radically increase the population through immigration. On the one hand, they advocate the simple solution of building more housing per capita; yet at the same time, they seek to make this outcome more difficult with feverish support of open borders immigration policy.

Another contradiction is that, when it comes to roads, for example, YIMBYs often argue that you can't build your way out of traffic congestion.[2] They see the equilibrium effect of more roads as lowering the price of driving and inducing more driving; they don't see that this arises in the housing market. Yet, as we saw in the rental and spatial equilibria, these are very real economic forces at play in housing too.

The YIMBYs have further hijacked housing debates by introducing terms such as 'housing abundance' and 'legalise housing', confusing debates rather than clarifying them.

Lastly, YIMBY culture frames the problem of high housing rents and prices as a *good-versus-evil* debate between NIMBYs and YIMBYs. It might make a good superhero movie, but it isn't telling an accurate story. The symmetry of property markets is real, with a conflict between property owners and non-owners, but I wouldn't call either side evil. As one commentator put it, the logical conclusion of the YIMBY movement is 'community input is bad, actually'[3]—a position we might associate more with a villain than a superhero.

YIMBY hypocrisy

Underneath the social signalling and cultural debate, everyone is a NIMBY; we just have different tastes and preferences. YIMBYs don't want new highways through the suburbs, and they hate new car parks. They are NIMBYs when it involves things they don't like. Often the two groups are indistinguishable, even on housing.

Harvard pro-density urban economist Ed Glaeser, for example, is a vocal critic of planning regulations and a key intellectual force behind the YIMBY movement. He lives on a 6.5-acre (2.6-ha) plot of land in Weston, Massachusetts. This suburb, on the outskirts of Boston, has not one, but three, massive golf courses, which are a symbolic 'enemy' of the YIMBY movement because they use land inefficiently. Although he grew up in New York City, the guy who could live anywhere decided to move here.

At a 2011 event, Glaeser was asked about this apparent hypocrisy: 'I can't get past the fact that you actually live in the suburbs. It's brave of you to admit to that. By working in the city, aren't you taking the best from the city and getting away from the worst of it? Although you say high density is the thing, it's not actually what you personally choose to do.'

Glaeser replied: 'I cannot tell you how acutely aware I am of what I am missing every day by living in the suburb. I count the hours until my last kid is out of high school and I can move back into a one room apartment. My five years in the suburb has not left me feeling as though I'm living some wonderful existence.'[4] I don't know where Ed Glaeser lives today. But, when given the choice, he went with the suburban oasis rather than the density that he says is desirable.

More telling is a 2011 article in which Glaeser argued that an area near the Walden Pond reservation in his neighbourhood should be protected from new housing and that new housing should instead be built in other people's neighbourhoods.[5] This just shows that NIMBYism or YIMBYism is a matter of taste. Sure, Walden Pond reservation has cultural significance, but does that mean nearby areas can't have housing?

A long-time research collaborator of Glaeser's, Joseph Gyourko, responded to an interview question from Columbia Business School professor Frederic Mishkin in May 2002 by saying that 'rich people like you and Ed Glaeser' are always trying to 'keep people away from your mansions and your houses'.[6]

Glaeser is an intellectual guru of the YIMBY movement and its case against town planning regulations. His followers worship city growth and argue for new housing in every nook and cranny. Yet all the while he has been living the suburban dream on acreage and lobbying to keep new housing out of his own neighbourhood.

Unfortunately, this classic 'Do what I say not what I do' position is common in debates about planning and housing, and the YIMBY movement has simply turned it into a broader cultural issue rather than a niche issue among planners and property professionals. Take for example former Sydney northern beaches federal Liberal MP, Jason Falinski. He chaired the 2022 parliamentary inquiry into housing supply and came down firmly in support of taking away the ability of local residents to influence the way their suburbs develop though their input on planning regulations. Yet, when new development plans for his electorate threatened his chances of retaining his seat, a different position emerged, as reported in the *Australian Financial Review*:

> The state government and the local council are on board. The local federal member [Falinski]—battling to hold his seat against independent candidate Dr Sophie Scamps—is not.
>
> 'This development can't go ahead until we get real upgrades to our roads, transport systems and cellular towers,' a petition on his website states.
>
> A video message on the issue laments the plan to put in 'hundreds of homes and thousands of cars' without a plan for 'more roads, better infrastructure and how to maintain the character of this area'.
>
> Note to Falinski: that's what they all say! [7]

Former Brisbane Lord Mayor Jim Soorley promoted densification across the city during his time in office, and on behalf of property developer clients as a consultant after his political career.[8] But he hates density in his own neighbourhood, even for not-for-profit aged care housing. In 2020 he labelled a plan by a non-profit organisation to build a six-storey retirement facility in his inner Brisbane neighbourhood of New Farm as 'greedy rubbish'.[9]

Rebecca Matthews, who sits on Wellington Council in New Zealand and describes herself as the 'oldest YIMBY' in town, lives in a 'heritage-protected railway cottage, along a character street, in hilltops dense with native bush'.[10] Her preference is to live in the very place created by the planning regulations she wants to remove.

Even many property developers hate living near the type of buildings they build and promote to others. In a hilarious turn of events, Matthew McNeilly, the managing director of the Perth property development company Sirona Urban, got very upset that a four-storey luxury aged care home was set to be approved for development across the road from his home.[11] He warned of planning 'civil wars' on the horizon if communities were stripped of their voice.

Personal experience

My perspective on the entry of YIMBY culture is also informed by my lived experience. I live in a detached house in the dense inner-city suburb of West End in Brisbane, one of the fastest developing suburbs in the state, with more than a tripling of the population since I moved here eighteen years ago. I've been involved in local community groups, trying to make sure that the changes are incremental and facilitated with public investments like parks, schools, bike paths, bus services, traffic lights and more, to enable densification in a way that creates a net benefit.

I have lived through quite radical gentrification and densi-fication. I can now see into dozens of new apartments from my lounge-room window, and they can see into mine.

When density comes with public investment in better trans-port and parks, and other upgrades, people often support it. Jim Soorley's period as Brisbane lord mayor really did start densification in a way people seem to like. He was re-elected three times. He created a separated bus-way system, started building bike lanes, began a tree-planting push to make all the suburbs feel like the older rich ones; he enabled footpath dining on council footpaths. Many of those changes persist today and are being expanded upon, with new electric metro-buses using the bus-way, and the shade of trees planted in the 1990s keeping walkers and cyclists cool.

But when the process of densification looks more like an ad hoc giveaway to certain private developers to allow them to exceed planning rules without any public support for density, then you can see why people often don't like it. That is why even those with YIMBY views feel the need to push back and choose for themselves quite different housing options.

In my area the state government decided that more parks and schools would not be needed even if the population more than tripled, on the assumption that kids don't live in apart-ments. The state government sold to a private housing developer a state-owned property where a distance education school had been located. Instead of using this site to make complementary investments in public services to accommodate the planned density, the government did the opposite.

A decade after the government sold that site, the enormous number of new school students in our area meant that the state had to acquire private land to massively expand the primary school and also acquire a whole suburban block to build a new high school.

In the meantime, new parks are missing because the state says it can't spend money on such frivolous things, even though the suburb is accommodating an extra 20,000 people.

The reality of how urban growth and change happens is very different from the simplified NIMBY versus YIMBY culture war. Aligning community expectations is important. When that doesn't occur, you get: 'The town plan said this and now you are changing it on me'. After all, people move to a location because they like it how it is. If they wanted to live in a higher density place, they would be living somewhere else. If we want to get the housing debate back on course, the last thing we need is a new culture war. There are enough distractions and distortions without it.

Distractions and distortions

12 ◆ Mismeasuring manors

Why falling house prices aren't the good news that first home buyers think.

—A headline in *The Sydney Morning Herald* that epitomises the confusing public discussion on what makes housing affordable (article by Kate Burke, 7 July 2022)

In late 2021, an enormous amount of media attention was on the plight of first home buyers due to rising prices. In late 2022, this reversed. Prices then were falling, but the cost of buying wasn't falling because interest rates were rising. According to many reports, 'mortgage prison' was awaiting those recent first home buyers whose loan balances were going to become higher than the value of their home if their home value continued to decline.

It is very confusing to read that rising prices are bad for first home buyers, then a year later to read that the exact opposite is true. But do you see where the rabbit was put in the hat for this little bit of deception?

In 2021, 'first home buyers' was the name given to people who didn't yet own homes but wanted to buy one. In 2022, it was the name used for people who already did own homes.

Falling prices are good for the first group but bad for the second, due to the symmetry of the property markets.

As we saw in the asset price equilibrium, housing asset prices are a poor measure of the cost of housing. They increased in 2020 and 2021 because interest rates fell. In many places it was cheaper to rent money than rent a home, and a record number of new first home buyers did that.

Because asset prices are not a good measure of how much it costs to occupy housing, the price-to-income ratio, sometimes called the 'median multiple', is meaningless. A distraction. That is why the economic analysis of commercial property doesn't mention price at all, just yields.

A puzzling popular statistic

Price-to-income ratios are unfortunately widely reported in the media and often cited as evidence in academic works. I suspect this has a lot to do with Demographia, a private research organisation that releases an annual report summarising the price-to-income ratio for the housing markets of many cities around the world. These reports claim that a median dwelling price of more than three times the median income means that a city is 'unaffordable' and they imply that local regulations are the cause of these ratios. This logic must seem sensible and intuitive to the many people who use these figures. They cite them despite the lack of transparency and poor research quality; there is no description of data sources used, no clear definition of dwellings (whether detached houses only or apartments), and no explanation of how income is measured.

But the economic logic is also wrong.

We don't compare the price of industrial properties, company shares or other assets to median household income. And we shouldn't. Even though rents track incomes, housing asset prices can diverge because of changes in yields.

For example, a dwelling with a $1 million asset price and an annual rent of $35,000 has a 3.5 per cent gross yield. A household with an income of $175,000 would be paying 20 per cent of their income on rent in this situation and the price-to-income ratio would be 5.7. But if they wanted to purchase this house, rather than rent it, whether the price-to-income ratio is 'unaffordable' depends enormously on interest rates. If the mortgage interest rate is 8 per cent, and this household borrowed the full price of $1 million, they would pay $80,000 per year interest, or 46 per cent of their income on interest, more than double the cost of renting the home. But if the mortgage interest rate is 3 per cent, then borrowing $1 million costs just $30,000 per year in interest, which is less than the cost of renting and 17 per cent of income.

———

If housing asset prices grow while rents don't, this must be due to changes in the yield, or capitalisation rate, or other changes that affect the costs of ownership, like taxes.

In Australia, home prices have diverged from rents significantly since the 1990s. The graphs in Figure 4 show that rents, in this case using real rents adjusted for inflation, were flat over the two decades to 2023, though with a large 2010s surge. In Perth, a temporary sharp effect of the 2010s mining boom on rent can be seen, which fits the logic of rental equilibrium being

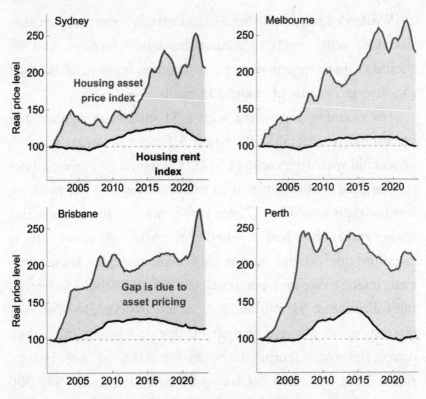

Figure 4 ◆ Housing asset prices do not reflect 'affordability', whatever that means

the result of extra demand from higher incomes and population during that period.

If we look at Melbourne in 2003 and again in 2023, the rental price index has seen no net change. But the price index (also adjusted for inflation) has risen 150 per cent. Since rents over this period have tracked household incomes, using the price-to-income ratio as a metric of house price affordability would imply that the affordability of housing in Melbourne is two-and-a-half times worse in 2023 than it was in 2003. But that is not true.

Researchers at the Bank of England also noticed that price-to-income ratios were being used uncritically and they decided in 2019 to write an article arguing exactly the same point I have made here: a deviation of asset prices from rents can't be explained by variations in the physical stock of homes compared to the number of people. They wrote the following:

> Many commentators attribute rises in house prices to a lack of supply. Indeed, if dwellings get more scarce, an asset price model would predict a rise in the spot price of housing service, i.e. rents.
>
> Other things being equal this would also push up house prices. But house prices can be affected by lots of other things (interest rates, the financial frictions mentioned above), so rental prices should be a 'cleaner' measure of relative scarcity: at least in markets where rents are unregulated and free to adjust to market forces. If rental prices don't move in the same way as house prices then this suggests something else must be at play.[1]

Other costs of ownership change asset prices too

For the same reason that price-to-income ratios make little sense, comparing housing asset prices between locations is also tricky, especially when making international comparisons. Not only do local incomes, rents and asset market yields vary substantially, but property tax settings also differ enormously. Since the value of an asset depends on its net income relative to other assets, different taxes levied on property owners can significantly affect the net incomes and values.

Here's an example from the United States, where tax settings and city income levels differ more than in Australia.

I'm often told that large homes in Houston, Texas, are cheap compared to other major cities because of different planning regulations. Houston famously has no zoning codes in its planning law, and it is often thought that Australian cities could learn from this.

One example given to me to make this case was to compare two homes listed for sale. First, a 150-square-metre two-bedroom, two-bathroom home in a nice suburb of Arlington, Virginia, had a price of $825,000. Second, a much larger five-bedroom, five-bathroom home with a pool in a nice suburb of Houston, Texas, had an asset price of $440,000.

These asset price differences don't seem to make sense from a physical perspective, but from an economic perspective, these price differences make perfect sense.

First, the rent of each home depends on the desirability of the location and the incomes of people there. Arlington, Virginia, has a median household income of US$128,000, while Houston's is less than half at US$56,000.[2] The rental equilibrium says that rents reflect incomes, so the same quality of dwelling should get roughly twice the rent in Arlington. If the Houston home is twice the quality, but the local incomes are half as high, it is reasonable to expect that the rent would be roughly the same in dollar terms as the home in Arlington.

A second big difference is property taxes. The annual tax payable on the Houston home was US$15,000, while the Arlington home was US$7000, or less than half. The cost of paying an extra US$8000 per year in tax is a liability that reduces the net cashflow and hence the asset price for the Houston house. The high upkeep costs (also known as depreciation) of the larger Houston home also reduces the net income to a property owner.

Putting some numbers to this example, we might get the following annual figures for the Houston mansion.

- Gross rental per year: $35,000
- Property tax: $15,000
- Ongoing/upkeep per year: $5000
- Net income: $15,000

For the Arlington home, with lower costs of upkeep and lower property taxes, but higher local incomes that provide the same gross rent, the numbers might look like this.

- Gross rental per year: $35,000
- Property tax rate: $7000
- Ongoing/upkeep per year: $2500
- Net income: $25,500

Once we look at the details needed to determine an asset price for each home, we discover that the net income going to the owner is about 70 per cent higher for the small Arlington home. If we apply a 3 per cent capitalisation rate to this net income, assuming that growth expectations are the same in both locations, the price we would expect for these two homes is $500,000 for the Texas property and $850,000 for the Virginia property, which is roughly in line with the advertised prices. Yet I was told these prices were evidence of the effect of planning regulations.

If the price was $500,000 for the Virginia home, then this wouldn't be an asset price equilibrium as the owner of the Texas home could sell it and buy the Virginia home and get a much higher rate of return. These asset pricing details matter and mean that price-to-income metrics are a distraction.

13 ◆ Skipping the cycle

By 2007 Britain and most of the other industrially advanced economies will be in the throes of frenzied activity in the land market ... land prices will be near their 18-year peak ... on the verge of the collapse that will presage the global depression of 2010.

—Fred Harrison, in his 1997 book *Chaos Makers*,
predicting that a frenzied property market cycle in the
2000s would precede a global depression in 2010.[1]

May 2020 was near the peak of Covid-19 policy panic. Australian banks had released analysis showing the possibility of 30 per cent declines in the price of housing assets, worrying many. At this exact time, in a podcast entitled 'Australia housing market: Bear vs Bull debate', I argued they were wrong. I explained why prices were more likely to rise 20 per cent than fall 20 per cent, despite concerns about unemployment, lockdowns and enormous economic disruption.[2]

I was called mad. People on social media asked if I had got my university degrees from a cornflakes box. I was going against the forecasts of the Reserve Bank of Australia, the guidance of all the major banks and just about every media housing analyst you could poke a stick at. That same week, *ABC News* ran the headline 'CBA warns Australia risks 32 per cent house price crash in a "prolonged downturn", flags $1.5 billion coronavirus-hit to bank'.[3]

But I was right. Housing asset prices for all dwellings across the five biggest capital cities boomed by 20 per cent in the next 18 months. On the dot. To their peak in 2022, housing asset prices were up 43 per cent in Brisbane and 42 per cent in Adelaide, with far greater price gains in many regional centres and lifestyle towns.

There were a few elements to my argument, but the three big ones were these.

1   An upwards impact from recently reduced interest rates.
2   Even a rise in unemployment and decline in household incomes would have a small percentage effect on total household incomes, and hence rents.
3   Property markets move in cycles.

The last point confused people. If you understand the asset pricing equilibrium, the first makes sense. If you understand the rental price equilibrium, the second makes sense. But what many miss is the third part, the property cycle. All the equilibria move in a surprisingly regular economic cycle, or heartbeat.

I knew that after a bust comes a boom, not another bust, and that rents and prices had both already fallen for two years and were starting to rise again. But in the hijacked housing debates, ignoring the property cycle is all too common.

The long history of property cycles and forecasts

The property market pulse is well documented by the housing development industry. For decades, industry analysts have produced 'property clocks' to place each city at its point in the recurring cycle. They aren't always right, but they fundamentally understand that the property market is tightly linked with the boom-and-bust cycle of the macroeconomy.

In fact, the boom-and-bust nature of the property cycle was a huge political and economic concern in the nineteenth century, which had seen periodic crashes disrupt economic activity and investment.

Homer Hoyt tracked the 1800s boom-and-bust cycle in real estate with his book *One Hundred Years of Land Values in Chicago: The relationship of the growth of Chicago to the rise in its land values, 1830–1933*. Roy Wenzlick in 1936 wrote a book entitled *The Coming Boom in Real Estate*, in which he predicted with great accuracy property boom-and-bust cycles over the next decades. If you had been around and able to follow the advice in Ohio farmer Samuel Benner's 1875 book *Benner's Prophecies of Future Ups and Downs in Prices* about when to buy property in the late nineteenth and early twentieth century, you would have made millions.[4] And more recently, if you had taken seriously Fred Harrison's predictions, quoted at the start of this chapter, you would have navigated the 2000s financial crisis with your wealth intact.

All of these approaches recognise that, even if it is not clear why, there are property cycles. And ignoring these repeating patterns leads to bad predictions and housing policy prescriptions.

It's a modern mystery

The causes of property market cycles are somewhat of a mystery to modern economics. The standard explanation is that prices should be stable over time and any change must be due to an external cause acting at random—maybe a collective panic, or a technology change, new trade routes or border closures during a pandemic.

Samuel Benner noticed this even in the 1870s. Experts back then thought that market declines were a random occurrence, driven by a sudden panic. At that time, panics in the commercial and financial world were compared to comets in the astronomical world, which were then thought to have no regularity of movement, no cycles, and hence were beyond the domain of astronomical science.

My view is that, just as gravity generates regular and predictable patterns among the planets and stars, the economic equilibrium forces in the property market also generate regular and predictable cyclical patterns.

Like our solar system, where each planet is in an equilibrium but still moving over time, the five property market equilibria must always exist but are not always fixed in place. Though it is not a perfect analogy, we can think of an asset price cycle as like the movement of the Moon around the Earth, which causes rising tides, raising the level of the water (the density equilibrium) and the flow of water into rivers and streams (the absorption rate). Renters get a boost if they are paddling upriver when the tide comes in (the rental equilibrium falls a little), but then, when the tide goes out, their paddling becomes more difficult. We know that these natural forces cause tides and cycles everywhere on the planet and we don't look for any local explanation of this phenomenon.

The five housing market equilibria are tied together in a system. In every property monopoly, whether it is Australia, Canada or the United Kingdom, or whether it is in a board game or the virtual world, these same economic equilibrium forces generate the same system-wide cycles.

The Speculative Index is a tool to monitor cycles

My preferred method for monitoring the property cycle is to track the asset price equilibrium with a measure I call the Speculative Index. It is the ratio of the mortgage interest rate to the gross yield (or capitalisation rate, being a year's current gross rent divided by price) of housing. Since the force acting on the asset pricing equilibrium is the relative return of swapping the yield on non-property assets for property assets, this gives a feel for the state of that equilibrium at a point in time.

I call it the Speculative Index because, when it is high, the mortgage interest cost is much higher than the rental income. It only makes sense to buy housing at this time if you expect plenty of capital gains, even for owner-occupiers, who could be better off renting temporarily and investing their money in other assets. You are speculating on those gains more than buying the current rental income flow.

Figure 5 shows the Speculative Index for Australia for the past four decades. You can see the tidal nature of it. In late 1989, for example, gross housing rental yields were much lower than yields on money in the bank. Bringing these yields closer could only happen via lower housing prices or lower

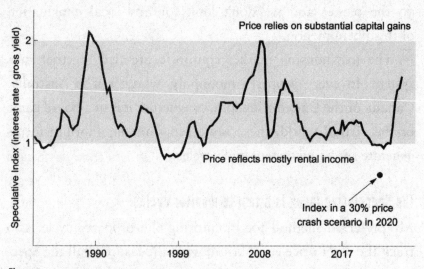

Figure 5 ◆ The Speculative Index, 1983–2023

interest rates, both of which occurred in the early 1990s and brought the Speculative Index back down to one by the end of that decade. A similarly high Speculative Index occurred again in 2007, after mortgage interest rates increased from 5 per cent to 9 per cent, while yields on housing stayed below 5 per cent. And you can see that in 2023 we were heading towards another peak.

Just as the tide has a limited range, so does the Speculative Index. It has never really exceeded two, where the mortgage interest rate is twice the yield. Neither has it ever fallen for long below one, where the mortgage interest rate is equal to the gross yield. These appear to be the bounds of the pricing equilibrium system.[5]

Because I was monitoring property cycles with the Speculative Index, I could predict that house prices were unlikely to fall substantially during Covid-19 disruptions in 2020 and 2021. Gross housing yields were above 4 per cent, and the interest rate had been dropped quickly so that mortgage interest rates were around 2.5 per cent and falling. That meant you could borrow your total property value and pay less than 3 per cent interest while earning nearly 5 per cent in rent. Sure, there are ownership costs to include, but that would mean an ability to leverage into housing with a positive cashflow. For renters, it meant that borrowing 100 per cent of the property value to buy the house they lived in would lower their total housing costs. That's why first home buying shot up to record highs at this time.

It was foolish to predict a 30 per cent price decline from this point. That is like predicting that the tide will go out after it already has. Maybe it is possible this time but, based on the historical record, you would bet against it. I have marked in Figure 5 a point in 2020. It is where the Speculative Index would have been if the widely predicted 30 per cent price decline had combined with a 10 per cent rental decline. That point is in uncharted territory, yet it was the majority view.

Property cycles drive housing policy debate cycles

During the 1880s Victorian land boom, banks were inclined to raise rates to push back on these cyclical extremes, just as central banks do today with monetary policy. But it never seemed to work. Michael Cannon, in his book on the land booms of this period, describes these events of the 1880s as follows:

In 1886 it appeared to some of the associated banks that the land boom had reached its zenith and would now plunge downwards. They became alarmed at the large withdrawals being made to meet land payments, and increased the interest rate on deposits and overdrafts by 1 per cent. Money lodged for twelve months could now earn 6 per cent. The land companies were compelled to follow suit and increase their interest rate on deposits. For a year land speculation became less profitable. Sales fell from about £12 million in 1885 to about £2 million in 1886. Then in 1887 there began a new wave of speculation, the land boom proper, so forceful that it over-rode all considerations of interest rates.[6]

The last phase of the asset price cycle seems to be one where high interest rates and rising prices go together, which sends the Speculative Index sharply upwards for several years before an inevitable crash. This occurred after the 2003 Sydney house price peak, with a new wave of rising prices before the financial crisis. In 2023, renewed housing asset price rises in Australia and globally, in the face of high interest rates, shocked many people and led to debate about the effectiveness of monetary policy in achieving its economic stabilisation objectives. Yet at a similar point in the late 1880s, property asset prices increased not by 10 per cent or 20 per cent a year, which is fast by modern standards, but by 10 per cent to 20 per cent a month!

Calls for regulation and intervention in the housing market track the rental and price cycles, but they usually come too late. For example, public concerns about rising rents reached their zenith during the May 2023 federal budget. A Council of Australian Governments (COAG) meeting was convened to look at standardising tenancy laws across states and putting a percentage limit on rent increases for sitting tenants. A senate inquiry into this matter was announced in July 2023. All this political action happened after the biggest cyclical rent increase in more than a decade, not before. It is a repeat of the 1912 New South Wales rental inquiry that similarly was triggered after rents had suddenly increased, as they do near the end of the asset price cycle. The inquiry cycle lags the property cycle.

The example we saw earlier of the ACT's discounted land purchase scheme came at the end of the price cycle. It began in 2008, when asset prices peaked. By the time the next asset price cycle had started, the scheme had been disbanded. Other schemes, like the Victorian government's shared equity scheme in 2022, were also launched immediately after cyclical asset price rises, not before them. The policy cycle lags the inquiry cycle.

Two policies stand out as effective in dealing with the property cycle. First is counter-cyclical public housing construction. This type of fiscal policy was enacted by the Rudd government in 2009, which quickly spent $6 billion on new public housing construction, with positive outcomes for the construction sector during that cyclical downturn. The second is boosting home-ownership, which insulates more households from the effect of rent and price changes. No doubt the extreme property cycles from the 1800s all the way until the 1930s were a factor in promoting homeownership as a major policy objective.

14 ◆ Proper planning

In Tura Beach, on the NSW far south coast, residents learned in June last year that an area of bushland, which they say is of high ecological value, had been approved for subdivision for housing in 1989. The residents have been challenging the council, which is in favour of the development.

Further up the coast in Coila Lake, residents have been advocating against a DA approved in 1983 to develop 60 residential buildings.

—Jordyn Beazley, in *The Guardian* , 30 April 2023,
reporting on 40-year-old 'zombie' planning
approvals, showing that property owners choose
when to build new homes, not planners

A common view is that governments 'release' land to the market. But the 'new land release' signs I see beside the highway are all from private property developers who own the land, not the council or the state government, who don't own the land. Yes, governments have planning and zoning rules about what can be built at each location. But only property owners can decide when and if to build new housing.

The planning system and its zoning rules do not regulate how fast new homes are built. There are no speed limits. What town plans do is regulate where different types of immobile buildings can go, just as lane markings on the road regulate where mobile objects can go. Regulating the spatial use of roads improves coordination and, if done well, planning rules improve coordination by regulating the spatial use of property when it comes to erecting buildings, but also developing major works like mines, ports and roads, among many other projects.

The creation of planning—and zoning in particular, which is a set of rules that describe the as-of-right building types and activities allowed on property in certain areas—happened in the early and mid-twentieth century. Before this, owners in the property monopoly were able to create similar regulations using covenants. Property owners could attach a covenant, which is a type of contact, to their property title to restrict what future owners could do with the property.[1] These pre-zoning rules offered legal protection from nuisance to nearby property owners, and they also regulated the location of housing and other land uses.

United States housing researchers John Quigley and Larry Rosenthal explained that the emergence of planning and zoning there was partly to override existing legal protections and to enable large-scale land development. They wrote: 'Before the 1920s, experimentation with planning and zoning in U.S. cities and towns was sparse and arose primarily as a consequence of the desires of large-tract residential developers to eliminate industrial and commercial activities in their path.'[2]

In Australia, modern planning and zoning emerged from the slum conditions seen in the early twentieth century through to the 1930s Great Depression, and from later efforts to coordinate large-scale catch-up development in the cities after World War II.

The idea that planning regulations and zoning constrain the absorption rate of new housing and lead to higher rents and prices is based on a distorted view of how the planning system operates and interacts with the economic choices of property owners.

Who builds homes

A first part of the misunderstanding is to confuse construction with property development. Construction companies build for property owners, and their interests are to build as many homes as possible. Property owners have a choice about when and how fast to build to maximise their return over the long term from owning property. Since you need a location to build, it is property owners who make that choice, not builders or construction companies.

The process of development starts with property ownership, whether that is direct ownership, a joint venture between a property owner and a development company, or an option contract that enables a property developer to buy a property in the future, once they have reduced their risks by assessing the market and the planning system.

A planning approval comes next. This checks whether what the property owner proposes to build, based on their assessment of the market, complies with the rules of the planning system. After this planning approval, most housing developers will try to sell dwellings before they decide to build.

If the project doesn't pre-sell well, or market conditions change, then approved projects don't have to be built. Property developers can wait for better market conditions—in some cases, for many decades. Or they can seek a different planning approval for a new project design. If they sell the undeveloped project, the next property owner faces these same choices.

Only at the very end, when all these pieces are in place—the planning approval, the pre-sale purchase contracts and any financial arrangements—will a developer commit to a construction contract with a builder. And it is only at this last step that a separate building approval is sought, which assesses the building design against construction codes.

It is no surprise that most buildings with building approvals get built, because seeking building approval usually happens after a new dwelling is already sold. But planning approvals, which come at the start of this process, are different. Market risks mean that it is sensible for property owners to keep a buffer stock of planning approvals. They can then respond quickly to new market conditions by selling and starting construction; or they can delay without having committed significant capital; or they can vary the approval and seek a new one for a different project that meets new market preferences.

Unfortunately, many property analysts and media commentators do not know there are two types of approval in the housing development process. They see the Australian Bureau of Statistics (ABS) publishes data regularly on building approvals, and wrongly think that these are planning approvals, and blame the planning system any time these approval numbers fall.

Strangely, they never credit the planning system when building approvals surge at other times in the property cycle.

Limited planning approval data

There is little data collected on planning approvals, the stock of undeveloped land that could have approved development, and the buffer stock of current planning approvals. But there is some, and it reinforces the picture that the planning system regulates the location, but not the pace, of new housing development.

Government statisticians in Queensland estimate that, in the south-east corner of the state, there is land currently zoned for detached housing that could produce more than 400,000 new housing lots, and that does not include small subdivisions of less than 2500 square metres. Yet only around 10,000 detached housing lots per year are developed, though this varies with market cycles. This data also shows a buffer stock of projects with planning approvals that are not yet developed of more than 60,000 detached dwellings and 120,000 apartments and attached dwellings.

It is stunning to compare these enormous figures with media reporting about planning and zoning. In 2003 a scary headline ran in the *Financial Review*: 'Brisbane running out of land for housing'. It quoted statements by the then Lord Mayor-elect Tim Quinn about how 'Brisbane's land shortage is escalating and its greenfield sites are expected to be exhausted by 2015 to 2020'.[3] Two decades later we can check the accuracy of that headline. According to Queensland government data, the Brisbane City Council area in 2023 was still producing new detached housing at a similar pace to 2001—about 1800 new detached homes per year, while the number of attached dwellings had boomed.[4]

In Sydney, where planning and zoning is a fierce battleground, far more approvals are granted than are developed. Only recently has data been collected and it showed that in 2022 there were planning approvals granted for 64,000 dwellings in Greater Sydney but building approvals for only 37,000. In 2023 it was 56,000 planning approvals and 33,000 building approvals.[5]

In Auckland, New Zealand, there are about 550,000 existing homes. The council there estimates that, if every property in the city was built to scale allowable in their planning regulations, a million additional homes could be built.[6] Taken together, this limited data shows that planning and zoning regulations usually allow for a huge number of potential housing projects to be built. But for the vast majority of these properties it is more profitable to wait to develop, as the absorption rate equilibrium regulates how quickly these feasible opportunities get taken up across the market.

It should also be noted that zoning rules, which prescribe requirements for density, use, setbacks and so forth, are almost always flexible; projects that exceed these limits can also be approved. If a new project design exceeds height or density limits, but has more merit and better design quality, planners will usually approve them.

Which is great. It means that where the density equilibrium is above the zoned density limit, there is an economic incentive to invest in better building designs to be allowed to exceed zoned density limits.

A recent application in my neighbourhood is a good example. The site is 37 Boundary Street, South Brisbane, and a planning application was made for a 25-storey apartment tower in an area with a zoning code allowing for 20 storeys. The property owner argued in their planning report that an extra five storeys were reasonable, given the surrounding conditions, and I think that's true. But the choice to design a 25-storey building and apply for this more difficult and slower approval, instead of a 20-storey building that would comply with the zoning codes, means they have chosen a slower and riskier approval option.

This is a 154-dwelling project that would have been 123 dwellings if it complied with the zoned height limit. I expect it will be approved and that the suburb will have 33 extra dwellings on that site that apparently the planning regulations did not allow, or 22 per cent more. This zoning flexibility is underappreciated.

Density limits and spatial equilibrium

Perhaps counterintuitively, zoning rules can restrict density on a property below the density equilibrium without binding (constraining) the absorption equilibrium. This is because of the spatial equilibrium—substitute locations can be used to meet the absorption rate equilibrium. After all, whether a new dwelling is above or beside another is just a vertical dimension to the spatial equilibrium; apartments on different levels of the same building have different rents and prices too.

If the absorption equilibrium is ten dwellings per year, zoning determines whether a city sees development of these possible options:

1   ten buildings with single dwellings under low-density zoning, or

2   two buildings of five dwellings each under medium-density zoning, or

3   one building of ten dwellings under high-density zoning.

If the planning system doesn't change the rate at which new homes are developed, but changes their location, can that have important rent or price effects? Perhaps we can start with an explanation from Bank of England researchers about how spatial equilibrium deals with this:

> Another common refrain is that the houses are 'in the wrong place' and so this mismatch of houses and people has the same effect as limited supply in pushing up prices. But an asset pricing approach contradicts this view: Assume that houses . . . are permanently fixed in one place but people can move. If a shock hits (say jobs move from one region to another [and] it's too far to commute), that raises the relative demand for housing services . . . in one region and reduces it by the same amount elsewhere. Rents go up in the region with the inflow and down in the other. But assuming the sensitivity of demand to rents is the same in both places, then they should exactly offset.
>
> The asset price mechanism should move local house prices in lockstep with local rents. For prices and rents, the dispersion rises across different places, but the national average of each should be unchanged. This mismatch might bring with it other important issues and challenges (e.g. wealth inequality, labour mobility and others) but it shouldn't raise aggregate prices.[7]

How zoning interacts with the density equilibrium

I try to convey the logic that zoning regulates what is built where, not how fast, in Figure 6. The grey curve is the density equilibrium, which as we saw, is higher when local rents and prices are higher, and hence has a spatial dimension. Under the density equilibrium are drawn the existing dwellings, which are mostly far from the current density equilibrium, with plenty of locations able to be developed into new housing.

The dashed line represents the zoned density limits in a planning scheme. Sometimes this limit is below the density equilibrium, and sometimes above. In addition to these zoned limits in the planning system, many other things limit housing at a location. Sometimes it is other land uses, environmental regulations, public lands, roads and thoroughfares, and sometimes it is physical constraints like rivers, mountains or roads. Zoning merely adds a regulatory element to the physical and economic geography of cities that the spatial equilibrium navigates so well.

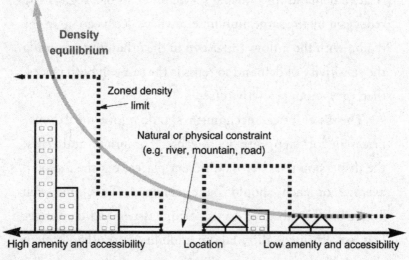

Figure 6 ◆ How planning limits interact with the density equilibrium

Often, the zoned density limit is far above the density equilibrium, which is visible in the middle of Figure 6. We saw earlier the cases of Wyndham and Beenleigh, but this situation is common in many cities and towns across the country. Even when zoned density restricts the number of dwellings at a location below the density equilibrium, housing will be built if there are feasible options that comply with the density limit.

An extreme case

You may not be convinced. After all, planning rules really do restrict where different types of dwelling can be located. Surely if a city went to the extreme and banned new dwellings, this must a) be quantity restriction across the whole city and b) cause a lack of housing, and c) cause rents and prices to rise.

We have a case study of that outcome at Noosa, the Sunshine Coast council renowned for its restrictive town planning requirements. In the 2000s, Noosa had a buffer stock of between 500 and 900 detached housing lots with planning approvals. In 2022, it was down to between 50 and 80, a 90 per cent decline. There were 634 new housing lots from 2003 to 2008, but only 72 from 2018 to 2023, and a decline from 600 to 400 apartments completed between those five-year periods.[8]

You might expect this to have had a large effect on rents and housing asset prices.

Before I show you the data, let's think about the question differently. Imagine that Noosa, a relatively small council, was a single property development project of a single company. The project was developed over many decades into this physical form, which the company thought maximised its returns, and then they stopped building.

Would anyone think this company is causing a housing shortage? Or would they merely observe that, after buildings have been developed, they have a lifetime during which they cannot be profitably redeveloped.

This is the case with every new housing project, whether it is an apartment building or complex, or a detached housing subdivision. For decades afterwards it is uneconomical to put more housing on the same location. It quarantines the space from more housing.

This is why we need to always think about spatial equilibrium and substitute locations. Even without planning regulations, the historical legacy of previous development creates large economic constraints on new housing in addition to planning and zoning regulations.

Spatial equilibrium is also why apartment rents in Noosa, despite so little new housing developed there, increased by exactly the same 50 per cent from 2019 to 2023 as Caloundra, the fastest developing area in the Sunshine Coast and one that has planning regulations with few density limits.[9] These are substitute areas and spatial equilibrium applies between towns and cities too.

Had Noosa had different planning regulations, more dwellings would have been built there, but fewer across the rest of the Sunshine Coast region. I can't say which is better from an urban design or transport investment perspective. What I can say is that, from a pure rental market perspective, the fact that one part of a region has no housing development doesn't lead to higher rents in aggregate, just as the cessation of housing construction for decades after a major subdivision is completed does not affect the greater market.

15 ◆ Immigration inspection

I actually believe in a big Australia—I make no apology for that. I actually think it's good news that our population is growing.

—Former Prime Minister Kevin Rudd, explaining his view that rapid immigration to grow the population is politically desirable, seemingly ignoring effects on rental and labour markets, *ABC News*, 23 October 2009

Property speculators and landlords love high rates of immigration, even though they constantly argue that there is a shortage of housing.

No one seems to care about this contradiction.

I was at a meeting in 2019 hosted by Maha Sinnathamby, the developer of Springfield, a massive master-planned suburb between Brisbane and Ipswich. The topic was population.

I made the comment about how weird it is that property developers think that it is the government's job to bring new customers to their projects through immigration policy, especially high-income immigrants who can splash out on expensive rents and prices, rather than the job of developers to compete on price and quality.

There was little substantive response to this. But then the discussion moved to dealing with a possible future scenario where Australia needed to support a sudden refugee inflow, perhaps due to a catastrophe in the Pacific. In this scenario, most participants at the meeting changed their story. The housing needs of these immigrants were a problem that the government should sort out. They said: 'Oh, where would we house them all? What a disaster. The government would have to do something.'

I was puzzled. I said something along the lines of: 'You just said you want the government to bring in lots of people because you have thousands of homes to build. Can't you just house refugees too?'

Stunned faces followed, then weak excuses. Apparently, those new suburbs and subdivisions aren't appropriate for these types of people. Property lobbyists have hijacked housing debates when it comes to immigration by arguing that it's the government's job to ensure plenty of new wealthy immigrants arrive to buy homes, but also the government's job to house poor immigrants, so they don't end up living in their snobby new housing subdivisions.

Recent immigration experience

The post-Covid period from late 2022 has seen a record number of new immigrants arrive in Australia, a pattern repeated in the United Kingdom and Canada. A lot of this was catch-up immigration, squeezing the 2020 and 2021 years into 2022 and 2023. But this incredibly high immigration also looks similar to the step-change in our immigration system that happened in 2006 and has mostly persisted since. In the decade before 2006, net immigration to Australia was around 100,000 per year, but it jumped suddenly to become roughly 215,000 per year over the next decade, with a brief peak of 300,000 in 2009.[1]

For reference, the population of Canberra in 2021 was 450,000 people. The immigration rate from 2006 onwards has meant building a new Canberra's worth of homes, roads and public services every couple of years to accommodate the additional people.

The past two high immigration decades have created a broad coalition of vested interests that rely on high immigration for their business—from universities to landlords, property developers and the Australian media. The interests of this coalition are now reflected in the positions adopted by the Treasury and other government agencies like the Productivity Commission.

I want to be clear that, when it comes to immigration, as in many things, moderation is the key. It is perfectly fine to desire a bigger Australia. Any negative outcomes from Australia's immigration program are not the fault of immigrants, who are simply following the rules, but of our rule-makers. You can comment on immigration policy, both costs and benefits, without blaming immigrants personally for any negative outcomes. Apart from the Middle East, Australia has the highest proportion of foreign-born residents and, despite this, essentially no social conflict. That is something to be proud of.

Many politically active younger people who consider themselves left-leaning support open borders or high rates of immigration. Which is a little strange, as the left-leaning Greens Party had a population policy in the 1990s that stated that a stable population or a low rate of growth was best because of environmental considerations. The party scrapped this policy when immigration debates gained a racial undertone after Pauline Hanson's election to federal parliament 1996—it became culturally too difficult to separate race from immigration policy.

This is part of the history of a strange new political alliance. The property industry loves property buyers queuing up, and the business lobbyists want competition for jobs rather than competition for workers. But the modern political left also sees high immigration as a top priority.

The immigration policy question is not about how many Australians there will be at some unspecified future point in time, just as the 3.8 million Australians in 1901 were right not to worry about the future 'Big Australia' of twenty million a century later in 2001. The policy question is about managing how quickly the population grows. And when it comes to the growth rate of the population due to immigration, one of the unintended costs for existing residents, which can last for some years, arises from the adjustment of housing market equilibria.

Immigration and adjusting equilibria

It is intuitive that high rates of immigration mean high rents. But this logic isn't compatible with the rental equilibrium, whereby rents are determined by household incomes, unless immigrants have much higher incomes, which they don't.[2] It is also incompatible with the fact that from 2017 to 2019 rents were falling across Australia's capital cities, especially in Sydney, despite a near record high level of 250,000 net immigrants per year.

So how does high immigration interact with the rental market?

The short answer is, temporarily, but often substantially.

The housing market equilibria evolve slowly—much more slowly than financial markets, and especially slowly in rental markets. All adjustments in price and all changes in occupancy, or who lives where, happen only via homes that are traded or homes where rental contracts expire. Most of the time, most homes are occupied by the same people as were there the previous year: they aren't sold, they aren't leased to new renters and the number of occupants doesn't change.

On average, residents of the three million private rental properties move every two-and-a-half years.[3] At any given point in time, there are about 75,000 dwellings nationally in the pool of rentals available in the market.[4] These available rentals are not just empty homes waiting for new immigrants. They are advertised because renters are moving from one dwelling to the next. If renters move less frequently, the number of rental homes available each month falls, like it did in 2021 and 2022, down to a record low 30,000 per month.

Any immigrant household must find housing among this small number of homes and compete with other relocating households to rent them. If there are 20,000 or so new immigrants per month, requiring 8000 dwellings (for households containing 2.5 people on average) that is a big squeeze relative to the 75,000 homes turning over in the rental market that month. New immigrants, relocating renters and newly formed households must all squeeze into these same homes. This can lead to a temporary squeeze where demand for this small number of homes leads to a rapid rental price increase. Households choose in the short term to give up more non-housing consumption simply to get a home and pay the higher rent, shifting the rental equilibrium.

But these higher rents can't be sustained. Over time, renter households will respond by forming bigger households to share the costs, such as by young people delaying moving out of their parents' home or moving back in with family. Some renters might buy a dwelling and move out of the rental market.

Property investors also respond to these higher rents by buying more property, including new housing, which changes the absorption rate equilibrium and adds new homes that also become active rental listings and absorb some of those renters.

When immigration is stable, even at a high level, investors adjust and buy more new housing, increasing the absorption rate. Often it is investment by immigrants themselves or the purchasing of new homes by foreigners that increases the absorption rate equilibrium. From 2012 to 2016, for example, foreign buying of new housing was high, contributing to a higher absorption rate.

But it takes years, not months, for all these adjustments to happen.

We can gauge how long by observing the same adjustment process after a natural disaster, when there is a sudden effective increase in population compared to the number of homes. The 2022 floods in and around Lismore in northern New South Wales led to a huge number of homes being destroyed and many people needing to be quickly re-housed. The small nearby rental market, as well as their friends and family, had to absorb these people. It was like an enormous immigration wave.

What happened?

Rents spiked by around 25 per cent in nearby areas. But by late 2023, rents had returned to their 2021 levels as more household adjustments and relocations were slowly made. The effects were large but temporary.

Macroeconomic limits to immigration

If we want to keep getting more and bigger, better dwellings per person over the long term, high rates of population growth can make that more challenging. During the 2010s population boom, about 174,000 dwellings per year were constructed. Building them required 6 per cent of the workforce for housing construction alone, or 1.3 million people, taking up 5 per cent of the nation's gross domestic product and 25 per cent of all investment in the economy.[5]

Every new person doesn't just need a dwelling. They need roads, parks, schools, hospitals and other modern urban and public services to go with it. The post-war boom was the last period of rapid growth comparable to the 2010s and the post-Covid 2023 period. New housing subdivisions at this earlier time had no sealed roads, drainage or sewers. Even in 1965, 45 per cent of homes in the capital cities did not have an internal toilet or sewer connection. Public services like hospitals and schools were stretched, with children taught in church halls or outdoors.

One of former Prime Minster Gough Whitlam's greatest achievements during the 1970s was to 'help resolve the many problems of the swollen, new suburbs of the capital cities', which also meant getting complete public sewerage systems built in the capital cities.[6]

Modern infrastructure standards are much higher, so more investment is required to maintain these per capita standards. Doubling the rate of immigration to 400,000 in a sustained way would require 2.8 million people working directly in new housing construction and a need to spend 16 per cent of resources in the economy on this building binge—an impossibly large challenge when a sudden increase in construction during Covid, as a result of subsidised renovations and new home buying, led to huge delays and construction-cost blowouts.

There is a real economic cost to the existing population when accommodating high population growth. But that doesn't mean that Australia won't, can't or shouldn't get bigger. It doesn't mean that Australia should get smaller either. When a population grows or shrinks by moderate amounts, of less than 1 per cent per year, there is little effect.

Small rates of change are easily accommodated in the housing market equilibria and by the productive capacity of the economy. What is a big deal is how fast the population change happens, since that change must be accommodated via slow-moving property markets and the reallocation of resources from other productive uses to build housing and to expand other infrastructure services.

16 ◆ Vacant villages

National vacancy rates hit record low as affordability
starts to impact rent hikes

—A headline from property data provider CoreLogic
(10 October 2022) implying that low advertised
rental vacancies cause higher rental prices,
but they are in fact due to a common cause

According to the last census, about one in ten dwellings in Australia, or a million homes, are vacant on any given night. About half of those are because the residents are absent on census night—on holidays or travelling for other reasons—and about a quarter are second homes or holiday homes. Another 10 per cent are vacant rentals, either in the long-term rental market or the short-term holiday rental market.[1] Most of the remainder are either for sale, or newly completed and yet to be occupied.

This suite of underused extra homes across the housing market is how, during the Covid-19 pandemic, people were able to reallocate themselves among unoccupied dwellings and reduce the number of people per household from 2.55 to 2.49.[2] It doesn't sound like much, but for 26 million people that's nearly 500,000 unoccupied dwellings that became occupied nationwide, of which only about 180,000 were new dwellings completed in that period.[3]

Looking abroad, in Taiwan, for example, about one in six dwellings is vacant at any one time. In China it is more than one in five dwellings.[4] Those 65 million built-but-unoccupied homes in China are enough to house 140 million extra people, or about the population of Russia. In Japan there are more than eight million unoccupied homes, or nearly 14 per cent of the housing stock.[5]

In Spain in 2023, the government took steps to take control of 50,000 homes that had sat empty and in the possession of banks for over a decade following the 2008–09 financial crisis, with the intention of making them available for rent.[6]

Vacant property in every nation is a buffer stock to accommodate flexibility. For its owners, there is value to that flexibility and in waiting beyond the income immediately available from leasing the space to the first comer at a rock-bottom price. This is more obvious in retail and commercial buildings, but rarely are there policy discussions about the fact that, for example, 20 per cent of the less premium B-grade quality space in Perth was vacant in 2021.[7] But it is less obvious in housing, where there are heated policy debates about vacant property.

Vacancy is not unoccupied housing

Two vacancy concepts are often conflated: vacant and unoccupied. In Australia, what is called the rental vacancy rate is the number of rental advertisements that have been posted online longer than three weeks in a month divided by the estimated stock of rental homes. If you read in the media that the 'national vacancy rate is back at its lowest point on record in

January—0.8%'[8] then you can interpret it as 'Of the nation's estimated 3.1 million rental homes, 24,000 of them were advertised online for more than three weeks based on website statistics over the past month.'

Unoccupied homes are a different concept. While vacant homes might be occupied while being advertised, unoccupied homes are empty. The main data on unoccupied homes comes from the census each five years in Australia and measures how many homes were empty on census night. As earlier noted, the bulk of these homes are unoccupied on census night because the residents are travelling temporarily, they are second homes, or they are for sale or rent.

The think tank Prosper Australia has used water meter data from Melbourne water providers to estimate the number of homes unoccupied for a whole year. They found that suburbs with large numbers of new dwellings also have a large number of long-term unoccupied dwellings. For example, in the dense and rapidly growing inner-city Melbourne suburb of Docklands, 17 per cent of all dwellings had no water use for twelve months straight in 2013. In their 2020 analysis, the twenty suburbs with the highest rate of unoccupied dwellings had about 5 per cent of all dwellings using no water over twelve months, being continuously unoccupied. Only a small number of homes nationally are unoccupied long term, and the bulk of these are newly constructed dwellings.

Unemployed homes and unemployed people

The best way to understand vacant and unoccupied homes is to think about housing markets in the same way we think about the labour market. The unemployment rate measures the number of people currently not working but actively seeking work, while the rental vacancy rate measures the number of dwellings soon to be unoccupied and actively seeking a new tenant. They are both measures of the state of the current market, either for jobs or for tenants.

We also know the unemployment rate does not measure the number of people without jobs, only the number of people actively looking for jobs. In the same way that people can be 'out of the labour force' for many reasons, dwellings can be unoccupied and not looking for a tenant for many reasons and be 'out of the dwelling force'. A booming labour market brings people into the labour force, and a booming housing market brings unoccupied homes into the rental market, which is what happened during the Covid-19 pandemic.

In keeping with this analogy, economists think there is a rate of unemployment that is necessary for the job market to function and allow for people to switch in and out of jobs without pushing up overall wages. They call this the 'non-accelerating inflation rate of unemployment', or NAIRU for short, or sometimes just the 'natural rate'. When unemployment is below the 'natural rate', wages tend to rise, and, when unemployment is above it, wages tend to fall.

Since the average stay in a rental home is a touch over two years, if every rental dwelling changed tenants every two years or so, and all were advertised online for more than three weeks, then we would expect to find 75,000 rental advertisements at any given point in time, or about 2.5 per cent.

That 2.5 per cent rental vacancy rate is what we might call the 'natural rate' of rental vacancy, where rents are neither rising nor falling.[9] When the rental vacancy is above this rate, rents tend to fall, and when rental vacancy is below this rate, rents tend to rise.

The Sydney rental vacancy grew to 2.5 per cent in 2018 and stayed above that level until the end of 2021. During that time, rents paid by tenants of the same dwelling—measured in the Australian Bureau of Statistics surveys of real estate agent rental rolls—fell over 5 per cent in nominal terms, and estimates of advertised asking rents across houses and units fell from $610 to $520 per week in that time, or nearly 15 per cent.[10]

Just like in the labour market, dwellings move from being unoccupied to occupied, or vacant to rented, or unoccupied to vacant and so on. The similarity between rental markets and labour markets helps us understand whether the causal stories that are often assumed to explain the rental vacancy measure make sense.

It is common to hear that low rental vacancy causes rents to rise. But low rental vacancy rates are the mechanism by which rental prices adjust, just like low unemployment is the mechanism by which wages adjust. Rising wages and falling unemployment are the same thing, measured differently. Rising rents and falling rental vacancy are the same thing, measured differently. They are both symptoms of the same equilibrium adjustment in the respective labour and rental markets.

This similarity also explains why a 'rental crisis' is a predictable part of the business cycle and usually coincides with a booming labour market. We can look, for example, back to the 1880s property boom and then the early 1890s bust in Victoria.

The number of unoccupied dwellings in Melbourne rocketed to 14,000 in 1893, which is equivalent today to 150,000 unoccupied dwellings. But as the economy recovered in 1894 and 1895, this fell to 10,000 and lower. The vacancy rate for housing tracked the unemployment rate for people in that cycle.[11]

Rental vacancy rates, like the unemployment rate, are useful for understanding which way the rental equilibrium is adjusting. But these metrics are not very useful for telling us whether there are physically too many or too few homes, or the state of unoccupied housing.

Low rental vacancy is not quantity driven

To show that low rental vacancy is a symptom of rental market equilibrium adjustment, and not an indicator of a shortage of dwellings, imagine the following scenario. Every household gets a 25 per cent income boost—imagine the government simply credits everyone's bank accounts with extra money in proportion to their previous income.

Some households will spend the money on new cars, holidays or fancy clothes. Others will spend some of it on better located or better quality homes.

What 'better quality homes' often means is fewer people per home—couples move in together, young adults move out of the family home and student share-houses break apart. The advertised stock of rental dwellings will quickly be taken up by these new tenants faster than it can be replaced. That boost in demand from higher incomes will reduce rental vacancy and increase rental prices, despite there being no change in the physical quantity of people or dwellings. Queues at rental inspections will be indistinguishable from a boost in demand due to high immigration, for example, where additional income competes for rents via additional people.

This scenario would also see a sudden increase in buyer demand for new cars, holidays, fancy food and restaurants. Restaurant vacancy will decline. Hotel vacancy will decline. Queues for new cars and trendy doughnut shops will increase. These markets will adjust too.

Higher incomes of renters are a big part of the reason for low rental vacancy in 2023. The Reserve Bank of Australia's published estimates reveal that the lowest income households saw 15 per cent nominal increases in employment income in the year to March 2023, an astonishing rate of income growth, and one that should lead to rising rents.[12]

Vacancy and rental absorption

But surely low rental vacancy also signals to property owners that, if they build new homes faster, they can easily find tenants without having to reduce the rental price. Why doesn't low rental vacancy trigger more housing development?

The short answer is that it does. And it also brings unoccupied dwellings into occupancy, just as high demand for workers brings non-workers back in the workforce. But none of this happens instantly and the logic of the absorption rate equilibrium still applies.

In one of Australia's first major build-to-rent estates, the Smith Collective on the Gold Coast (the former 2018 Commonwealth Games athletes village), the 1251 already-constructed dwellings took nearly four years to be fully leased to renter households, despite low rental vacancy on the Gold Coast. The managers of the project explained to me in 2021 that 'the precinct has been on a staged release strategy so as to not flood the rental market'. They held hundreds of dwellings vacant for many years from the rental market, at a time when the vacancy rate in the area was around 2.5 per cent, near the 'natural rate'. Only in 2021 and later, when local vacancy fell to 0.7 per cent, did they accelerate renting the last buildings in the project.

This is completely normal property market behaviour. Most of the dwellings unoccupied in Melbourne for more than a year based on water use data were newly constructed and waiting for tenants.

The office market provides another example. In Australian cities, the amount of unleased empty office space is between 8 per cent and 18 per cent most of the time, and was about 16 per cent at the end of 2022. This figure doesn't even include the lack of occupation due to working from home. To get that space occupied quickly would mean large reductions in rental prices. But here's the catch. If getting that 16 per cent more office space occupied means dropping rents by more than 16 per cent, then total rents earned by building owners falls under higher occupancy. Only if reducing rental price to reduce vacancy increases the total income (price times quantity of space leased) will it be worthwhile to lease those vacant spaces.

In addition to rental vacancy and unoccupied homes, there are also undeveloped property rights to consider. Unbuilt homes are always vacant. We already know from the absorption rate equilibrium that there is an optimal rate at which land will be converted to housing. If the Smith Collective project hadn't had to be built all at once to house Commonwealth Games athletes, it would have been built in stages over many years, so that fewer dwellings were vacant at any point in time, but more land was vacant. The same market forces that dictate the equilibrium rate to rent already built homes also dictate the equilibrium absorption rate of converting vacant property into housing.

Vacancy taxes

In Victoria, Australia, and British Columbia, Canada, vacancy taxes, or more accurately unoccupied home taxes, have been recently introduced. Property owners with homes held unoccupied for periods of more than, say, six months in a year, must pay for the privilege of excluding people from existing homes.

The motives behind this policy are admirable. There is a commonsense logic to it, as captured by a 2022 article in the *Investigate Europe* magazine that noted: 'Europe has reached a point where there are too many people without homes and many homes without people.'[13]

The British Columbia empty homes tax began in 2017 and applied at 0.5 per cent of the market value of the property; for foreign property owners, the tax rate was 2 per cent. More than $231 million in revenue was raised in the first three years, mostly from foreign owners, and about 20,000 unoccupied homes were estimated to have become occupied over that period out of a total housing market of roughly 2.1 million dwellings, or nearly 1 per cent.[14]

While often difficult to administer, taxing unoccupied homes can be a useful revenue source. Equilibrium adjustment, however, would suggest that any effect on rents in the housing market is small and temporary. We know from the rental and spatial equilibrium that a 1 per cent change in the total stock of occupied housing won't reduce rents or prices much at all, as households adjust to fill these extra homes and continue to pay roughly the same share of income on rent. The initial outcome in British Columbia was to add about 1 per cent extra occupied dwelling space for each person on average, but there were likely also countervailing effects on the absorption rate because of people occupying empty homes rather than renting or buying new homes. This is why, so far, there is no analysis showing a noticeable reduction in rents after the tax was introduced.

17 ◆ Rental rules

What's the point of a rental commissioner who can't control rents? If you just want someone to tell you to increase housing supply then there's plenty of property industry lobbyists doing it for free.

—Housing researcher Alistair Sisson noting on X/Twitter that, although politicians pretend to want lower rents, they avoid any action that creates the power to control them (12 April 2023)

In early April 2023 the Queensland government floated the idea of limiting how fast rents could be increased each year for sitting tenants. Within hours of their public announcement, the real estate industry was in panic mode. The 9 a.m. announcement by the premier, Annastacia Palaszczuk, led quickly to dozens of response articles in the online media, and the six o'clock news that day was clogged with property lobbyists explaining with a straight face how bad rental protections for tenants are for tenants. The Victorian government a month later proposed similar limits on rental price increases, and within hours the 'real estate experts . . . savaged the move, saying it will decimate the industry'.[1]

So many property owner interest groups have for decades voiced their opposition to any regulation of housing rents that it is now widely thought to be 'inefficient' or 'distortionary' and famously believed to be so detrimental to a city's housing market that 'next to bombing, rent control seems in many cases to be the most efficient technique so far known for destroying cities'.[2]

The reason that rent controls attract such a response from property owners is not that they are ineffective and cumbersome. Or that they backfire.

It's because they work.

Homeownership is rent control, but popular

Imagine for a moment that a whacky new political party imposed the most extreme rent control possible—freezing rents at today's prices in perpetuity and prohibiting the removal of the current tenant. They allowed tenants unlimited rights to sublet the property but obliged them to pay council rates and property taxes. This would be one of the most extreme versions of rent control imaginable. Yet, it is exactly what happens when someone buys a home to live in.

The whole point of homeownership is to control the rent, rather than be continually exposed to market pricing, by finding a favourable landlord. Yourself. The asset value of a home is, after all, just the financial representation of all future rents paid at a fixed upfront price. The only difference with rent control is that the occupant and the name on the property title are different.

Because rent control is one of the benefits of homeownership, wealthy cities and countries with stringent rent controls often have low homeownership. Countries like Switzerland and

Germany have strong rental protections and the majority of people live in rented housing. The lure of escaping the rental market is much lower when the future cost of renting is curtailed. Additionally, because there are so many renter households, there is an influential voting bloc that provides political support for maintaining strict controls.

The problem with rent control is that it works, and hence it confronts the symmetry of property markets. The distraction is to pretend that it doesn't.

How rents can be regulated

'First-generation' rent controls, or rent freezes, fix rents at a certain point in time and prohibit the owner of that property from raising rents above that level. These have been enacted during wartime in Australia (through World Wars I and II) and in much of the world. These first-generation rent controls usually allow for higher rents only if landlords renovate or improve the property.

The problem with first-generation controls is that the rental equilibrium still exists. When tenants want to move, new tenants want to outbid each other up to the rental equilibrium, so some kind of non-price mechanism for choosing to whom to allocate the home must be used. In Vienna, Austria, after World War I, rents were controlled in this way and relocations happened via a government clearing house. Those who wanted to move would submit their property and their desired new area, and when appropriate matches were found (in pairs or larger indirect swaps) tenants would swap homes and pay the regulated price at their new home.

'Second-generation' rent controls allow for rents to reset to the market equilibrium between tenancies. They are better described as tenant protections that limit how quickly rents can be increased for a sitting tenant and are usually coupled with protections so that landlords cannot evict a tenant to boost the rent for the next tenant. Typically, the limit on rent increases is related to a price index in the broader economy, either the consumer price index, or a local housing rent index. For example, consumer price inflation plus 3 per cent is the current limit in the Netherlands. Spain, Austria, Switzerland and Germany all limit the rate of rent increases.[3] Even in our own backyard, the Australian Capital Territory has a soft limit on how fast leases can rise to a touch above the local rental inflation measure, though it allows tenants to agree to higher increases.[4]

If this ACT rule was a strict limit, it would mean that, if the local rental equilibrium adjusted 15 per cent in a year, whereas the local inflation measure increased only 5 per cent, then a rent increase to match the market must be smoothed out over three years at a maximum of 5.5 per cent per year rather than a single 15 per cent rent increase.

The benefit of second-generation rent controls is that they smooth out sudden shocks to tenants when the rental equilibrium changes quickly, reducing forced moves by renters due to rent price increases. In fact, they perform a similar function to the way land taxes are smoothed out for landlords in Queensland and New South Wales. In these states, land tax is levied on the average of the past three years of land value in their land tax assessment, not just the land value in the last year. If land values jump 20 per cent in one year after being flat for two years, then that 20 per cent increase in land tax is smoothed out over three years because of this averaging process. Landlords don't like sudden increases in their costs either.

Economic consequences and arguments

The temporary periods where second-generation rent controls create a gap between paid rents and market rents come at a cost to landlords of exactly the value of this gap. But unlike first-generation controls, these gaps are relatively small and temporary, minimising the negative effect on property asset values from these regulations.

Minimising doesn't mean removing. The symmetry of property markets still applies, and this is why the arguments about even minimal rent regulations are fierce.

In 2022, roughly $60 billion was paid by Australian renters to landlords. If new rental regulations reduced rents from rising by just 5 per cent on average for one year, this would save renter households $3 billion, but cost landlords the exact same $3 billion.

That small changes to rents scale up so dramatically to have large financial effects on property owners is the motivation for ongoing lobbying by landlords against regulations that make rents even a little cheaper. A favourite argument used in this lobbying is that rent control in any form reduces new housing supply, both from landlords selling and from fewer new developments, meaning it backfires and 'in the long-run drives up prices'.[5]

These arguments don't pass even rudimentary scrutiny.

First, the claim that landlords will sell, and this will result in fewer homes, confuses swapping names on a property title with bulldozing homes. Landlords can only sell to other landlords or to first home buyers. That's it. When they sell to another landlord there is no change to the stock of rental homes or rental households. If they sell to a first home buyer, then that household is no longer renting and is now owning, and hence the stock of rental homes falls by one, and the stock of renter households falls by one as well. Even if the first home buyer is a new household, formed from previous homeowning households and not coming directly from the rental sector, this still removes demand for rental homes by that household, which would have otherwise rented.

In fact, the only way to increase homeownership is for landlords to sell their properties to renters. A widely acknowledged benefit of wartime first-generation rent controls was that they encouraged landlords to sell to renters, who became owner-occupiers, as landlords could get better returns if they invested their cash elsewhere.

Second, if rent control backfires and leads to higher rents and prices in the long run, then property owners should lobby for more rent control, not less. After all, if they can forgo a little rent today for much more later, that would be a great investment.

Finally, if lowering rents really does have the major effect of lowering the lower absorption rate equilibrium, then a favourite story of the property lobby, that allowing more supply will push down rents, can't also be true. If lower rents slow down new supply, then it can't be true that property owners will supply new homes so fast as to cause lower rents and remain unaffected by those lower rents.

Trust me, I was a landlord too

I was a landlord for seventeen years and had all the nasty experiences that landlords complain about when tenancy protections of any sort are proposed. So I have little time for these sob stories.

In 2002, when I was nineteen, my dad gave me and my siblings $30,000 each and made us each buy a home as an investment. It was his way of securing our financial future after battling a life-threatening cancer.

At the time, I paid $161,000 for a modest house at Ferny Hills in Brisbane's north-west, which seemed expensive at the time. The green shag-pile carpets and brown 1970s wall cladding were tired after decades of rough treatment. But the home had a long-term tenant paying $160 a week and he wanted to stay.

Only after many years did I raise the rent on my first tenant. When I did, I was acutely aware that I had no real reason to do so other than the fact that I had the bargaining power because the rent was so far below the rental market equilibrium. I made the usual landlord excuses for bumping up the rent by $20 a week. That tenant moved out seven years later, having saved enough to buy himself a home.

Though I was losing money each year in a strict accounting sense, the whole enterprise felt like free money as the value of the house kept rising.

In 2003 I bought another house, this time in Bellbird Park, west of Brisbane. It cost $118,000 and the tenants paid $170 per week. Again, its market price grew quickly. After the first tenants vacated, I rented to an organisation that housed children whose parents were in prison. This worked out fine for a few years until one day I got a call about some repairs. It turned out that one of the children staying there was getting up to mischief. I later heard from a neighbour that this child had broken into their house, taken their car keys and stolen their car.

The final straw was the kid running away. They left the bathtub filling up and, muffled by the sound of the water, they snuck out of the house. In the heat of the moment, the guardian didn't turn off the tap. A bathmat covered the floor drain, and, so, as they were chasing the kid around the suburb and getting police help, the house was slowly flooding.

When I first inspected the property after this event, I felt the sadness that all houseproud investors get when they see their properties in disarray. The carpet was destroyed throughout, as well as the vinyl in the kitchen; the kitchen cabinetry had soaked up the water. All the wall plaster was swollen. But that wasn't all.

Recent weeks and months had not been easy on the old house. The letterbox had been smashed with a bat. All the timber logs used for garden edging had been ripped out and used to make a bonfire in the middle of the yard, along with about half the timber fence panels. The classic Aussie Hills Hoist clothesline had been ripped out of the ground and bent and broken; it must have taken the weight of a few big kids hanging and swinging violently. The front door and most of the bedroom doors had been kicked in, and half the kitchen cupboard doors were dangling off or missing. Light fittings had been pulled out of the ceiling. Troubled kids and tough times had combined in a destructive way.

What's my point? Is it that landlords have enough to worry about?

In fact, the opposite.

I had landlord insurance for exactly this situation. It covered the cost of repairs (though I did many smaller repairs myself) as well as most of the rent while the house was vacant. Within a few months I was made whole, financially speaking.

The worst treatment a home could suffer at the hands of a tenant didn't really affect me financially as a landlord. And the whole time, the value of the house was rising.

Maybe, because I was a young landlord, I didn't have an expectation of making a lot of money with no effort. Or maybe it was my dad's advice: 'If it was easy, everyone would do it', which ensured I understood that managing property is a real job. What it did show me is that, even for landlords, there is a benefit from stable tenants that can outweigh the cost of lower rent. Although property investment is risky, that risk comes with rewards too.

But what about all those economic studies?

Study after study has shown that rent control makes housing cheaper for tenants, yet there is a monumental effort by property owners to pretend that these studies find the opposite. A 2021 report about the Berlin experience with rent control—rents were frozen there at €9.80 per square metre per month on the 70 per cent of dwellings built before 2014 for two years—is a great example of the way the beneficial outcomes of these regulations are widely and intentionally misrepresented.[6]

That report showed an enormous benefit for Berlin renters, with its total city-wide rental price increase being 60 per cent lower than in the thirteen next-largest German cities. New apartment listings outpaced peer cities. To give some indicative figures, average Berlin rents were about €800 per month and around 700,000 renter households were benefiting from the controls. Rents stayed flat for two years for those households, while rents in the unregulated sector increased by about 10 per cent. This saved renters in this one city €340 million over two years, before the rent control was deemed unconstitutional and removed.

Instead of being reported as a success, lower rents were reported as a bad thing because they resulted in lower asset prices. The finding of higher new apartment listings was also labelled a bad thing in the press because they were 'only slightly outpacing' other cities. Two good results twisted into bad ones.[7]

A study on the removal of rent control in Cambridge, Massachusetts, found that rents increased 40 per cent over three-years for formerly rent-controlled tenants after the rules ended in 1994, compared to 9 per cent for the uncontrolled market, and the process increased the value of these formerly rent-controlled properties by $1.8 billion.[8]

Even in Canberra in the mid-1970s, a short period of rent controls there saw rents rise only 6 per cent over two years, compared to 25 per cent in neighbouring Queanbeyan.[9]

A now famous study on San Francisco rent controls found that 'landlords treated by rent control reduce rental housing supplies by 15 percent by selling to owner-occupants and redeveloping buildings'.[10] But these are good outcomes—they increased homeownership and the quality of the dwelling stock—not bad ones, as they were reported to be. The idea that rent control means that landlords won't invest in their buildings is wrong. In fact, most rent control laws are written so that rents can only be increased above the limit if dwellings are extensively renovated or improved.

This San Francisco study found that rent controls stopped the displacement of poor people when rents were rapidly rising. But this was described as a negative because poor people staying in their homes while richer people moved in nearby 'contributed to widening income inequality in the city'.

Other rental rules

There are some final comments to make regarding rental regulations.

Regulations that limit Airbnb are also a form of rent control; they limit renting to the long-term tenant rental equilibrium and restrict the often more lucrative short-term holiday-maker equilibrium.

Shifting homes into Airbnb, instead of into long-term rental, certainly affects some local areas, but these are usually areas that always had a holiday rental market. No one argues that allowing Airbnb increases housing supply or discourages landlords selling; clearly, allowing unrestricted Airbnb is not good for tenants. We know that restricting Airbnb makes the homes affected by such regulations cheaper, just as with all rent controls.

As a final observation, I've encountered several people who grew up in rent-controlled housing or public housing, and who have now turned against it. I was once interviewed by a United States resident who grew up in rent control and said that he and his family were 'stuck there' as children, because of the higher rents if they moved. But, because of the low rent, his mum was able to send him and his siblings to private middle school.

The puzzle for me is that, although he felt stuck, living in rent-controlled housing gave his family more options than an alternative scenario without rent control. Instead of the two options—market rent or market purchase—they had market rent, market purchase *and* rent control. The fact that this option was so much cheaper that they felt stuck shows just how financially beneficial it was.

Hoax housing policies

18 ♦ Supply superstitions

Build build build build build build build build build build build build build build build.

—*The New York Times* headline arguing that 'unleashing'
housing supply by changing zoning rules is the key to
affordable housing, Conor Dougherty, 13 February 2020[1]

The main hoax housing policies in Australia stem from what I call the supply myth. Readers from Canada, the United Kingdom, the United States and New Zealand will also no doubt be sick of hearing about a shortage of land, or that governments must release land, or that regulations are stifling supply, or that taxes on property are inhibiting supply. The variations are endless.

The supply myth fills a beautiful niche. It doesn't question the distribution of property ownership. It doesn't annoy property owners, as they stand to benefit from less regulation and lower taxes. And it sells a believable story to renters—who can disagree with the idea that more homes are better than fewer?

If there isn't an obvious shortage of homes today, then the trick is to stoke fear by claiming that one is just around the corner. The supply myth works at all points in the property cycle. Rising rents or prices are a story of current shortages;

falling rents or prices are a story of impending shortages. You can never lose.

Planning academics Nicole Gurran and Peter Phibbs tell a classic tale of the lobbying efforts behind the supply myth:

> Some people liken houses to bananas. When the supply of bananas drops, prices rise. The Property Council of Australia has called this 'banana-nomics'. In 2017, the Property Council of Australia lobby group sent plastic bananas to state and federal MPs with a crib sheet on housing affordability. Recalling Cyclone Larry, which devastated fruit farms in Northern Queensland, its message was simple—when there is a shortage of bananas, the price goes up. With housing, the disaster wasn't a cyclone but rather 'excessive delays', 'inconsistent planning' and inadequate land supply.[2]

It would be a great relief if this were true. I'd love to not write this book. But the economics or the five market equilibria show why it's not. And so does the money.

Imagine for a moment that the story was true and that letting the market rip by removing taxes and regulations really could achieve the outcome of, say, 25 per cent lower rents and prices over five years. Where is the lobbying to protect the trillions in asset values and the billions in rental income that are at risk from up-zoning? It doesn't exist. In fact, the Real Estate Institute of Australia (REIA), the lobby group for landlords, supports mass up-zoning.[3] The Property Council of Australia, representing property developers and major investors, argues that 'National Competition Policy-style supply and housing incentives could boost state housing supply and spur state housing production within 3 years.[4]

It's a puzzle that property owners and the development lobby, who make money from selling and renting property, claim that land use regulations decrease housing supply and should be removed, despite standing to benefit financially from higher prices and less competition.

Only one of three options can resolve this contradiction:

1 housing supply does not operate the way they imply, or
2 the industry puts the interests of the community before their own shareholders, or
3 they are incompetent.

Option 1 it is.

No industry lobbies for deregulation if it genuinely believes stronger competition and lower prices would be the result.

The taxi industry, for example, did not seek deregulation to facilitate more supply and competition and lower prices from Uber. Instead, they argued for more regulation. The Australian Taxi Industry Association (ATIA) called Uber 'a political manipulator'[5] for its successful drive to deregulate the industry and the Taxi Council of Western Australia (TCWA) pushed for more regulation—'instead of deregulating the industry, [we] would maintain and heighten regulation, creating a Smarter Taxi Service for Perth'.[6]

The Pharmacy Guild of Australia argues that competition is not in the interests of its pharmacy-owning members, producing material like 'Supermarket pharmacies . . . bad for health?' where it states that the 'Guild does not believe it is in the best interests of patients to allow pharmacies in supermarkets'.[7] They further support laws that restrict competition from new pharmacies through location rules that prohibit too many pharmacies from locating close together to improve options for customers, and ownership rules that require qualified pharmacists to own the business.

Although we associate big business with a deregulatory agenda, because of how they portray themselves in the media, no business that makes monopoly profits will want less regulation. They want less regulation for themselves, and more regulation for their potential competitors.

Returning to the property market, you will find that, when surveyed, landlords are far more likely to support up-zoning, allegedly against their own financial interests, whereas renters are the opposite.[8]

In the 2022 parliamentary inquiry into housing supply, chairman of the inquiry, Liberal MP Jason Falinski, was good enough to take up my idea to ask some of the country's biggest property developers under oath if up-zoning would reduce property prices. He first asked, 'If a new competitor established themselves beside your major residential projects and sold similar dwellings for 25 per cent less than what you sell them for, would that be a good or bad thing for your business financially?'

The housing developers all said that this would be bad: 'It would be significantly bad. There's no doubt about it.'

Falinski then asked, 'Do you think if state local governments rezoned more land to allow greater supply, that you could see dwelling prices drop by 20 per cent?' Which was especially relevant since prices had risen 20 per cent in the previous year.

They all said no. That wouldn't happen.[9] Implausible. Quickly realising their story was unravelling, they pivoted to the idea that prices would rise more slowly than otherwise, a weaselly claim. If prices rise 5 per cent instead of 25 per cent over the next year, then that really does reduce prices 20 per cent compared with the alternative. You can't switch from levels to rates of change so as to hide the fact that you don't really think that what you are advocating works the way you claim it will.

Indeed, if building lots more houses was both profitable and would reduce rents and prices more broadly, then a public housing developer would be a way to achieve the same thing— make money and make rents cheaper! Yet this obvious solution is never part of the debate.

Searching for evidence

In 2022 I received an out-of-the-blue phone call from the United Kingdom's Office of Innovation. This office was tasked by its government with validating the supply myth and finding examples from around the world where changing planning and zoning regulations had resulted in cheap housing. They called me because after calling all their local housing experts, they had not yet found any examples. They were hoping that maybe there were some Australian examples. I had none to offer.

Tokyo is one place the YIMBYs will often point to as evidence that changing planning regulations can lead to cheap housing via faster new housing development. It came up as a topic of conversation on that phone call, but it is not a valid example.

Tokyo is famous for its expensive real estate and tiny homes. In fact, if you compare Japan to Australia in terms of dwelling areas, not dwelling numbers, there is three times as much housing space per person in Australia. A typical Tokyo resident has 19 square metres of dwelling space per person while the typical Australian has about 80 square metres of dwelling space.[10] On many metrics of housing costs, Tokyo is more expensive than all Australian cities.

Another city we discussed was Auckland, which in 2016 removed many planning and zoning regulations to allow three-storey townhouses across most of the city. The spatial pattern of development since 2016 did change, as expected, and a construction boom that had begun before this zoning change continued. But the construction boom was merely part of the normal property cycle, which hit a low in 2010 and reached its next peak in 2022. It's the same cycle that Sydney saw in the 2010s, which was also followed by declining rents for a period. In 2021, despite the new planning rules, Auckland house prices still rapidly boomed, like they did in most cities around the world, with the median price increasing by over $100,000 in February 2021 alone.[11]

We can also search back in time, before modern planning regulations and taxation. Perhaps housing was cheap and abundant then.

Nothing is further from the truth. The property market before the mid-twentieth century was a terrible time. An 1897 newspaper article noted the following:

In the City Court, yesterday, four children whose ages ranged from 11 to three years, were handed over to the care of the Institution for waifs and strays. They lived in a den in Latrobe-street, which was in a disgustingly filthy condition and the [last] resort for young people of the vagabond class.[12]

By the 1930s and the Great Depression, the slums of Australia's major cities were a major social and political issue. Repeated disease outbreaks—due to overcrowded, cold and damp living conditions over the previous decades—triggered a push for minimum housing standards and public housing programs. Methodist social reformer F. Oswald Barnett, learning from European experiences, pushed hard for re-housing people from slums with public housing programs.[13]

No one at the turn of the twentieth century thought free markets were going to provide better housing for the poor; all they had were free markets and only the smallest amount of charity and philanthropy, but it wasn't working. Governments in Australia were less than 5 per cent of the economy in 1900, compared to more than 30 per cent today; it was the epitome of an unregulated free market outcome.

It is also the case that the number of people per dwelling declined for three decades up until the early 2000s, down from over 5 people per dwelling to around 2.6 people per dwelling. The number of adults per dwelling has been flat since the 1980s at 2.1 per dwelling, even as the size of dwellings has grown.[14] There are now more large and high-quality dwellings per capita than ever and yet, despite the evidence, the supply superstition persists.

19 ◆ Zoning zealots

*It is costly and inefficient for developers to hold
inactive land.*

—Former Stockland CEO Andrew Whitson avoids focusing
on the gains made from owning undeveloped property:
Su-Lin Tan, 'The free market has failed to provide
affordable housing in Sydney & Melbourne', *Australian
Financial Review*, 2 August 2016

A popular hoax housing policy is to remove the zoning and
planning regulations that put local limits on density and to
up-zone to allow higher housing densities. One of the major
selling points is that this policy costs governments nothing, so
why not do it?

But up-zoning is not free. It is unpriced. That is why the
property owners are so fond of this policy.

To understand this, recall that property rights to invisible
boxes of three-dimensional space are the emergent result of
many interacting laws, including zoning and planning laws. Just
as property can be carved up horizontally into lots, it can be
carved up vertically too. Zoning laws that limit density are a
tool that carves out some of this airspace property to reserve it
for the public.

Sometimes, planning regulations explicitly regulate property in a way that separates the rights to airspace from the rights below so that airspace can be traded independently. New York famously has a system where 'air rights' can be traded among property owners at different locations, so that unused rights to density can be traded to owners of another lot to allow them to build to higher densities than would otherwise be the case.[1]

In the board game Monopoly, the rules about how many houses and hotels can be placed on each property are like planning regulations. Up-zoning in Monopoly would be like the 'bank' giving all the current property owners the right to build even more hotels—like stacking another level of the board game on top and handing the new level to each of the owners below. It's great for the players who own the most property, as it gives them new property, but it doesn't help the players who own the least, or none at all.

Imagine you can build an apartment complex with 100 apartments under currently defined property rights, including planning and zoning laws. You could build 200 apartments if you were given the property rights to the publicly owned site next door. You could also build 200 if you were given property rights to the airspace above. Both options have roughly the same value to you and are hence economically identical. But you can get airspace rights for free if you lobby for up-zoning, while you would have to pay the market price for the property next door.

Rights to airspace are as real as other property rights, and up-zoning changes the rules so as to hand this property right for free to the owners of the property below. No wonder there is a huge incentive to lobby for up-zoning and foster supply superstitions.

These property rights could be priced instead. It would be economically irresponsible for a government to give away property like a public park to a neighbouring private property owner so they could build more homes. That property would be sold at market prices. But when that property right is in the air, we all too easily give it away. Since these rights could be priced instead, the lost revenue is an invisible cost to government budgets and a gift to property owners. No wonder they lobby for it.

Pricing up-zoning property is possible

It is not always true that a property right created by up-zoning has a value. Existing limits on density can be higher than the density equilibrium, and often are. But it is also true that the value of changes in the density equilibrium over time that go unused can be priced, even without zoning regulations. Creating a system of separable development rights that need to be purchased by property owners who want to change the density of their property above its current density is a way to price the value of increases in the density equilibrium over time and any extra rights created by up-zoning.

This idea might seem strange at first, but the Australian Capital Territory has successfully priced development rights like this for half a century. A change-of-use charge (CUC) is levied at 75 per cent of the market value from the increase in the density of use when redeveloping property.[2] For example, if a property is worth $1 million when the existing detached home is the only allowable use, but the property would be worth $5 million as a development site for apartments, then the property owner would pay 75 per cent of the $4 million value difference to take up the right to redevelop, or $3 million in this case.

Pricing the value of development rights also happens in São Paulo, Brazil. Property owners in designated development areas there are granted a default right to erect a building with an internal area equal to the area of the site.[3] To build above this density, they must buy additional development rights from the city government at regular auctions. Prices around US$400 per square metre of additional building area are normal, and the city has raised more than US$2 billion in twenty years of operation.

Back in the 1970s, Sydney had a 'betterment levy' of 30 per cent of the additional value from converting rural to urban land, raising over $12 million in its four years of operation.[4] Tellingly, the government that got elected on the promise to charge this fee had to go to the next election promising to unwind it, such was the political pressure from property owners.

I studied the property values of just six up-zoned areas in south-east Queensland between 2008 and 2012, and found that, compared to adjacent property that hadn't been up-zoned, the value of the up-zoned land increased by more than $700 million.[5] More interestingly, I could predict where the up-zoning boundary was drawn by analysis of the social and corporate networks of the property owners.

Of note is that in Queensland there are mechanisms for property owners to seek compensation for down-zoning in the planning laws, but they must be sought within a certain time period. But there are no general mechanisms to price up-zoning (though with a few exceptions in some state-controlled priority development areas). This asymmetry makes little sense.

After years of my own personal lobbying, the Victorian government in 2022 announced a plan to charge for new development rights, called the Windfall Gains Tax of 50 per cent of the market value arising from certain types of planning changes. This new law was passed in 2022, to be implemented in 2024. Given my assessment of the politics of housing and the experience of Sydney in the 1970s, I am wary that this policy will stick. I hope my fears are unfounded.

'Inclusionary zoning' is a policy that recognises the property value created by planning rule changes that allow more density. Instead of paying in cash, property owners are required to pay in the form of providing some housing at a below-market rent for a period of time in their project. In 2023, New South Wales Premier Chris Minns announced that new housing developments could get a 30 per cent increase in density if 15 per cent of the dwellings are rented at 20 per cent below market rent for fifteen years.[6]

This is a complex way to get below-market rentals, and it often fails. These requirements only work for large projects, so property owners have an incentive to break projects into smaller ones that fall just below the cut-offs. Because building costs are similar, but prices vary across locations, it is hard to create rules that work broadly and not just in a few high-value areas. The complexity of combining a funding program, in the form of charging for development rights, with a non-market housing scheme, is not necessary. Why not sell development rights and use the revenue raised to build or buy homes to rent at below market price?

In fact, since undeveloped property increases in value, it is often a good investment for governments to develop housing directly. In the ACT, a public land agency owns all the non-urban land and subdivides it into new housing lots, generating public profits that were $165 million in 2019–20 alone. In the Netherlands, this is known as Active Land Policy. Councils there acquire land at a market value reflecting the previous use only, and then change the zoned use and density via a public developer, and they earned more than €600 million per year in the 2000s boom from this.[7]

Charging property owners to accelerate the absorption rate

Because up-zoning provides an economic gain if property is undeveloped, it provides an incentive to delay development at locations where future up-zoning is likely.

There is a milk-bottling factory on a 2-hectare riverfront inner Brisbane site, adjacent to the glamorous Gallery of Modern Art and near to a glass bottle factory and concrete plant. These old industrial facilities are nestled on prime waterfront land near a major cultural precinct with its art galleries, museums and theatres. These are clearly outdated uses of this valuable, well-located property.

Brisbane Council has attempted to incentivise Parmalat, the French owner of this property, to relocate by up-zoning the site's height limits from 12 storeys to 20 storeys, and then a few years later to 30 storeys. In 2023 the council proposed no height limit at all. In the meantime, the company was making plenty of money by land-banking that site. Had they sold and relocated two decades earlier, they wouldn't have made those tens of millions of dollars of gains in the value of their property rights from upzoning.

A logical end point, once you realise that the planning system is regulating locations but not the absorption rate, is to seek ways to incentivise faster housing development. A popular policy idea in Australia in 2023 was for the federal government to pay councils for every additional new home in their area. Another idea is to offer temporary up-zoning in targeted areas, so that property owners must rush to develop before their right to build higher density housing expires. Another is to have fees on development that rise over time, so that they add to the cost of delay. Another is to have short expiry periods for planning approvals.

Although not widely acknowledged, these concepts are more common in systems of mining property rights, where 'use-it-or-lose-it' provisions are often used to ensure property owners do not delay investment in extracting minerals.

A recent analysis of Zimbabwe's[8] mining policy notes that use-it-or-lose-it provisions need to be more rigorously applied to 'free up vast tracts of mining locations that have been sterilised for speculative purposes . . . Some mining houses have held on to title of mining locations from as far back as the 1960s, more by reason of paying inspection fees and less due to real mining activities.' This reminds me of the 'zombie' New South Wales planning approvals we encountered earlier, which were issued in 1983 but still not developed in 2023.

The idea of providing a timing incentive to develop housing is good. But there are two issues that make these approaches far from the ideal housing policy. First, in practice there are strong political motives to do the opposite. Laws have mostly shifted in the opposite direction, rewarding waiting. In Queensland, for example, there are exemptions from land taxes for newly subdivided residential land so that the property developer is not financially punished for selling these new lots more slowly.

The more problematic thing is that enforcing timing rules must happen in the future and possibly by a different government. And practically, enforcing mechanisms to squeeze property owners into building homes faster will look a lot like compulsory acquisition of property by the government if they fail to comply. After a property has been up-zoned for residential uses because the government wants faster new housing supply, the property owner may claim they cannot fund home construction. So the state fines them. The property owner refuses to pay. The result is that the state will compulsorily acquire the property so as to recover the penalty and to force new homes to be built. 'You must build homes even if you lose money' is a challenging policy stance.

The enormous cost of up-zoning as a housing policy is widely ignored because it suits property owners, who benefit from billion-dollar giveaways that have no effect on the absorption rate equilibrium. Australian cities have taken this idea seriously and been madly up-zoning for decades, with nothing to show for it.

20 ◆ Financial fixes

I get the impression that every time the residential building industry is under pressure, some crises are concocted: rent crisis, house price affordability crisis, intergenerational inequality, boomer wealth bashing; justifying straightout corporate welfare.

—Rabee Tourky, Professor of Economics at ANU, summarising the political games at play when it comes to tax changes that rely on the supply myth, posting on X/Twitter, 18 June 2023

Because of the financial dimensions to property assets, policy attention gravitates towards financial fixes, and the best hoax housing policies are those where financial fixes are used to create the illusion that housing will become cheap.

The financial-fix class of policies extends to tax settings, loan guarantees and funding tricks for state and federal budgets that all serve to achieve very little and can come at a big cost to public budgets with no benefit to renters. Plenty of places around the world have tried all sorts of different tax settings, and none really makes a difference to housing rents.

I'm going to ruin the surprise and tell you that, although some of the tax changes discussed in housing policy debate may be worth doing to improve the efficiency and fairness of the tax system, this class of financial fixes isn't going to make housing rents and prices cheaper or solve other inequalities in the property system.

Funding tricks

In 2022 the federal government proposed a $10 billion Housing Australia Future Fund (HAFF). The idea is to sell Treasury bonds and use the cash from that sale to buy a range of higher-yielding assets like company shares. Because of a differential return between the low interest cost of borrowing and the higher returns on these financial assets, the net gain from the fund over time can pay for future housing subsidies.

It sounds bland and innocuous, which means it is easy to miss how economically backwards the policy really is. On the funding side of the government ledger, it is a balance sheet trick of swapping two assets with different risk profiles. This can be done at any time for any reason, and if it is a good idea to swap $10 billion as a public revenue exercise, then why not $100 billion? Why shouldn't the government own all the shares and raise money from the profits rather than taxing? If getting more housing is a policy concern, why not invest the fund in developing new homes and renting at market prices? Every Aussie and their dog know that housing is the best place to invest your money. Doing this would also directly expand the housing stock.

Had Australia's existing Future Fund directly invested in Australian housing instead of the financial products it did invest in, it would have made more money. Since the Future Fund was established in 2006, Australian dwellings increased 7.7 per cent in value each year and earned about 2.5 per cent in net of rental income in addition, for about a 10 per cent total return per year. The non-housing assets in the Future Fund have only managed to earn 7.8 per cent per year.

Even housing that is rented at a discounted price is a decent investment. The New South Wales Land and Housing Corporation (LAHC) owns the public housing stock in that state. In 2012 its stock of dwellings was worth $32 billion. After selling many of its assets, by 2019 it owned $54 billion worth of public housing assets. That's a 7.8 per cent annualised return while at the same time providing cheap homes to tens of thousands of people.

To show what a good investment public housing is, LAHC announced in March 2014 it would sell 296 public housing units in and around Millers Point in Sydney for an estimated $500 million. But the sales were delayed and only finalised in 2019. They achieved sales revenue of $762 million, a $262 million gain, due to the appreciation of Sydney residential property values during the four-year delay.

You only concoct a financial trick instead of funding existing agencies that build new public housing if you don't want to spend money building housing. After the 2008 financial crisis, the then Rudd-led Labor federal government gave $6 billion to the various state housing agencies to build new homes: the biggest increase in public housing in Australia since the early 1970s. This was done for the macroeconomic benefits of higher construction activity, as everyone knew that up-zoning and other hoax policies weren't going to do the job of faster homebuilding.

Instead of spending tens of millions a year managing a financial fund, the fund's board members could simply go and buy new dwellings, sometimes in bulk, at a good price from private developers, as mystery shoppers. This would put housing equity into the fund, increase the absorption rate of new housing construction, and immediately grow a pool of housing to allocate to state public housing agencies or—my favourite—by lottery to non-homeowner households.

Tax tricks

Two major tax reforms suck up a lot of policy energy: 1) changing the settings on negative gearing and capital gains taxes, and 2) swapping stamp duties for land value taxes.

Unfortunately, neither of these reforms changes anything fundamental about the five property market equilibria, and hence neither makes homes cheaper.

To understand why, recall the asset value of housing is a conversion of future cashflows into a single price today. Lower cashflows mean a lower asset price because there are other assets that you can buy instead of housing to sustain the equilibrium rate of return. Adding or removing a tax on ownership also doesn't change the rental equilibrium, which is determined by the incomes of households. So the effect of a tax on property ownership is to push down asset prices by the exact capitalised value of the future flow of taxes, leaving ownership costs unchanged.

This means that, for example, a tax paid in the form of an infrastructure contribution, which is levied upon development of new housing or other buildings, doesn't add to the market price of those buildings. Asset values aren't a summation of costs. These taxes reduce the residual value of the undeveloped property because the net future cashflow from development is lowered by the amount of the tax. In short, taxes on property ownership serve as a way for the government to share in the economic gains from the property monopoly.

In general, the tax settings on property should be considered as a government funding exercise and compared to alternative taxes, not considered a housing policy exercise. On these terms, they can be quite beneficial.

Negative gearing and the capital gains tax discount

You won't find the phrase 'negative gearing' in tax legislation. Negative gearing is a feature of Australia's tax system whereby individual incomes from all sources are pooled together to generate a single taxable income. If I make a loss on one type of income-generating activity, but a gain from another, like a wage income, then I can subtract the loss from my gain and pay tax only on the net income. Interest on borrowing for an investment property, capital depreciation, maintenance and management costs, local rates, charges and insurance all are tax-deductible expenses for property owners. Often, these costs will exceed the rental income, even in a rental and asset price equilibrium, generating an accounting loss from the property, which when pooled with other incomes, decreases taxable income and hence tax paid.

What makes negative gearing interesting is the reason that landlords will pay a price for a home that is so high that it generates an accounting loss. They are willing to incur this short-term loss on the expectation of future increases in the value of the property asset, known as capital gains.

Since September 1999, capital gains on assets owned for more than a year have been taxed at a 50 per cent discount compared to other incomes. This means that there is an incentive to buy a loss-making asset today in the hope of a lightly taxed capital gain in the future. If capital gains were taxed like any other income, with no discount, the incentive to pay a higher price and take the ongoing loss would be greatly reduced.

Say, for example, you buy a residential property asset for $600,000 and make $20,000 of rental income over the year and have $40,000 in costs, including depreciation and mortgage interest. That would be an income loss of $20,000 that you would deduct from your other taxable income. If the tax rate on that $20,000 of income that you now don't have to pay tax on is 37 per cent, then you pay $7400 less in tax, giving you a net after-tax loss of just $12,600.

If you sell this property for $700,000 after a year, net of selling costs, this is a $100,000 capital gain, but it only adds $50,000 to your taxable income because of the discount. If you pay a 37 per cent tax rate on that extra $50,000 of income, you pay $18,500 in tax.

In total, you've made a $100,000 capital gain and a $20,000 loss, or $80,000, and paid only $11,100 extra tax, or just a 13.9 per cent tax rate on your net economic gains from the property. Your tax rate is about a third as much as earning income any other way.

Even if the capital gain was only equal to the losses incurred, the tax advantage would still exist. If this property was instead sold for $620,000 after costs, then only $10,000 of the $20,000 capital gain would be taxable, giving a $3700 tax bill. The $20,000 income loss plus the $20,000 capital gain means there is no gain from that investment. But the shift between types of taxable income still made this person $3700 better off—by saving $7400 of tax due to the negatively geared income loss, and only paying $3700 on the capital gain of the same value.

In 2020–21, 1.2 million landlords reported an accounting loss from their rental property.[1] This about 6 per cent of the adult population, or a little over half the 2.2 million landlords in the country.

———

Owner-occupiers are even more tax-advantaged on capital gains, getting a 100 per cent tax discount. Any value gains on your own residence are tax-free. But the difference is that costs like mortgage interest, maintenance, rates, and insurances must be paid with after-tax income.

Like all tax settings the main effect of negative gearing and capital gains tax discounts is distributive—does value go to the property owner or the tax office? That's why the real estate lobby groups hate the thought of tax changes that go against them.

Regardless, the price effect of these tax settings comes mostly from the capital gains tax discount, not the fact that property income losses can be deducted from other personal income. It is hard to know exactly how large the price effect of removing the capital gains tax discount would be on the equilibrium asset price of housing. If we look at our previous scenario where only a $20,000 capital gain was made, this had the effect of saving the owner $3700 of tax. If this benefit is added to the future cashflow when pricing the asset, then removing it would reduce the asset price by about 0.6 per cent.

The larger the expected capital gains, the larger the effect on asset prices from removing this tax discount. Some researchers have modelled the effect of removing the capital gains tax discount on the asset price equilibrium under a variety of scenarios, and most estimates fall in the range of 4 per cent to 8 per cent.[2]

It's not nothing, of course. It gives first home buyers, who don't pay any capital gains tax, a slight financial head start on investors. And it redirects the value of the tax discount from landlords to the tax agency.

For landlords collectively, a 4 per cent to 8 per cent reduction in asset value makes an enormous difference. If removing the capital gains tax discount led to a 5 per cent reduction in asset prices, landlords would lose $125 billion in value across their $2.5 trillion of housing assets. This is why lobbyists for property owners find it financially worthwhile to lobby full-time for years to ensure that even modest tax changes like this are unlikely to be enacted.

Notably, New Zealand had no taxes at all on capital gains until recently, and housing rents and prices there were not clearly favourable compared to Australia. In 2015, the 'bright line' rule was introduced so that if you own a property for less than a certain period, then capital gains are added to your taxable income. This had no noticeable effect on housing outcomes.

––––––

Whether the capital gains tax discount is a good policy is mostly a question about the equity of the tax system, not about the cost of housing. On these equity grounds, it doesn't stack up well. Analysis in the *Journal of Taxation* back in 2002 noted the following:

> It is difficult to justify the introduction of the CGT discount and other changes on any tax policy grounds. The changes have considerably reduced the equity of the tax system, may be of dubious benefit on efficiency grounds, and do very little for the simplicity of the Australian CGT regime.[3]

Fighting a tax equity battle is probably a distraction for those seeking cheaper housing, as these tax settings don't change the rental equilibrium, and hence don't make housing cheaper. Remember Susan Lloyd-Hurwitz, the ex-CEO of property developer Mirvac who in December 2022 was appointed to lead the federal government housing taskforce? She made the mistake of commenting on these tax settings, saying: 'My personal opinion is that negative gearing and capital gains tax concessions do contribute to Australians investing in real estate for capital gain rather than for income.'[4]

It immediately cost her. The Real Estate Institute 'called for her removal from the federal government's new National Housing Supply and Affordability Council as a result of the comments'. Her former organisation, the Property Council of Australia, was more moderate, 'merely dismissing discussion of such issues as a "distraction" from housing supply issues'.[5]

Of course, had Lloyd-Hurwitz suggested increasing the capital gain tax discount, she would have been knocked down in the rush of support from the property lobby.

Stamp duty for land value tax

Among think tanks, academics and government agencies there is near universal agreement that swapping stamp duty, a once-off tax on property transactions, for a land value tax, an ongoing tax on property ownership, is going to radically improve the housing market.

I'm here to tell you that, unfortunately, they are all wrong.

The first time I questioned the idea was in 2015, after I realised one of the popularly cited benefits of removing stamp duty—that it would reduce costs for home buyers—was plainly wrong. If you remove a cost to owning an asset, you increase its price.

Stamp duty is a state transaction tax payable by the buyer of a property asset to get their name stamped on the property title (or so to speak). The tax liability is calculated based on the contract price of the sale, with a rising marginal tax rate applying as the value of the asset traded increases. For example, a stamp duty of 4 per cent might apply to the first $1 million of property value, while a rate of 5 per cent applies to the portion of value above $1 million.

Land value taxes are annual tax paid as a proportion of value of the property assuming there is no building on it—as if it was vacant land. That value comes from a residual value calculation, being the market value of the property with the current building, minus the cost of replacing those buildings.

If the value of your land is $1 million and the land value tax rate is 1.5 per cent, you pay $15,000 that year, regardless of the value of replacing the house itself. If the market price of land rises to $1.5 million the next year, you pay $22,500 the following year, though as we saw earlier, in practice property owners in some states get their tax liabilities smoothed out by paying based on the average of the last three years' land values.

You can't avoid land value taxes by building or demolishing on a property or by selling, but you can avoid stamp duty by not selling. This lack of avoidance is why economists widely agree that land value taxes are an efficient source of public revenue. But that doesn't mean they make housing cheap.

The most popular, but wrong, argument for reducing or removing stamp duty is that it adds to the price of buying a home. Property prices are determined by net income flows, and stamp duty is just an immediate negative income flow, meaning the value of the asset falls by the exact amount of the stamp duty. Stamp duty doesn't change how much is paid by buyers of property assets; stamp duty just changes how much sellers get and how much the tax man gets.

This is why, during the height of the Covid-19 pandemic, the United Kingdom enacted a stamp duty holiday to help 'kickstart the stalled housing market'.[6] It's a good way to keep prices up and create an incentive to trade more. The effect of stamp duties on reducing prices is also why Singapore in 2021 instituted additional stamp duties to curtail the rapid price rises that were especially being driven by foreign buying.[7] Singaporean citizens buying a second home now pay 20 per cent of the purchase price as a stamp duty, and 30 per cent for their third and subsequent property. Foreigners pay a whopping 60 per cent stamp duty and corporate owners 65 per cent.

———

Another argument in favour of the tax swap is that lowering the cost of trading homes means that more homeowners will upsize and downsize to suit their family situation and relocate more regularly for work opportunities. This will better match the housing stock with the needs of households. But the evidence is that any effect is small.[8] Which it should be, since most households who plan to move regularly choose to rent.

The forgotten side of this argument is that landlords own a third of properties and they too will trade more frequently. Most of their extra trades will involve forcing a renter household to move who didn't otherwise want to. New Zealand hasn't had stamp duties on property trades since 1999,[9] and the one big difference between their housing market and Australia's is that New Zealand renters are more likely to move because of their landlord selling the home.

Since property markets allocate ownership by income and wealth, more trades don't necessarily mean a better matching of households and homes. The Australian Capital Territory has been decreasing stamp duties and increasing land taxes since 2012. Dwelling prices there have grown roughly in line with Sydney, and the effect of higher turnover and 'loosening up' the market is hard to see. In fact, when the Territory created an over-65s stamp duty exemption in the hope of older households selling bigger homes and moving into new apartments, they found it was common for older people to take advantage of that exemption to buy an even larger home. The benefit to doing this was to shield more funds from the age pension asset test, as pensioners can own a home of any value and not lose their age pension, but if they hold that value in other assets, their pension will be reduced in proportion to the value of those assets. The Territory soon capped the value of the over-65s stamp duty discount to avoid this outcome.

What should be clear is that all the homes occupied by over-65s will be reallocated to other households upon the death of current residents in any case. Downsizing is at best a shifting forward in time of the inevitable reallocation of homes.

Another argument is that land value taxes are a stable source of revenue for state governments compared to stamp duties, which vary over time in accordance with both transaction volume and price, while land taxes vary by price alone. This is true, but it is not clear that stable taxes are desirable. States should manage the economy, not the budget, so when there is a boom they should tax more, and when there is a bust, tax much less. Stamp duties stabilise the economy more than land value taxes, which is the flipside of being a more volatile revenue source.

Indeed, stamp duties raise a lot of revenue. In New South Wales, half a billion dollars per month for the past decade, and nearly $10 billion in 2020–21 (of which $7.9 billion came from residential property asset trades). In Victoria, it is $9 billion and about 30 per cent of the total tax revenue. Removing stamp duty is not a trivial change from the perspective of state budgets and comes with the risk of being removed without a commensurate increase in land value taxes. In fact, in 2023 the New South Wales government announced the no–stamp duty trick but forgot the land value tax part.

Like capital gains tax, stamp duties and land taxes should be assessed based on whether they are a good tax, not whether they are a good housing policy. Unfortunately, here too there is much confusion, with claims that stamp duties compared to other taxes are an economic disaster. Stamp duty is apparently 40 times more economically costly per dollar of revenue than council rates,[10] which are also levied on property values. As you might have guessed, this is nonsense. The computational general equilibrium (CGE) models used in these exercises cannot account for transaction taxes because there are no transactions in these models.

Build-to-rent to the rescue

Build-to-rent is the name given when a single entity builds and owns a complete apartment building, rather than each apartment being owned by different individual owners. Of course, ownership of the single build-to-rent entity can be split up— as property shares and company shares are equivalent ways to divide up ownership—but the tax treatment will be different if you own a share of the company that owns the building via a company share, or a share of the building via a property title.

The main policy changes to encourage build-to-rent have been to a) provide land tax and stamp duties discounts;[11] b) change requirements that managed investment trusts, a legal pass-through structure to share ownership, no longer have to retain 30 per cent of the profits of foreign investors, which will be changed to 15 per cent;[12] and c) increase depreciation allowances, which deduct the use of the building from taxable income, from 2.5 per cent to 4 per cent of the construction cost per year. In short, encouraging build-to-rent in the Australian housing market is a tax policy.

Some argue that build-to-rent corporate landlords will offer something that individual landlords do not for the benefit of tenants. I'm not so sure. There are existing residential build-to-rent projects that can give an indication of what to expect. Mirvac's Liv build-to-rent project in Sydney is reported to be renting at 20 per cent above the local market because it rolls in various hotel-like features. The earlier-mentioned Smith Collective on the Gold Coast was Australia's first build-to-rent project. Rents there have increased in line with the rest of the Gold Coast, up from about $450 to $675 a week between 2020 and 2023 for a two-bedroom apartment.

Notably, the Queensland government facilitated the project, but instead of owning it, sold it to foreign investors, including the Abu Dhabi government's wealth fund. That owning housing in Australia was seen as a good investment for a foreign government, and that an Australian government felt obliged to reduce taxes for them, tells you a lot about the hijacked housing debate.

We also saw previously that this project chose not to flood the market with new housing, yet the core debate centres around using the tax setting and ownership structure of build-to-rent to somehow sidestep the absorption rate equilibrium. Best to file this under tax policy, not housing policy.

Mortgage lending regulations

Another financial fix involves regulating mortgages. It is common to hear that loose mortgage lending is pushing up housing asset prices.[13] It is also common to hear the completely opposing view: that tighter lending means some first home buyers miss out and that it restricts investor buying of new homes, lowering supply.

As we know, the asset price equilibrium is unaffected by who can access mortgages. If interest rates are low, housing asset prices will rise eventually regardless of who can access mortgages. The focus on regulating credit partly confuses the normal property cycle, whereby higher asset prices both require and justify larger mortgages, as a causal story of larger mortgages leading to higher housing asset prices.

I find the best way to understand the role of mortgages and finance in the housing market is as regulating factors that control who can participate in the market and how quickly the asset price equilibrium can adjust.

In 2017, the Royal Commission into Misconduct in the Banking, Superannuation and Financial Services Industry led to banks tightening their lending standards in the form of more detailed assessment of borrowing capacity for homebuyers and by increasing their interest rate margins on investor mortgages.[14] The main result was to shift lending away from investors and towards first home buyers, changing the pattern of who could get a mortgage and buy a home. Prices nationally also peaked immediately after this royal commission, falling 8.6 per cent from the December quarter in 2017 to the June quarter in 2019.

Did these changes also cause the price declines? It's not clear. Rents were also falling during that period, due to low income growth and the enormous number of new dwellings being completed from the 2013–16 construction boom. But there was a noticeable shift in who got finance, with a bump in first home buying and less investor buying.

One reason financial regulation exists is that there are strong incentives in banking to make risky loans during cyclical booms. Slowing the speed of asset price adjustments may also dampen the asset price cycle, even if it doesn't change the level of prices on average. Because of the importance of property markets to the macroeconomy, stabilising the property asset cycle is desirable for economic and financial stability reasons, even if it will not directly make housing cheaper.

Part of that stability regulation is the requirement that lenders assess borrowing capacity at a 3.0 percentage point buffer above the loan interest rate. If a borrower was offered a 5 per cent interest rate, they would need to also be able to afford the mortgage repayment if the interest rate was 8 per cent. This also means borrowers near their income limits are disadvantaged compared to other borrowers, perhaps those who benefited from selling a previous home and hence have lower leverage, as well as investor borrowers. Clearly, such rules mostly determine who gets to borrow money and buy homes.

Another element of financial regulation concerns the absorption rate. Regulations on lending change who can access a mortgage, but they can also change which types of homes can be financed. The 2012–16 apartment building boom, for example, was driven by high demand for new apartments and off-the-plan sales from foreign buyers.[15] Since regulations limit foreign buyers to only new homes, this had the effect of increasing demand for new property and increasing the absorption rate.

If borrowing money to buy a new home was cheaper or easier than borrowing for existing homes, then demand for home-buying at any point in the cycle can be shifted towards the new and off-the-plan market, increasing the absorption rate equilibrium.

This is certainly much better than the alternative and advisable in general to ensure that the power of mortgage credit adds to the housing stock as much as possible. But, since the stock of homes changes only slowly, even if the absorption rate is substantially increased, as occurred with the help of foreign buying in the 2012–16 boom, the effect on the rental equilibrium will be small and temporary.

Subsidising landlords

A final financial trick illustrates the degree to which property owner subsidies can be presented as cheap rental programs by hiding behind financial complexity.

Australia's National Rental Affordability Scheme (NRAS) was enacted in 2008 during the Rudd Labor government and was disbanded six years later by the Abbott Liberal–National Party government. It was a policy that gave subsidies to property owners to build dwellings and rent them out to eligible tenants at 20 per cent below market rent for ten years. The estimated total cost of the scheme was $3.1 billion, and the per-dwelling value of the subsidy was set at $11,000 per year. But the value of a 20 per cent discount below market was far less, so the extra amount of the subsidy was a windfall gain to property owners. In fact, Grattan Institute analysis shows that the 20 per cent rental reduction was worth less than $4000 on average for NRAS properties, meaning that of the $11,000, only $4000 was a rental discount to the tenant, and over $7000 was given to property owners.[16]

Rather than give twice, or three times, as many renter households a cash payment of $4000 per year, a financial trick that subsidised landlords and came with enormous administrative costs was chosen instead. Relatively little attention was paid to the fact that this scheme was predominantly a landlord subsidy.

———

Because taxes on property have enormous effects on asset pricing and wealth, they generate enormous and ongoing political battles. If you are in the business of writing and analysing tax settings and property markets, then you are likely to always have customers. But do taxes make homes cheaper? No. Housing is usually included in these debates for political leverage.

21 ◆ Favoured first home buyers

The starting point for a first home buyer is to get a good job that pays good money. If housing were unaffordable in Sydney, no one would be buying it.

—Joe Hockey, former federal Treasurer, June 2015,
touching a cultural nerve of first home buying,
quoted in Latika Bourke, 'Joe Hockey's advice to first
homebuyers', *The Sydney Morning Herald*, 9 June 2015

Joe Hockey understands the property market. First home buyers who make good money *do* buy homes every year. He also understands that the concept of affordability makes little sense. Hockey's comments generated a media backlash because he touched a cultural nerve. Buying a home in Australia is sacred and subsidising first home buyers hits a political sweet spot. Whether it is lump sum payments, matched savings accounts, free public mortgage insurance or shared equity, subsidised rent control in the form homeownership is politically advantageous.

The history of first home buyer subsidies is long. Renowned Australian economist Saul Eslake describes that history this way:

The federal government began giving cash grants to first home buyers in 1964 when, at the urging of the New South Wales division of the Young Liberal Movement (whose president at the time was a young John Howard), the Menzies government began paying Home Savings Grants of up to $500 to 'married or engaged couples under the age of 36' on the basis of $1 for every $3 saved in an 'approved form' (generally with a financial institution whose major business was lending for housing) in the three years before buying their first home, provided that the home was valued at no more than $14,000.

This scheme was abolished by the Whitlam government in 1973 (in favour of an income tax deduction for mortgage interest payments by people with a taxable income of less than $14,000 a year); reintroduced under the name of Home Deposit Assistance Grants (without the age or marriage requirements and the value limits and with a larger maximum grant of $2500) by the Fraser government in 1976; replaced by the Hawke government in 1983 with the First Home Owners Assistance Scheme, initially with a maximum grant of $7000 (later reduced to $6000) and subject to an income test; abolished by the Hawke government in 1990; and then reintroduced as the First Home Owners Grant by the Howard government in 2000, without any income test or upper limit on the purchase price of homes acquired, ostensibly as 'compensation' for the introduction of the GST (even though the GST only applied to the purchase of new homes, and not to existing dwellings, which the majority of first-time buyers purchase).[1]

Despite the decades-long policy approach, homeownership has declined from its 71.5 per cent peak in 1971 to 66 per cent in 2021, with only minor cyclical variation.

————

The political logic behind subsidising first home buyers is clear. There are relatively few first home buyers per year, typically around 100,000. Out of the eleven million total dwellings, only 0.9 per cent of homes, new and existing, are sold to first home buyers each year. Compared to this, there are 3.1 million renter households in the private market.[2] A first home buyer subsidy only needs to go to a very small number of households and it leaves the broader rental market unchanged.

Of course, there are some political drawbacks. If I were a renter not in a financial position to buy a home, I would wonder why I am paying taxes to subsidise the home-buying of others who may be financially better off than me.

How is it, though, that subsidising a thing, in this case first home buying, hasn't generated more of the thing, in this case homeownership?

Before we consider that puzzle, I will briefly describe some recent first home buyer subsidy schemes and their economic effects, though I am wary of getting into too many details since they change with great regularity.

First are the cash grants, the most famous being the $7000 grant that was available in the 2000s. Most states also have stamp duty discounts for first home buyers, which are economically equivalent to a cash grant the size of the discount.

Then there are the deposit subsidies, like loan guarantees and savings schemes. For example, there is the First Home Super Saver scheme, which allows extra pre-tax income to be saved into a superannuation retirement account and then withdrawn to contribute to a home purchase.[3] (The idea of using compulsory superannuation retirement savings for housing, which are more lightly taxed than wage incomes is a form of first home buying subsidy.) There is also the First Home Guarantee, whereby the federal government takes on the risk of default for first home buyer loans with high loan-to-value ratios, saving on mortgage insurance and interest costs.[4] These offer relatively small financial advantages to first home buyers. Compared to the low interest rates in the 2020–22 period, for example, which halved the interest cost of a mortgage, these subsidies are extremely small.

What do all these first home buyer subsidies have in common? They advantage first home buyers slightly, and in proportion to their existing income, compared to other buyers in the housing markets. Like our supermarket queue analogy, they change the order of the home-buying queue, which is sorted by wealth and income, and put the qualifying first home buyers a few places ahead. But since there is a limit to how many households can become first home buyers in any period of time, jumping the queue only brings forward in time decisions that would be made later.

If the subsidies are large, they can also generate temporary bumps to the asset price equilibrium. Imagine two first home buyers bidding at an auction where the price stalls at $500,000. Before the gavel drops, the bidders are notified that the government will now give them $7000 in cash if they buy the home. So the two bidders each now are able to continue bidding up another $7000 to get back to exactly where they were before.

Of course, first home buyers aren't all the buyers across the market. They vary between 20 per cent and 35 per cent of buyers in any given year. So this price effect is probably not the full value of the subsidy, and it is probably not sustained for long in the asset price cycle. As queue-jumping grant-recipient first home buyers are exhausted, the asset equilibrium will return to its previous level.

Why haven't first home buyer subsidies increased homeownership?

The main problem with first home buyer subsidies, and the reason they haven't increased homeownership, is that even grant-receiving first home buyers must pay the asset price equilibrium, which is set by the broader market of buyers and rate of return on alternative asset classes in the economy. A general rise in wealth and income inequality means that lower income households, which are predominantly younger households, are less able to compete for these assets against others.

This is the rub.

First home buyers compete with landlords. Because of this, many of the financial fixes in the previous chapter work against higher rates of homeownership because they benefit landlords. Small first home buyer subsidies are not enough to shift the balance.

To boost homeownership back to the 71 per cent peak level that Australia saw in the early 1970s would require 500,000 landlord sales in net terms—whether that is landlords not buying new homes or selling their existing homes.

Competition between landlords and first home-buyers is why rent control policies that reduce the net income of landlords have historically resulted in higher homeownership rates.

Shared equity

A special mention must go to shared equity schemes for first home buyers. In these schemes, a government agency provides funding in exchange for an equity share of the property instead of a loan. The government equity share is repaid from future capital gains if and when the property sells. The Labor federal government's 2022 proposal was tried before by state governments and other nations like Canada and the United Kingdom. While there are clear benefits of bringing forward homeownership for those who do participate, many schemes fail to attract as much interest as anticipated. This is because a home is both a place to live and an asset. First home buyers who can afford to participate in these schemes usually prefer to hold more of the housing asset with a larger mortgage to get the untaxed future capital gains for themselves.

In practice, two offsetting effects can reduce the net benefits to participants. First, few private banks usually participate in these schemes. Those that do usually only offer higher interest rate mortgages, undermining resident benefits. Second, because the schemes have income limits and home value limits, the few housing markets and locations that could be popular under such schemes can see temporary price effects due to the additional financial resources of buyers.

But shared equity policies offer important lessons about how governments can capitalise on the fact that housing is an asset. If owning 30 per cent or 40 per cent of the equity in a home without charging any rent on that equity share is a good idea, then it is a good idea for a government to own housing equity in general. A more expansive approach to shared equity would acknowledge that state public housing departments own 100 per cent of the equity in their public housing assets. The federal government could fund these agencies and call that funding an equity stake, while offering rents at far below market prices. This hints at how to course correct our housing policy debate.

Course corrections

22 ◆ Managing monopolies

Doctors are keen to preserve the lucrative advantages of the fee-for-service system, and private hospitals and private health insurance funds are eager to stay in business.

. . . Most doctors who vehemently opposed the introduction of Medibank now accept the inevitability of Medicare. The arguments now centre on terms and conditions. Doctors remain wary of any attempts to encroach on their professional privileges or to limit their incomes.

—From a 1984 article in the *Age*, announcing the arrival
of Medicare national health insurance against the
protest of doctors and private health insurance funds[1]

If a natural economic force of competition or innovation could be unleashed to combat the property monopoly, I would want it unleashed. Unfortunately, it is not possible.

This is not unusual. Many other sectors of the economy produce market outcomes that fail to meet our expectations. We can learn from them. Elsewhere in our economy, whether it is roads, education, healthcare or retirement, there have been similarly hijacked policy debates and political conflicts among interest groups, but also effective system changes that improved on market equilibrium outcomes. Better outcomes have been achieved by sidestepping the monopoly and creating non-market alternative systems. These examples reveal the true scope for system change when there is a political will.

Medical monopolies

At the start of this chapter was a quote about the push-back from doctors and their unions (the British Medical Association, which is now the Australian Medical Association) during the political debates of the 1970s about the healthcare crisis that ultimately led to Australia's universal Medicare system. Doctors came out against public health insurance because, by increasing supply and lowering prices, it would affect their income.

Prior to universal public healthcare, medical treatments could be bought privately, with insurance companies pooling risk for their members, or help could be sought from churches and charities. Queensland had state-run and Catholic church–run hospitals funded by the Golden Casket lottery, while other states relied on charity and taxation. Public hospitals run by the states were generally not free. Except for those who fell below tight means-tested income and wealth thresholds, patients paid fees for public hospital services. Funding for general practice doctors in working-class areas relied on a minimal insurance pool, where each resident's 'lodge payment' premium was pooled to cover the fees charged by local doctors providing limited services.

It took decades and a world war to get the modern universal public hospital and Medicare system of today. As early as 1939, then Health Minister Robert Menzies expressed a desire for a national insurance scheme, but his efforts were overruled by the national cabinet and he resigned in protest. His scheme was designed to cover health insurance and age pensions by pooling compulsory contributions from the broadest national level. But there was political fear about the huge amount of funding needed to administer such a system.

Then there was war. General taxes were raised to pay for it. Governments got into just about every business, and the old political barriers disappeared. Returned soldiers had high expectations of social support, including housing and healthcare; leaving them homeless and broken would have created a political crisis. A universal public healthcare system was gaining political support, as 'the middle classes began to demand that they, too, should share in the benefits provided by public hospitals'.[2]

The post-war Chifley Labor government fought many battles with doctors and pharmacists, with its *Pharmaceutical Benefits Act 1947* challenged in court on a technicality, and its *National Health Service Act 1948* immediately disbanded by the Menzies government after election in 1949.

It was ultimately the Labor Whitlam government, elected in 1972, that introduced a federal health insurance system, with funding granted to the states for public hospitals. It wasn't easy politically and took multiple attempts to pass the legislation in the senate. Even then, another decade of political battles lay ahead before the system became irreversibly stitched in the country's institutional fabric.

We quickly forget the political battles that changed our health system. A public health system is now taken for granted as sensible, effective and politically untouchable.

Before Australia's public hospital and medical system, medical bankruptcy was off the charts, a situation not unlike that in the United States today. As one report recalls: 'Hospital and medical expenses were one of the largest reasons for personal and non-business-related bankruptcy before Medicare. After Medicare they actually removed it from the published list of reasons because it fell so low.'[3]

Healthcare debates in the United States are rehashing the 1970s debates in Australia. They centre around a similar economic symmetry, trying to maintain the profitability of private insurers and pharmaceutical companies, and keep up the extravagantly high pay of certain doctors and specialists, but also somehow obtain lower prices and more services from these same groups.

You can argue that there are inefficiencies in the Australian public health sector. But that is true of every large complex organisation. Detailed research has shown that common medical treatments in public hospitals are cheaper than in private ones.[4] This makes sense, as there are financial incentives to sell non-medically required services, resulting in outcomes such as longer hospital stays for comparable medical events. You might also argue that the low price of public health services, often free for users, creates queues and inefficiencies. But the alternative is to have higher prices and next to no queuing—much like outcomes in the private housing market that are widely thought to be undesirable.

Retirement

Retirement income policy also has lessons for housing. The old-age pension is the simple solution for those elderly who have saved insufficient money to lead a socially acceptable lifestyle. It is generously means tested, though not universal; around 62 per cent of all people aged over 65 receive the pension in part or whole, so it enjoys broad support in the community.[5]

In contrast, private provision for old age through savings—even if compulsory, as superannuation is—doesn't really help low-income earners. Private retirement provision merely amplifies the inequalities of working life into retirement. For the bottom 25 per cent to 30 per cent of households by income, for example, when they grow one year older and get the age pension, it is a pay rise for them.[6] They were earning less money *before* getting the age pension!

We must reallocate wealth to solve the problem of poverty in old age, and no serious person argues differently. We know that many retirees cannot pay for rental housing, so we give them extra money for this. We don't pretend that competition from landlords will make their rents cheap or that competition from pharmaceutical companies will make their medicines cheap. It is obvious that solving retirement problems requires creating non-market ways to access income and healthcare.

Meanwhile, there is a group who makes a living from managing other people's superannuation savings for a private retirement system who pretends this is not the case. As in housing, when a policy change is promoted to improve the retirement income system—such as by raising the old-age pension rate, or lowering the age pension age, or giving people their superannuation money to spend when they are young and poor—they fight hard against it. Like the doctors who fought against cheap healthcare, and the pharmacists who fight against cheap medicines, they claim to be helping poor grandma with her retirement, while at the same time fighting against improvements in the more effective and robust universally provisioned age pension that helps all grandmas.

Schools

Similar problems of mismatched income and spending arise with education of children, which is huge cost for families that is borne unevenly. Schooling is an essential spending need. Religious-based private schools that operated in Australia before public intervention in the 1840s 'failed to instruct half of the colony's children who were of school age'.[7] A colonial New South Wales government report argued for the adoption of a national system of schools but the Anglican Church opposed it, only to agree to the public system if their schools were also subsidised.

This approach, combining public schools with subsidised private schools, was further cemented when the Menzies government passed the *States Grants (Science Laboratories and Technical Training) Act* in 1964. Previously all financial support for private schools was from state governments, but Menzies' pioneered federal funding to private schools (so-called State Aid). It was triggered when the private Catholic schools in the New South Wales city of Goulburn went on strike in 1962 because they could no longer accommodate students without raising their fees and the local public schools could not be enlarged quickly enough to meet the surge in demand that this strike created.[8]

The tension between private and public education options continues today, with the debate about public funding for private schools being repeated regularly in the media cycle. Public and private schools compete for students. The more that private schools attract better students, the more difficult this is for the public schooling system, which is forced to carry the load of a concentrated proportion of poor students and students who lack academic skills. But this competition also creates a schooling system that tends towards self-correction—each is a check on the other.

A similar tension occurs between public and private hospitals. Private insurance is effectively subsidised through the tax system via the Medicare Levy Surcharge, which taxes people more if they don't have private health insurance, meaning there is universal funding of both private and public hospitals.

The coexistence of public and private systems adds value and public support. The public school system is available to every child, no matter their financial means, but it doesn't eliminate private schooling options. The public hospital system is available to anyone from any class and wealth background, but it doesn't mean that private healthcare and hospitals cannot also operate. A public pension doesn't mean people can't save for their own retirement. The radical socialist creation of public parks doesn't mean we eliminate private backyards (I bet you never thought about them like that before). These are all universal public options that provide an option outside the private system.

Roads

To get deeper into the concepts at play here, imagine a world carved up by a property monopoly but with no spaces left for public thoroughfare. No roads anywhere. A chessboard of private lots with no spaces in between.

Private property owners would need to cooperate with each other to designate space for thoroughfares and decide how and if to charge people for passing through their space. Would this result in a low-cost travel utopia that provides universal road access?

Many libertarian thinkers have proposed that a free market in roads is more desirable than the almost universal system of publicly and collectively building and managing road space.[9] They say it would reduce congestion (i.e. use of roads) and the main reason for this is the use of prices: there would be fewer roads and higher prices for using them.

I can only speculate that in this world people would argue about road shortages and high prices. Instead of homeless people, there would be *moveless* people: those who would opt out of moving around and simply stay put because the price of doing otherwise was too high.

We know the interests of private road owners match those of private property and housing owners because we have many privately owned roads.[10] Australian private toll-road owners *want* congestion in the road system and *hate* competition from public roads, just like private property owners hate competition and love high demand.

In contracts with private toll road owners, state governments and councils are often obliged *not* to improve alternative roads so as to force drivers on to toll roads. Some contracts stipulate that other roads will be closed, to push traffic onto the toll road, even though this means less throughput of the entire road network. Private roads mean lower travel supply and higher prices.

These realities are why no one suggests privatising all the roads for cheaper travel. But imagine for a moment we were in a situation that had only private roads. Would people say we should nationalise roads to provide a public alternative, or would we have a hijacked transport debate that would avoid this obvious solution because of a taboo about reducing the income and value of owners of toll roads, and a Roads Cheer Squad instead advocate for things like tax breaks and less regulation on road standards?

———

The lessons from other sectors of the economy are as follows.

First, change is not easy. It often relies on a political crisis, where enough electoral pressure is generated to overturn the financial interests who seek to preserve their privilege.

Second, these vested interests will fight viciously and hijack the debate with myths and stories to protect their profits.

Third, if access to public provision of services is universal, it gets broad support from the community compared to targeted solutions, and that makes them difficult to remove later.

Fourth, creating an alternative system to access goods and services requires some form of redistribution compared to the market equilibrium benchmark. Either redistributing the right to these services (hospitals, schools, roads) or redistributing money (retirement) to overcome the inequality of buying power in private markets.

This last point can be a real barrier to change. When I suggest giving a homeless person a free home, I hear things like 'It's not that easy' and 'What about the signal you send?' But then, when the same homeless person is sick or injured, everyone agrees that they should get world-class healthcare for free. During Covid-19 we saw how easy it was to end homelessness by accommodating people in hotels. We also rapidly built quarantine camps that could accommodate thousands of people, with the full support of the public.

23 ◆ Perfecting property

*I hope you will understand that, when I speak of the
land monopolist, I am dealing more with the process
than with the individual landowner. I have no wish to
hold any class up to public disapprobation. I do not
think that the man who makes money by unearned
increment in land is morally a worse man than anyone
else who gathers his profit where he finds it in this hard
world under the law and according to common usage.
It is not the individual I attack, it is the system. It is
not the man who is bad, it is the law which is bad. It
is not the man who is blameworthy for doing what
the law allows and what other men do, it is the State
which would be blameworthy were it not to endeavour
to reform the law and correct the practice. We do not
want to punish the landlord. We want to alter the law.*

—From a speech delivered by Winston Churchill at
King's Theatre in Edinburgh on 17 July 1909[1]

History shows us that lower income households are always
financially squeezed by high rents and prices when a property
monopoly interacts with unequal household wealth and income.

This financial squeeze does not depend at all on the physical design, materials or shape of the buildings enclosed by the property system. Even board games and virtual online computer game worlds suffer.

This means that there is no shortage of places and times to look at for solutions—in the past and the present, in Australia and abroad. Correcting course starts by acknowledging the symmetry of property asset markets, and looking for systems that have successfully navigated its political realities. These usually involve creating a housing system that bypasses the property monopoly. The bypass strategy is akin to improving the housing outcomes on the Monopoly board, not by changing the rules, but by starting another board game in parallel to give players more options. Although simple conceptually, real countries don't have a spare Monopoly board with unowned but accessible locations. So it is worth learning how these systems were created.

Europe

In Vienna, Austria, in 1928 the average household paid 5 per cent of its income on rent. At the same time in the United States, the average household paid 26 per cent of its income on rent, and Australian renters in urban areas paid around 20 per cent.[2] Rents in Vienna were fixed at their 1918 levels for many years and rental relocations took place through a central public clearing house that rationed homes based on need. This depressed property prices, as did the 1923 housing construction taxes, which funded mass homebuilding by the city government, which has continued to be renewed in the century since. Today half of Viennese households live in more than 400,000 homes at a below-market regulated rent, and tenants save around €700 million compared to private sector rental.[3]

Access to these homes is broad, but not universal. Controversially, a politician living in one of these homes caused a stir when people argued that other more needy households should get the low rent.[4] But regardless of such minor controversies, there is broad public acceptance that providing cheap non-market housing is part of the basic function of a city government.

Sweden's 'One million homes' program was an ambitious endeavour that got a million new homes built in Sweden between 1965 and 1974. It followed plans first espoused in a post-war 1945 report from the Royal Commission on Housing and Re-development, which argued that socialising housing construction was necessary because private risk-taking was thought to be incompatible with the large-scale low-return investment required for massive investment in housing and city construction.

Prior to this program, only 35 per cent of Swedish homes were owner occupied, 10 per cent were employer provided and 7 per cent were public or cooperative housing.[5] The rest were poorly housed market renters in increasingly overcrowded urban conditions.

Today, more than 20 per cent of Sweden's housing stock is public housing, another 20 per cent or so is cooperatives, and 40 per cent is owner occupied, meaning that most renters access housing at regulated below-market prices.[6] This is a larger proportion than even in France, where 17 per cent of households live in public housing, which is 43 per cent of all renters.[7]

In Finland, there are about 63,000 state-owned apartments in Helsinki, a city with 370,000 dwellings, and they are available to households with a broad range of incomes.[8] In 2020, the average rental price of these was €12 per square metre compared to €21 per square metre for rentals in the private market, a 43 per cent saving. Rents are set on a cost-based, not market-based, approach. The country had also used its state housing institutions to build dwellings to stabilise the property cycle. In the 1990s recession, it ramped up production to the point where 78 per cent of all new homes that decade were built by the state's Arava housing company.

The United Kingdom tells a similar story. From World War II all the way until 1980, the public sector built half the new dwellings, but most have since been sold to tenants at heavily discounted prices, converting public housing to private owner-occupation.[9] In 1980, Prime Minister Margaret Thatcher introduced the 'right to buy' for public housing tenants, who could purchase their homes at a discount that recognised previous rents paid.

Some housing researchers think this was a bad thing. The sale of public housing has been blamed for causing a housing crisis, but this ignores the symmetry of property markets.[10] Those households who bought the homes still benefit from cheap housing. The problem is not that these homes were sold cheaply, but that they were not replenished with more homes for future tenants to be offered a cheap purchase option.

In Poland, more than 70 per cent of households outright own their home with no mortgage, and only 5 per cent rent at market prices. This is the result of communist-era mass home-building. That housing was mostly poor quality, as were many goods produced under that political regime. But these housing investments meant that, after the 1989 political transition, market reforms were able to convert these housing cooperatives into freehold property rights, creating an instant and nearly universal home-owning class, who have since enjoyed all the accompanying benefits, such as avoiding market-priced housing rents.

Asia

Japan in the post-war era began a major program of public housing development and enacted policies to promote home-ownership. The Government Housing Loan Corporation was established in 1950 to boost mortgage lending at discounted interest rates to low- and middle-income borrowers to support housing construction on private property. The *Public Housing Act* of 1951 enabled local governments to build new housing for low-income people, and the Japan Housing Corporation was created to manage large-scale housing development.[11] This radically improved housing options in Japan.

When Lee Kuan Yew became the first prime minister of a newly independent Singapore in 1965, his party faced concerns about their legitimacy and the challenge to house people who expected improvement in their material conditions. Only 20 per cent of households owned the property they lived in at the time, and slum conditions for workers were a problem with a widespread lack of running water, flush toilets and electricity. Thirty years later, the homeownership rate was an astonishing 90 per cent and Singapore had the biggest and best-quality housing in the region.

The Housing and Development Board (HDB) was created at that time of independence, when Singapore's economy was only 7 per cent of the size it is today in per capita terms. It was tasked with reallocating property to non-property owners, starting with rebuilding slums and allocating new homes to residents. The HDB re-housed a quarter of the entire population in new apartments over its first five years.[12] As of 2020, 78 per cent of households live in a home that was built by the HDB public housing developer and bought below market price. This is a 'right to buy' scheme that has been well managed and well funded, and its universal accessibility has created political and social buy-in.

Any Singapore permanent resident can buy a HDB home at a heavily discounted price if they are over 21 years old and apply as a couple. One resident I interviewed paid about SG$350,000 for their brand-new apartment (one Singapore dollar is worth about one Australian dollar). They told me that to buy a similar dwelling on the private market would cost around a million dollars. They also said that, because compulsory retirement savings can be used as a home deposit and to repay the mortgage, for most buyers of HDB homes there are no out-of-pocket costs for the home. They merely redirect their compulsory savings into paying for the home. This is by design, as the first goal of Singapore's retirement system is to have all residents attain a fully paid-off home before they retire.

In short, Singapore's HDB is a little bit like the public school or hospital systems in Australia—anyone who needs to use them can. The homeownership nature of the system helps with administration, since internal maintenance and refurbishment decisions are made by the residents who can also trade these homes in a parallel HDB market.

HDB also has long-term cheap rental housing options for the elderly and the poor, which range in cost from an astonishingly low SG$23 per month to SG$275 per month with multi-year leases available.

Australia

In Australia in the 1930s, no one thought that the private property market was a solution to high housing rents. Across Melbourne, for instance, a huge number of renter households could not store food in their homes because of rat infestations due to nearby stables and factories, and disease spread widely due to the unsanitary slum conditions of the urban poor.

Some of the oldest people alive today experienced these slums as children. More recently, my baby boomer parents remember the nightsoil man who collected buckets of human waste from the thunderboxes of suburban Brisbane in the 1950s and 1960s because few parts of the city had sewer connection even then.

The Housing Investigation and Slum Abolition Board of the Premier's Department in Victoria clearly understood the problem. Here is an excerpt from their first report, in October 1937:

> Private enterprise in housing is engaged mainly in the building of houses to sell, and, when that demand is satisfied, houses are built for letting at a full economic rent which thousands of persons in this State are unable to pay.
>
> The present system, under private enterprise provides houses for letting only when it is profitable for the investor to provide them, and then only to the extent that those who need them can afford to pay a full economic rent.

The demand is for habitable houses at a rental commensurate with capacity to pay. If it had been profitable commercially, private enterprise already would have met the demand. As private enterprise has failed to remedy a condition of affairs which is rapidly becoming more grave, the nature and urgency of the situation calls for an appropriate State social service (which cannot be self-supporting) planned to that end.

Until a solution of the problem through the channels of increased earnings and other means is found, it is futile to attempt to deal with the problem as a cold commercial proposition.

Consistent with the experience in many other countries, it was the political upheaval of wartime that created the conditions for major housing policy change.

After World War I, War Service Homes and Soldier Settlements radically changed Australia from both a housing and production perspective.[13] New suburbs, farming communities, and businesses developed. War Service homes were funded with discounted interest rates or rent-to-buy provisions. Soldier Settlements involved giving large land lots to returned soldiers in new frontier areas conditional on payment by sweat equity—soldiers got land, but they had to work that land, clear the trees, and attempt to farm it. If it worked out for them, they could keep it. Many soldier settlement plots failed, often because the lots were uneconomically small for farming, but also because of collapsing prices of agricultural commodities and debts taken on to invest in land improvements. Despite the many failures, it is not clear that property market equilibrium outcome would have been a better alternative at the time.

I remember staying with my wife at a homestay in the Gold Coast hinterland during the 2000s housing boom. We met an Italian couple at breakfast who marvelled at the expansive estate, which included beautiful rainforest and lush rolling hills, with views to the ocean. They asked our hosts 'How do you come to own such a lovely part of the world? It would be impossible to buy such a large and beautiful estate where we come from.'

The answer was that this was originally Solider Settlement land that had been given to the host's grandparents on the condition that they started farming it. Had that scheme never happened, three generations of this family would have struggled as non-property owners instead of productively investing in the property and having secure housing.

After World War II, soldiers again benefited from War Service Homes, but broader schemes arose too. Over 15 per cent of all dwellings built from 1949 to 1970 were built or funded by public housing agencies. As in Europe at this time, there was an enormous push by governments to house people in better conditions after housing construction had ground to a halt in the war years and there was catching up to do. It was believed that private property owners would not build as quickly or comprehensively as required.

The post-war transformation of Australia's housing system was facilitated by a series of Commonwealth State Housing Agreements (CSHA) that empowered the federal government to get an enormous number of new dwellings built by funding states to use their administrative powers over housing and land to build homes.

Both sides of politics were on board. In his 1949 election speech, Robert Menzies, as the then leader of the Opposition, declared he wanted any government he led to use its vast financial resources to 'aid "little Capitalists" to own their own homes'.[14] He saw enormous social and political gains from everyone having an ownership stake in the country.

Later, in his 1955 re-election speech, Menzies boasted about how many more homes his government had funded than the Labor Party:

In their five post-war years, the then Labor Government saw 202,000 houses and flats completed in Australia. This was good. In our five completed financial years, 388,000 houses and flats have been completed; a record unsurpassed anywhere.

In War Service Homes, the Labor Government's five-year record was 22,755 homes, our five-year record 68,162!

We have, in fact, during 5½ years, provided nearly 20,000 more War Service Homes than were produced under all previous administrations for the previous 30 years since the inception of the scheme.

But we look forward. The housing arrears, accumulated during the war, are being handsomely reduced.

But there remains the vital problem of homeownership. In April we passed a law enabling tenants of houses built under the commonwealth and States Housing Agreement to buy those houses on favourable terms.[15]

The gains to homeownership and housing quality during this period are unmatched before or since as Figure 7 shows. After World War I there was a boost, especially from soldier settlements in rural and regional areas, and after World War II another step up. Figure 7 also shows Singapore's homeownership rate, showing an increase from 1965 to 1985 twice as large as the one Australia achieved from 1945 to 1965.

The end of these mid-century housing policies has meant a return to normal private property market outcomes for most households. Today, only 4 per cent of Australian homes are public rental housing, and access to them is tightly means tested. And public housing is broadly stigmatised.

But certain groups are treated differently. The prime minister is provided the free use of not one, but two, homes at public expense that are conveniently located to suit the prime minister's job requirements.

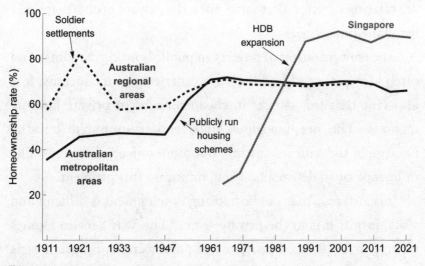

Figure 7 ◆ Direct policy programs can massively boost homeownership

Defence personnel can access non-market housing without tight means testing or stigma. Defence Housing Australia (DHA) operates as a public housing developer to ensure that defence personnel have affordable housing options near key military facilities. They sometimes sell those properties to private investors with a long-term lease in place (called a leaseback) and build more homes to replace them. Some of their projects even win architecture awards. We know how to provide quality homes at a fair price but do it only for politically favoured groups.

———

These non-market housing systems in Australia or abroad are never perfect. Despite this, a common complaint is that these discounted public housing schemes aren't available to enough people. On the one hand, they are claimed to be dysfunctional or ineffective. On the other, there are long waiting lists and people want more of them. Surely this shows that such housing systems are offering a better alternative than the private property market for many households.

The concentration of poverty in public housing dwellings and often low quality of buildings are other common concerns. It is also true that this occurs in cheap suburbs of private housing markets. The neediest households cluster in public housing because of tight means testing. But more universal systems, like in Europe or in defence housing, minimise this problem.

It is also true that public housing development is difficult and risky, just as it is in the private sector. The War Service Homes scheme in 1918 faced problems of purchasing appropriate sites at reasonable price, getting fair deals on building contracts, and meeting rapid construction rates without compromising quality.[16] These are still administrative challenges in public housing today. But there are lessons from all the examples provided here; in the next chapter we will piece together a workable 21st-century housing system.

24 ◆ HouseMate

Dad still can't work out how he got it so cheap. It's worth almost as much today as when we bought it.

—Dale Kerrigan, talking about his beloved family home in the film *The Castle*

We now take the lessons of the previous chapters and turn to what I propose as a housing policy that can make housing cheap while minimising political backlash due to the symmetry of property markets and reducing the likelihood of the policy being hijacked.

Don't for a minute think I've solved the problem of the symmetry of property asset markets. No. This is still a very real problem, especially politically. And with so many contradictory views about what's wrong with housing, many will remain unpersuaded.

But if Darryl Kerrigan can be proud of his home being worth what he paid for it, then maybe we can find a policy compromise that provides residents the security of homeownership, along with the flexibility to add, extend and renovate, and trade, and that fits with the Australian cultural norms epitomised in *The Castle*.

What is HouseMate?

In 2022, frustrated by the hoax housing policies of a hijacked debate, I proposed a public homeownership system with a distinctly Australian flavour. I dubbed it 'HouseMate', to match the trend of giving new policies portmanteau names, like JobKeeper, Medicare and HomeBuilder. Though inspired by Singapore and Australia's housing history of successful direct public housing programs, it also draws lessons from the way we solved universal access to healthcare, roads and education.

A one-sentence summary is that HouseMate gives every non-property owner Australian citizen the option to buy a home from a public provider at a cheap price.

That's it.

All citizens above a certain qualifying age—in Singapore it is age 21 for couple households and 30 for singles—where no household member owns property would be eligible to purchase a new or second-hand HouseMate dwelling. HouseMate will sell new homes to eligible non-property-owning citizens at a price approximating building costs but not including the cost of property on which the dwelling sits.

HouseMate would be a parallel public homeownership system alongside purchase and rental in the private property market. It's like adding an extra board to the game of Monopoly, but one where the five property market equilibria do not dictate pricing, housing production and access. It creates a new system of property rules without directly changing the rules in the existing property monopoly or encountering the political and economic conflicts caused by the symmetry of property markets.

Just like any other property owner, HouseMate buyers will own the home with freehold title and be obliged to pay council rates, insurances and take responsibility for maintenance and body corporate representation in townhouse and apartment dwellings.

Sales of second-hand HouseMate dwellings will be limited to buyers who qualify to buy a new HouseMate home. This achieves flexibility within the system for households to relocate, upgrade or downgrade, but overcomes the problem of House-Mate buyers obtaining a subsidised home and immediately re-selling it in the private market. Since eligible buyers of a second-hand HouseMate home would also have the option of buying a new home from the system at a regulated price, this anchors prices in the second-hand HouseMate market and stops them from reaching the level of prices in the private property market. The rules restricting who can buy a dwelling and the price anchor from selling new homes at discounted prices mean that the asset price equilibrium of the private market does not spill over to this parallel market.

Another feature worth borrowing from Singapore's Housing and Development Board (HDB) system is the minimum occupancy period, which requires buyers to live in their discounted public home for five years before selling, encouraging stability.

To produce new homes the HouseMate agency would acquire sites across Australia's cities and towns at market prices but also use compulsory acquisition powers and existing public property. It would simply then build, like a massively scaled-up defence housing program, and manage the purchase process for qualifying buyers.

Ideally, a HouseMate system would offer apartments in inner-urban locations, townhouses in middle suburbs, and detached homes in outer suburbs, and feature a variety of dwelling sizes and designs to accommodate different household sizes. HouseMate can also sell vacant land for housing for a small administrative fee and offer discounted construction loans to these buyers.

These dwellings don't have to be cheaply built, nor clustered in 'ghettos'. We don't do this with public schools or hospitals, or public parks, or any such thing. A good example comes from Le Plessis-Robinson, a town on the outskirts of Paris, where a major redevelopment push in the 2000s by the city required physically indistinguishable public housing dwellings in the same buildings as privately owned dwellings.[1] The city used design competitions to help create desirable housing projects, and profits from the market-priced sales of property helped subsidise the public housing.

During the previous waves of public housing, prefabrication became popular because investing in these systems could be justified with the high guaranteed demand. Many historical public housing dwellings, before the switch to tower blocks in the 1970s, are desirable today for their durable, efficient and even iconic designs.

Today, HouseMate dwellings would be expected to be priced at around $400,000 on average. But these regulated prices should also be set so that larger or better-located HouseMate dwellings reflect the rental differences in the spatial equilibrium in the private market. This is an important detail. It doesn't make sense to sell a HouseMate dwelling for $400,000 at

Bondi Beach, when the market price of a similar dwelling is $2 million, and also sell a similar HouseMate dwelling for $400,000 at Campbelltown, where the market price would be $600,000. Buyers will queue for the biggest subsidy and the system will face a rationing problem that is likely to promote corruption and insider dealing. Although pricing will reflect building costs on average, prices must vary so that HouseMate buyers do not face obviously favourable options, so they will probably range between $200,000 and $700,000. HouseMate buyers will choose their location, size and type of dwelling from a limited menu, but must pay a premium for accessing better locations that matches the spatial equilibrium price gradient in the private market.

The HouseMate approach improves on merely expanding income-contingent public rental housing (though this should also be done and can be part of the HouseMate program of development). It avoids concentrating low-income households in certain housing projects, increases political buy-in and minimises ongoing management requirements. Like all homeownership, residents avoid facing the changing rental market equilibrium, and this value lasts in perpetuity down the inheritance chain. Unlike some subsidised housing schemes, residents will not be forced back into market rent if their income increases.

Housing for retirement

To maximise the benefits of cheap homeownership, HouseMate buyers, either new or second-hand, can use their compulsory savings (their superannuation) for both the deposit and ongoing mortgage repayments.

A home is the best asset to own in retirement, so it makes sense to use retirement savings to buy this asset. Using compulsory savings also helps to buy sooner in life, when there are also major benefits. Owning a home younger means less income used to pay mortgage interest or rent, and more income for spending during lower-income years of life, especially when raising a family.

HouseMate could further help young buyers by offering a mortgage option up to a high loan-to-price ratio of, say, 95 per cent. This has two benefits. First, undercutting bank margins means HouseMate buyers repay mortgages faster. Second, the small margin on lending is a revenue source for the HouseMate program itself. Australian housing policy already guarantees mortgages and Australia already has a public bank, the Reserve Bank of Australia, so it is a relatively minor administrative step to do this, though taking customers from private banks may pick a new political fight.

With the use of superannuation and discounted mortgages, HouseMate could reduce the out-of-pocket cost of purchasing an identical home by more than 50 per cent.[2]

One concern about using superannuation to buy homes in the private housing market is because of the likely short-term price effect from new buyers entering the market quickly, temporarily increasing the asset price equilibrium. But this is not a problem for HouseMate, where the price of new homes is regulated.

HouseMate in context

Since 66 per cent of households are homeowners in Australia's private housing market, HouseMate can offer major benefits without needing to house anything like the 78 per cent of the population that lives in HDB homes in Singapore.

Around 90,000 Australian households buy their first home in any given year (though in 2021–22 the number boomed to 170,000). Many households will still want to purchase existing homes from the private market because of the financial benefits and flexibility rather than buy a dwelling from HouseMate. They certainly can do that.

If, after a ramp-up period of around five years, half of all first home buyers took up the new HouseMate option, the expected size would be 40,000 to 50,000 new homes per year, which is twice the size of Singapore's HDB building program for a population five times larger. Australia builds about 150,000 to 200,000 new homes per year, so this is about 20 per cent to 30 per cent of new homes that could be supplied by the House-Mate program. That is nearly double the proportion of new homes for first home buyers funded by governments through Commonwealth State Housing Agreements during the 1950s and 1960s. A reasonable expectation would be that a House-Mate program would grow to over a million homes within two decades, with a reasonable expectation being 8 per cent to 10 per cent of the total housing stock. This could boost Australian homeownership in all forms from 66 per cent up to around 75 per cent, a record high, while at the same time freeing a million households from the cost of renting or buying in the private market.

Despite such a system being a relatively small part of the overall housing stock, it would create broader indirect benefits.

Because every renter household has the option to buy a HouseMate home, they won't be willing to pay such a high price to rent, since they now have a cheaper option. HouseMate will compete with the private property monopoly as a whole and indirectly influence rents and prices in the private market.

We saw this dynamic with public schools, roads and hospitals, which are free alternatives for customers who might also choose private suppliers in these sectors. This limits the ability for private suppliers to raise prices but also provides an opportunity for people unable to have their needs met by the public option. Singapore's experience suggests that this indirect effect could be quite small, as non-resident households will still compete for rental homes, creating a rental market equilibrium. But the fact that HouseMate only has an indirect effect on private property markets is a key selling point, as it avoids the political fights that arise from direct intervention with taxes or rental regulations.

Putting property in HouseMate

How easy will it be for HouseMate to find sites for new housing? I hope readers who have made it this far are convinced that there are plenty of places to build homes and that planning and zoning are not the problem. But let me show how easy it is when there is a political will.

In my hometown of Brisbane in 2019, the Queensland government made available 26 hectares of land it owned in the heart of the central business district for an important project. That is 10 per cent of the land area of Brisbane's city peninsula. That important project was a casino.

More recently, the Queensland government acquired 7.5 hectares of inner-city riverside land in my neighbourhood in South Brisbane for $180 million.

Why?

Because the government would like the international media to use a nice new building for a two-week period in 2032. Yes, Brisbane will be hosting the Olympics in a decade's time and that site was acquired for the official Olympic media centre.

Additionally, the Queensland government spent $39 million to relocate a greyhound racing track to make use of a 27-hectare inner-city site. The reason? More Olympic sports venues.

It is amazing how much valuable inner-city property can be quickly made available for important political priorities. If it is difficult and expensive to find places for public housing programs of any sort, then it should also be true for massive Olympic venues and casinos.

The 7.5-hectare site in South Brisbane mentioned above is a great example of what might be a worst-case scenario for getting sites into HouseMate—a large inner-city riverfront site in an expensive suburb. But how bad is it really?

At a purchase price of $180 million, if 2500 dwellings were built on the site the land cost would be only $66,000 per dwelling. If the site was to have other retail and commercial uses, and public parks that would use a quarter of the site, then the cost share for the residential use is only $125 million, or $50,000 per dwelling.

A nearby 2.6-hectare site has been recently developed into 1250 apartments and 18,500 square metres of retail and commercial uses on a site a third as large. So, at a land cost of

$50,000 per dwelling, this 7.5-hectare site could easily be developed into two of these projects, while leaving 2.4 hectares for parks, roads and open spaces.

This is a worst-case scenario. It is possible to get plenty of land at a reasonable price into a public homeownership scheme if we want to. But so far it has been a political choice to only use compulsory acquisition powers to get massive well-located sites for casinos, stadiums and other pet political projects like toll roads, and not for housing.

The cost of HouseMate

Surely a large-scale subsidised public homeownership scheme would too expensive for the government budget? Not at all. When I ran the numbers I found that at a rate of 30,000 new homes per year, the peak cost is less than $3 billion per year. This is in line with the SG$2 billion per year required in Singapore's system to build about 20,000 homes per year.[3] For 50,000 homes a year, that's a $5 billion budgetary cost. And for every home built and sold in the program, the residents get the benefits of cheap housing for the life of the home.

At any reasonable scale, this is an extremely cheap program.

By comparison, public spending on healthcare in Australia is more than $125 billion per year—about 25 times larger than the expected budgetary cost of HouseMate. Compared to the $100 billion Covid JobKeeper scheme, HouseMate is a rounding error. If just 40 per cent of that money had been set aside for a HouseMate-style program, that fund could have sustained HouseMate for a decade.

To put this in perspective, the New South Wales government sold WestConnex motorways for about $20 billion. In other words, it costs the same as one toll road to provide cheap home-ownership to 200,000 Australian households by operating a national parallel housing system for four years. And the benefits to these households last a lifetime.

Each year, $19 billion of value is given to private landown-ers through rezoning decisions—a value that could be recouped by pricing those development rights. Taxing those value gains could fund the budget cost of the HouseMate program each year, nearly four times over.[4]

The National Rental Affordability Scheme (NRAS), which began in 2008, has cost around $3 billion to provide at best a 20 per cent below market rent for 30,000 households for a little over a decade. For a similar budget expense, HouseMate could provide about 30,000 dwellings at much more discounted prices, with the security of homeownership for a lifetime.

How HouseMate would get hijacked

HouseMate minimises the cost on existing property owners by not attempting to change the price or rental equilibria in the private property market through tax changes or strict rental price regulations. Its impact is indirect and relatively small. How much better is it to tell existing landlords that 'You are doing a great job and are always going to satisfy most of the people's housing needs. We don't want to tax you to control you. We just want to provide an additional option for Australian citizens and add more supply, like you always say you want.'

But this symmetry of property markets is still very real, and these stories won't be enough to pacify vested interests.

When the United States began its public housing system during the depression years, private property owners pushed back hard. Housing researcher Rachel G. Bratt describes how 'conservative members labeled public housing a socialist program and opposed it on the grounds that it would put the government in competition with private property'.[5] Their successful lobbying meant that 'public housing legislation included an "equivalent elimination" provision requiring local housing authorities to eliminate a substandard or unsafe dwelling unit for each new unit of public housing built. Public housing could replace inadequate units, but it was not to increase the overall supply of housing, since that could drive down rents in the private housing market.' Despite the effect on private rents being small and indirect, they could not be hidden.

The lobbying was so relentless that in 1949, when the program was to restart, President Truman called out these deceptive campaigners in a speech where he noted:

I have been shocked in recent days at the extraordinary propaganda campaign that has been unleashed against this bill [*Housing Act* of 1949] by the real estate lobby. I do not recall ever having witnessed a more deliberate campaign of misrepresentation and distortion against legislation of such crucial importance to the public welfare. The propaganda of the real estate lobby consistently misrepresents what will be the actual effect of the bill, and consistently distorts the facts of the housing situation in the country.[6]

Ultimately, this lobbying resulted in public housing being only for the poorest households and led to its austere design to differentiate it from private housing and be less of a substitute.

This type of pushback against HouseMate needs to be carefully minimised. For property owners, advancing the idea that public housing should not be universal is a key lever to pull to undermine it. Imagine if public schools, or public roads and parks, were not universally accessible but instead were means tested and designed to inferior standards. Under those circumstances, political support for these public programs would fall away.

The universality of HouseMate is a benefit that needs to be promoted. Perhaps piloting the program on politically favoured groups, like police, teachers and nurses, could help sell, politically, the value of universal access. Piloting in this way would help avoid the expected queuing during early years. Alternatively, queuing could be managed using lotteries, which is how unexpected demand for new HDB homes is managed in Singapore.

Another concern would be that HouseMate can generate windfall gains to buyers if their subsidised homes rise in value over time on the second-hand HouseMate market, so that when they sell it second-hand in the future, they make money from it. This concern is amusing for two reasons.

First, no one cares that people currently make money on subsidised property. Up-zoning is a type of subsidy. Inheritance is a type of subsidy. Lowering interest rates, which increases property values during a cyclical downturn, is a subsidy. Home-Builder was a subsidy. First home buyer grants are subsidies.

The second funny part is that, in Singapore, the fact that everyone has the option to buy an HDB dwelling means that everyone *wants* the system to provide a small windfall over the long term. If the program is universally accessible, then everyone feels like they are going to get their fair share.

A final argument is cultural. I think owning a home via HouseMate, given the flexibility to renovate and tinker, and to trade, is something that the Darryl Kerrigan character in *The Castle* could be proud of, just as residents who bought their public housing rental home during the 1970s were proud of those homes.

———

I'm not claiming it would be simple to implement HouseMate or any similarly ambitious public homeownership program. I'm in fact saying the opposite. The administration of the private property system is complex—its own land court, titles office, planning department, roads department, and more. The administration of a parallel public homeownership system will also be complex and need to evolve through trial and error. But we must keep in mind that such systems exist, provide massive benefits to residents, and the main arguments against HouseMate simply don't stack up.

As with all major public investment programs there are risks around competency, incentives and corruption. Rolling in existing public housing agencies with their capabilities and property assets makes some sense. The Land and Housing Corporation in New South Wales has property assets worth $54 billion, four times those of Singapore's HDB; it also holds an enormous stock of land that can be redeveloped. But existing capabilities of the private housing sector can also be used by allowing developers to offer projects for tender to HouseMate to provision homes at a set acquisition price if they meet design hurdles.

25 ◆ Future foresight

Many people view homeownership and rising home values as something they can pass along to their children, but this is a dark and pessimistic view of the future. Wouldn't it be better to have a world where homes are abundant and affordable, where our children can afford a place to live without a financial endowment from their parents?

—Author Shane Phillips describing competing visions for how housing and wealth are tied up in society, in *The Affordable City*

It is unfortunate that war and political regime change seem to be the two reliable ways to achieve major housing policy change. David Lloyd George, Prime Minister of the United Kingdom at the end of World War I, in a speech eleven days after the armistice, explained how the shift from war to peace led to a political calculus in favour of major public housing programs.

Let us deal with one point affecting housing conditions. Slums were not, and are not, intended for the men who have won this great war. They are not fit nurseries for the children who were to make to [sic] an imperial race, and there must be no patching up of this problem.

The problem has got to be undertaken in a way that has never been undertaken before, as a great national charge and duty. It is too much to leave it to the municipality. Some of them are crippled by the restricted income which is placed at their disposal. Some are good and some not so good, just like the rest of us—therefore the housing of the people must be a national concern, and must be undertaken as such.[1]

Outside these abnormal times, there is political logic that sustains the private property system and its internal incentives towards the five market equilibria. It is the same logic that dictates that direct intervention to make private housing cheaper is a non-starter politically and economically. Crashing rents and prices in the private property market comes with enormous political and macroeconomic costs. Yet we far too often pretend this is a possibility, ignoring the symmetry of property markets and our national obsession with housing investment. Instead, we have a hijacked housing debate.

I feel these incentives to avoid effective housing solutions as much as anyone. As I write *these words*, I am aware that if a government enacted HouseMate, or a variation of it, and started solving housing issues I would have nothing to write about. My incentive as a writer and analyst is to sell problems more than to solve them. Nonetheless, I would hope that if a transformative housing program was enacted, I could still write a book about my role in making it happen.

It is also worth remembering that the private property market works well for a large share of Australian households. Most homeowners are content with their housing outcomes. Most landlords too. Homes today are bigger and better, with the fewest people occupying each. And every home will be passed down to the next generation soon enough.

The problem has always been that the distribution of ownership of the property monopoly is unequal, so low-income households without an ownership stake get a raw deal. Their options are limited, and when their location becomes popular and generates an influx of higher income households, they get squeezed out by rental and spatial equilibrium adjustments. Access to housing is inextricably linked to poverty and inequality, and because housing is the biggest expense for renter households and new buyers, it gets a lot of attention.

This is why I argue that a parallel homeownership system can sidestep the persistent supply superstitions while directly creating a culturally appropriate alternative form of homeownership. It helps tackle inequality in general and expands housing options without forcing any household to change their decisions. History also shows that this is the only approach that works over long periods of time to make housing cheaper for those who don't already own their home.

Change comes all at once

The best way to promote effective policy change is to promote continuously. It takes years of effort to coordinate and push in the same policy direction so that when the crisis hits and the political class is looking to 'do something', this policy is the obvious solution that can be quickly adopted.

An example of a crisis leading to positive housing policy change is when the rapid rise in rents and homelessness in 2023 led to action by state governments to directly expand the pool of subsidised public rental housing by quickly building and buying homes. This contrasts with the experience just a few years earlier during the Covid-19 crisis, where that crisis led to policies like the HomeBuilder grants that subsidised the home renovations of some of the country's wealthiest households to the tune of $2.3 billion. Let's not waste the next crisis.

As the saying goes, 'policy creates politics': reforms, once implemented, generally summon forth new constituencies who benefit from them. Even bitterly contested reforms become the norm; in health, doctors and other professionals became accustomed to new methods of being paid and locked into the system under the new conditions.

Better housing outcomes are possible.

Glossary

absorption rate the rate of new homes developed of any density at all locations in a region per period of time: like matching food to your appetite—you don't eat tomorrow's lunch today

absorption rate equilibrium the rate of new housing development where there are no extra benefits from developing faster or slower

agglomeration effects the benefits that arise when activities cluster together, such as in a city centre

arbitrage the ability to buy an asset at one price and immediately sell at a higher price in another market

asset price equilibrium the asset price of housing which reflects a point where there are no expected benefits from swapping non-housing assets (such as cash) for housing assets

asset price of housing the value of getting your name on a property title; a type of financial product. Its value comes not just from providing housing today, but from the fact that the property right lasts indefinitely and provides an ongoing profit stream from housing services.

capital gains or losses changes in an asset's value over time

capitalisation rate (cap rate) the first year's income flow divided by the asset price

density number of dwellings per area

density equilibrium the density of new housing on a property where there are no extra benefits from building denser housing at a certain point in time

economic price of housing the rental price, which represents the market price of being housed for a certain period relative to the prices of new goods and services you must forgo to consume housing instead

first-generation rent controls rents are frozen at a point in time

highest and best use housing development design that maximises the residual property asset value and hence determines the value of an undeveloped property in an asset price equilibrium

inferior goods households spend a lower percentage of their incomes on these goods—such as no-name brands of food—as their incomes rise

luxury goods households spend a higher percentage or their income on these goods—such as international travel—when their incomes increase

natural rate (non-accelerating inflation rate) of rental vacancy where rents are neither rising nor falling—about 2.5 per cent in Australia in 2023

normal goods households spend about the same percentage of their income on these goods—such as housing—whether their income increases or decreases

rental price equilibrium the housing rental price where there are no extra benefits from swapping non-housing consumption for more housing

rental price of housing   *see* economic price of housing

sale price of a house   *see* asset price of housing

second-generation rent controls   rent increases are limited to increases in a price index in the broader economy

spatial equilibrium   the gradient between the rental price at different locations where there are no extra benefits from households relocating

time density   *see* absorption rate

yield   *see* capitalisation rate

Acknowledgements

The Great Housing Hijack is dedicated to my dad, Keith.

Dad had a lifelong interest in property markets and investing. He and Mum tell the story of how in the weeks before my brother was born, Mum was stacking besser blocks at flats they were building near their house at Marcus Beach—one of the property projects that enabled Dad to send us three kids to private school on a teacher's salary.

Dad always had one or two investment properties. When I was a teenager, he subdivided the block of the house we lived in, knocking down the above-ground pool and replacing it with a small cottage designed to be ideal for the rental market. I spent many weekends as a teenager reluctantly helping Dad do repairs at his investment properties. I dragged my feet like any teenager, and it resulted in quite a few arguments between us.

Because of Dad's interest and property investment, I grew up with an abnormal taste for property markets, even by Australian standards. When I returned from a gap year abroad when I was twenty years old, I decided to ditch the aerospace avionics engineering degree I had begun and sell real estate instead. Despite being a top student at one of the top schools in the country, the temptation to make money led me towards property. Forget the aerospace industry. Such is the perversity of the housing market and its importance in Australian culture.

Ultimately, I did return to university, studying property economics, worked in the development industry for a short while, studied a master's degree and worked in the Queensland state government as well.

I nearly gave up on economics altogether in 2012 because of the political nonsense invading every aspect of economic policy. I decided that being a medical doctor might be a more satisfying career. Luckily, Professor Paul Frijters convinced me over beers after an economics society function one night that it is possible to do good things within economics, and he helped me get into a PhD program at the University of Queensland and ultimately put me on my current path of economics research and policy analysis.

The Great Housing Hijack wouldn't be possible also without Peter Phibbs, who saw value in my research and approach, and created room for me at the Henry Halloran Trust at the University of Sydney, and has offered guidance and opportunities that are far beyond what anyone could expect. I have spent the past four years with the freedom to research any property topic of interest, refining and enhancing my understanding of property markets. The current director of the trust, Nicole Gurran, has taken up that guiding role and I thank her for that.

It has been a lifelong journey of merging property market experience with economic theories to help communicate a coherent way to understand the market. I hope it makes sense and that Dad sees that his intuitions about property markets make economic sense.

Notes

Chapter 1: Dwelling dreams

1   R. Keynes, *Charles Darwin's Beagle Diary*, 1809–1883, Cambridge University Press, Cambridge, UK, 1988, p. 396. Available at <https://archive.org/details/charlesdarwinsbe0000darw/page/396/mode/2up>, accessed October 2023.

2   R.F. Irvine, *Report of the Commission of Inquiry into the Question of the Housing of Workmen in Europe and America*, W.A. Gullick, Government Printer, Sydney, 1913, <https://babel.hathitrust.org/cgi/pt?id=uc1.$b288234&view=1up&seq=18>, accessed 15 September 2023.

3   W. Bunning, W.H. Ifould, C.R. McKerihan and S.J. Juker, *The Housing Problem in Australia*, 1947, p. 3.

4   Cameron K. Murray, 'Marginal and average prices of land lots should not be equal: a critique of Glaeser and Gyourko's method for identifying residential price effects of town planning regulations', *Economy and Space*, vol. 53, no. 1, 2021, pp. 191–209, <https://journals.sagepub.com/doi/pdf/10.1177/0308518X20942874>, accessed 15 September 2023.

5   N. Stapledon, 'Long term housing prices in Australia and some economic perspectives, PhD thesis', 2007, Figure 4.14, <https://unsworks.unsw.edu.au/entities/publication/31bfff1e-c544-4cf6-bf98-dceb244c4fb5/full>, accessed 15 September 2023.

6   Josh Ryan-Collins and Cameron Murray, 'When homes earn more than jobs: the rentierization of the Australian housing market', *Housing Studies*, November 2021, <www.tandfonline.com/doi/pdf/10.1080/02673037.2021.2004091>, accessed 15 September 2023.

Chapter 2: Property principles

1   Winston Churchill, 'The mother of all monopolies', from a speech delivered at King's Theatre, Edinburgh, 17 July 1909, *The School of Cooperative Individualism*, <www.cooperative-individualism. org/churchill-winston_mother-of-all-monopolies-1909.htm>, accessed 27 September 2023.

2   Lars Doucet, 'Land speculators will kill your game's growth', *Game Developer*, 27 August 2021, <www.gamedeveloper.com/business/digital-real-estate-and-the-digital-housing-crisis>, accessed 15 September 2023.

3   Matt Bruenig, 'Can you sustain an economic philosophy solely by begging the question?', *Matt Bruenig Dot Com*, 2 October 2015, <https://mattbruenig.com/2015/10/02/can-you-sustain-an-economic-philosophy-solely-by-begging-the-question/>, accessed 15 September 2023.

4   David Mullan and Lesa Parker, 'Aboriginal Australian perspectives on share ownership', *Canterbury Law Review*, vol. 22, 2016, pp. 82–102, <www.nzlii.org/nz/journals/CanterLawRw/2016/6.pdf>, accessed 15 September 2023.

5   *The Code of Capital: How the law creates wealth and inequality*, Princeton University Press, Princeton, NJ, 2020, p. 29.

6   Dan Rys, 'A brief history of the ownership of the Beatles catalog', *billboard*, 20 January 2017, <www.billboard.com/music/rock/beatles-catalog-paul-mccartney-brief-history-ownership-7662519/>, accessed 15 September 2023.

7   'Company title', *NSW Land Registry Services: Registrar General's Guidelines*, n.d., <https://rg-guidelines.nswlrs.com.au/strata_schemes/miscellaneous/company_title>, accessed 15 September 2023.

8   Eric A. Posner and E. Glen Weyl, 'Property is only another name for monopoly', *Journal of Legal Analysis*, vol. 9, no. 1, 2017, pp. 51–123, <https://academic.oup.com/jla/article/9/1/51/3572441>, accessed 15 September 2023.

9   'Lizzie Magie's first known commentary about The Landlord's Game from The Single Tax Review, Autumn 1902', <https://storage. googleapis.com/production-bluehost-v1-0-4/144/946144/zBi5DElr/ 772a141cb873432b8c6c04b8f8826a2b?fileName=Lizzie%20 Magie%20on%20Landlords%201902.pdf>, accessed 15 September 2023.

Chapter 3: Asset price equilibrium

1   Benjamin Clark, 'Falling prices won't fix housing affordability. Governments still need to act', *Crikey*, 17 August 2022, <www.crikey. com.au/2022/08/17/falling-prices-wont-fix-housing-affordability/>, accessed 18 September 2023.

2   Plus the value of all other rights in that property bundle, such as the right to redevelop to other uses in the future.

3   For example, Andrew Ballantyne and Paul Chapko, 'Australian office market overview 4Q22', JLL, 9 February 2023, <www.jll.com. au/en/trends-and-insights/research/australian-office-market-over-view-4q22>, accessed 18 September 2023.

4   Brian Albrecht, 'There is no such thing as supply: it's demand all the way down', *Economic Forces*, 24 December 2021, <https://price theory.substack.com/p/there-is-no-such-thing-as-supply>, accessed 18 September 2023.

5   The calculation is 4.8 per cent yearly turnover since 2011 on average, and the calculation is the *total transfers* from Table 2 divided by the *number of residential dwellings* in Table 1 from the Australian Bureau of Statistics 'Total Value of Dwellings (June Quarter 2023)', <www.abs.gov.au/statistics/economy/price-indexes-and-inflation/ total-value-dwellings/latest-release>, accessed October 2023.

6   Ò. Jordà, K. Knoll, D. Kuvshinov, M. Schularick and A.M. Taylor, 'The rate of return on everything, 1870–2015', *National Bureau of Economic Research*, Working paper no. 24112, May 2019, <www. nber.org/papers/w24112>, accessed 18 September 2023.

7   Anthony Shorrocks, James Davies and Rodrigo Lluberas, *Global Wealth Report 2021*, Credit Suisse Research Institute, June 2021, <www.credit-suisse.com/about-us/en/reports-research/global-wealth-report.html>, accessed 18 September 2023.

8   Australian Bureau of Statistics, *Australian System of National Accounts*, 28 October 2022, Table 61, <www.abs.gov.au/statistics/ economy/national-accounts/australian-system-national-accounts/ latest-release>, accessed 18 September 2023.

Chapter 4: Rental equilibrium

1   Rebecca Lake, 'Rule of thumb: how much should you spend on rent?', *The Balance*, 15 June 2022, <www.thebalancemoney.com/what-percentage-of-your-income-should-go-to-rent-4688840>, accessed 18 September 2023.

2   Analysis by Ben Phillips of ANU using historical individual Survey of Income and Housing records from the Australian Bureau of Statistics with 2023 estimate relying on proxy data inputs for rent and income change since 2021. Personal correspondence.

3   Office for National Statistics [UK], *Private Rental Affordability, England: 2012 to 2020*, 6 October 2021, <www.ons.gov.uk/people populationandcommunity/housing/bulletins/privaterentalaffordability england/2012to2020>, accessed 18 September 2023.

4   BLS Data Finder 1.1, *BLS Beta Labs*, <https://beta.bls.gov/data-Query/find?fq=survey:[cx]&s=popularity:D> (search household type : renter) and income and rent costs. Note the 2013 series break due to change described here—Kevin Jones, 'Why does the BLS think that taxes tripled in 2013?', *Mother Jones*, 29 June 2019, <www.motherjones.com/kevin-drum/2019/06/why-does-the-bls-think-that-taxes-tripled-in-2013/>, accessed 19 September 2023—and here is the report: Geoffrey D. Paulin, 'Improving data quality in Consumer Expenditure Survey with TAXSIM', *Monthly Labor Review*, March 2015, <https://stats.bls.gov/opub/mlr/2015/article/improving-data-quality-in-ce-with-taxsim.htm>, accessed 19 September 2023. But since the break the ratio is a flat 25 per cent.

5   Patrick N. Troy, *The Evolution of Government Housing Policy: The case of New South Wales 1901–1941*, Working Paper no. 24, Urban Research Program, Research School of Social Sciences, Australian National University, September 1990, <https://openresearch-repository.anu.edu.au/bitstream/1885/116257/1/URU%20no.24.pdf>, accessed 19 September 2023.

6   Ian Mulheirn, James Browne and Christos Tsoukalis, 'Housing affordability since 1979: Determinants and solutions', *JRF: Joseph Rowntree Foundation*, 18 January 2023, <www.jrf.org.uk/report/housing-affordability-1979-determinants-and-solutions>, accessed 19 September 2023.

7   N. Stapledon, 'Long term housing prices in Australia and some economic perspectives, PhD thesis', 2007, <https://unsworks.unsw.edu.au/entities/publication/31bfff1e-c544-4cf6-bf98-dceb244c4fb5/full>, accessed 15 September 2023.

8   Madeleine Achenza, 'State government bans "rental auctions" from Saturday', *News.com.au*, 12 December 2022, <www.news.com.au/finance/real-estate/renting/state-government-bans-rental-auctions-from-saturday/news-story/21ecdf2286b381cd489d140a606b7251>, accessed 19 September 2023.

Chapter 5: Spatial equilibrium

1   Jim Malo, 'Brisbane councillor Jonathan Sri lives on a houseboat so he can donate half his pay', *Domain*, 4 December 2017, <www. domain.com.au/news/brisbane-councillor-jonathan-sri-lives-on-a-houseboat-so-he-can-donate-half-his-pay-20171203-gzse1x/>, accessed 19 September 2023.

2   NSW Productivity Commission, *Building More Homes where People Want To Live*, May 2023, <www.productivity.nsw.gov.au/building-more-homes-where-people-want-to-live>, accessed 19 September 2023.

3   Tim Helm, *Melbourne's Pandemic Rental Dynamics: An (un)natural experiment in excess supply*, Prosper Australia Research Institute, May 2023, <https://www.prosper.org.au/wp-content/uploads/2023/05/Prosper_Pandemic-Rental-Dynamics_MAY2023_web.pdf>, accessed 19 September 2023.

Chapter 6: Density equilibrium

1   Peet no. 1895 Pty Ltd v Wyndham CC [2023] VCAT 168 (23 February 2023), <www8.austlii.edu.au/cgi-bin/viewdoc/au/cases/vic/VCAT/2023/168.html>, accessed 19 September 2023.

Chapter 7: Absorption rate equilibrium

1   Steffen Huck, Hans-Theo Normann and Jörg Oechssler, 'Through trial and error to collusion', *International Economic Review*, vol. 45, no. 1, February 2004, pp. 205–24, <https://doi.org/10.1111/j.1468-2354.2004.00122.x>, accessed 20 September 2023.

2   Michael Bleby and John Kehoe, 'Does land banking push up housing prices?', *Australian Financial Review*, 1 June 2023, <www.afr.com/property/residential/does-land-banking-push-up-housing-prices-20230525-p5db6s>, accessed 20 September 2023.

3   Cameron Murray, 'What's the rush? New housing market absorption rate metrics and the incentive to slow housing supply', 21 November 2022, OFSPreprints, <https://doi.org/10.31219/osf.io/xscg5>, accessed 20 September 2023.

4   Letter from the Rt Hon. Sajid Javid MP to the Rt Hon. Sir Oliver Letwin, MP, 'Review of build out', n.d., <https://assets.publishing.service.gov.uk/government/uploads/system/uploads/attachment_data/file/673794/20180112_Terms_of_Reference_for_the_Review_of_Build-Out_.pdf>, accessed 20 September 2023.

5   Samantha Partington, 'Letwin finds no evidence of land banking by developers', Property Week, 28 June 2018, <www.propertyweek. com/residential-and-development/letwin-finds-no-evidence-of-land-banking-by-developers/5097359.article>, accessed 20 September 2023.

6   FKP Ltd, 'CEO report', *Shareholders' Report*, 2003, p. 4, <https:// www.aveo.com.au/sites/default/files/aveo-shareholders-report-2003-FKP.pdf>, accessed 20 September 2023.

Chapter 8: Politics and politicians

1   John Garnaut, 'Housing is a monster out of control', *The Sydney Morning Herald*, 21 July 2003, <https://www.smh.com.au/business/housing-is-a-monster-out-of-control-20030721-gdh450.html>, accessed 24 October 2023.

2   For example: in 1939 there was the Rents Inquiry, *Lithgow Mercury*, 9 February 1939, p. 1, <https://trove.nla.gov.au/newspaper/article/219631918>, accessed 21 September 2023.

3   Brett Thomas, 'Politician property moguls revealed: The federal MPs and senators who own a stack of real estate, *realestate.com.au*, 18 May 2022, <www.realestate.com.au/news/politician-property-moguls-revealed-the-federal-mps-and-senators-who-own-a-stack-of-real-estate/>, accessed 21 September 2023.

4   Parliament of Australia, Register of Members' Interests: Statement of Registrable Interests, 47th Parliament, for Julie Collins, 19 August 2022, <www.aph.gov.au/-/media/03_Senators_and_Members/32_ Members/Register/47P/CF/Collins_47P.pdf?la=en&hash= F4022E5CAB584EB4CB17CAE130C92EBDD0AE6328>, accessed 21 September 2023.

5   Michael Sainsbury, 'Scott John Morrison: Where the bloody hell did he come from?', Michael West Media, 13 February 2019, <https:// michaelwest.com.au/scott-john-morrison-where-the-bloody-hell-did-he-come-from/>, accessed October 2023.

6   <https://www.linkedin.com/in/jason-falinski-b59256/?originalSub domain=au>, accessed 24 November 2023.

7   See Susan's LinkedIn profile: <www.linkedin.com/in/susan-lloyd-hurwitz-bba091180/details/experience/>, accessed 24 November 2023.

8   See 'Asset Prices and Wealth Channel' at Reserve Bank of Australia, 'The Transmission of Monetary Policy', <www.rba.gov.au/education /resources/explainers/the-transmission-of-monetary-policy.html>, accessed October 2023.

9   City of Brisbane, 'Minutes of Proceedings: the 4687 meeting of the Brisbane City Council, held at City Hall, Brisbane, on Tuesday 9 August 2022 at 1pm', <www.brisbane.qld.gov.au/sites/default/files/documents/2022-08/Council%20-%20Minutes%20-%20Ordinary%20-%209%20August%202022.docx>, accessed 21 September 2023.

Chapter 9: Academics and policy wonks

1   <https://www.macrobusiness.com.au/2021/09/mb-submission-to-housing-affordability-inquiry/>, accessed 24 November 2023.

2   <https://www.consumeraffairs.com/news/goldman-sachs-warns-biotech-clients-that-curing-patients-may-not-be-sustainable-041318.html>, accessed 24 November 2023.

3   Not her real name.

4   Debra Gruszecki, 'Real estate: Lewis Group of Companies poised for the next wave of building', *The Press-Enterprise*, 7 February 2014, <www.pressenterprise.com/2014/02/07/real-estate-lewis-group-of-companies-poised-for-the-next-wave-of-building>, accessed 21 September 2023.

5   Robert W. Lake, 'Value magic', *Environment and Planning A: Economy and Space*, February 2023, <https://journals.sagepub.com/doi/abs/10.1177/0308518X231154254>, accessed 21 September 2023.

6   'Singapore's public housing with Chua Beng Huat', ep. 28, *UCLA Housing Voice*, <https://podcasts.apple.com/au/podcast/ucla-housing-voice/id1565240355?i=1000568102494> (from 41.30), accessed 21 September 2023. Singapore of course has its own unique housing issues, especially with quality of housing for temporary foreign workers who make up nearly 30 per cent of the population and often live in dormitory-style conditions.

Chapter 10: Muddled media

1   <https://twitter.com/StreetNewsAU/status/1665480266628522393 7?s=20>, accessed 22 September 2023.

2   Lucy Macken, 'Meet the 37-year-old who bought a $20.5 million house with no mortgage', *The Sydney Morning Herald*, 1 July 2023, <https://www.smh.com.au/property/news/meet-the-37-year-old-who-bought-a-20-5-million-house-with-no-mortgage-20230629-p5dkex.html>, accessed 22 September 2023.

3   Australian Government, 'Individuals—Table 14', *data.gov.au*, <https://data.gov.au/data/dataset/taxation-statistics-2019-20/resource/7314db1e-fa26-41e6-95e8-a709aae130f4?inner_span=True>,

accessed 22 September 2023; Emily Holgate, 'Top 20 property investors in Australia ranked by occupation revealed', *realestate.com.au*, 8 March 2023, <https://www.realestate.com.au/news/top-20-property-investors-in-australia-ranked-by-occupation-revealed/>, accessed 22 September 2023.

4   <https://www.couriermail.com.au/news/opinion/editorial-states-property-war-is-illadvised/news-story/4c12a9d9e9f76e6bdeba62efa678cd47>, accessed 24 November 2023.

5   ABC 'Going, Going, Gone', *Four Corners*, 2021, <https://iview.abc.net.au/video/NC2103H038S00>, accessed on ABC iView, October 2023.

6   <https://sqmresearch.com.au/asking-property-prices.php?postcode=2206&t=1>, accessed 24 November 2023.

7   <https://content.knightfrank.com/research/84/documents/en/global-house-price-index-q4-2021-8865.pdf>, accessed 24 November 2023.

8   IBIS World <https://www.ibisworld.com/au/industry/residential-real-estate-advertising/5512/#IndustryStatisticsAndTrends>, accessed 24 November 2023.

9   *Today*, c. January 2023, <https://9now.nine.com.au/today/rentalcrisis-australia-hopeful-tenants-battle-for-spot-in-pricey-market/fe48ab79-fe2c-4533-9870-7b7413dc79b3>, accessed 22 September 2023.

10 Osman Faruqi, 'Good news for everyone locked out of the housing market', *Junkee*, 7 July 2016, <https://junkee.com/good-news-renters/81533>, accessed 22 September 2023; Christine Long and Caitlin Fitzsimmons, 'Rents are falling', *The Sydney Morning Herald*, 12 August 2018, <https://www.smh.com.au/money/planning-and-budgeting/rents-falling-fiona-home-cheaper-sydney-20180810-p4zwrw.html>, accessed 22 September 2023.

11 Tawar Razaghi, 'The Sydney suburbs where rents are rising and falling the most', *Domain*, 14 July 2019, <https://www.domain.com.au/news/the-sydney-suburbs-where-rents-are-rising-and-falling-the-most-june-2019-858424/>, accessed 22 September 2023.

12 'Expert says there's no end in sight for Australia's rental crisis', *Sunrise*, n.d., <https://7news.com.au/video/news/expert-says-theres-no-end-in-sight-for-australias-rental-crisis-bc-6318525108112>, accessed 23 September 2023.

13 'New renter laws forcing residents out of homes', *9news.com.au*, c. June 2023, <https://www.msn.com/en-au/news/australia/new-renter-laws-forcing-residents-out-of-homes/vi-AA1bVx9d?ocid=msedgntp&cvid=c8c0b466f3e248efadf2892aae506a21&ei=7>, accessed 22 September 2023.

Chapter 11: YIMBY yammer

1   Erin McCormick, 'Rise of the yimbys: The angry millennials with a radical housing solution', *The Guardian*, 2 October 2017, <www.theguardian.com/cities/2017/oct/02/rise-of-the-yimbys-angry-millennials-radical-housing-solution>, accessed 22 September 2023. A useful reference is Guy Rundle, 'To build better cites, we need to build better YIMBYs', *Crikey*, 13 June 2023, <www.crikey.com.au/2023/06/13/housing-crisis-for-better-cities-build-better-yimbys/>, accessed 22 September 2023.

2   'Myth—Traffic will get worse!', YIMBY Denver blog, 23 June 2021, <https://yimbydenver.org/stay-informed/myth-traffic-will-get-worse/>, accessed October 2023.

3   Jerusalem Demsas, 'Community input is bad, actually', *The Atlantic*, 29 April 2022, <www.theatlantic.com/ideas/archive/2022/04/local-government-community-input-housing-public-transportation/629625/>, accessed 22 September 2023.

4   Michael MacLeod, 'The case against living in the country', *The Guardian*, 24 August 2011, <https://www.theguardian.com/books/booksblog/2011/aug/24/edward-glaeser-edinburgh-book-festival>, accessed October 2023.

5   Edward L. Glaeser, 'If you love nature, move to the city', *The Boston Globe*, 10 February 2011, <http://archive.boston.com/bostonglobe/editorial_opinion/oped/articles/2011/02/10/if_you_love_nature_move_to_the_city/>, accessed October 2023.

6   Brookings Institution, 'BPEA Spring 2022 Conference—Day 2 Pt. 3: What have they been thinking? Homebuyer Behavior', *YouTube*, c. March 2022, <https://youtu.be/GQdas7B_qqI?si=zB5Yc05d8Jei M91T>, (1hr 4 mins), accessed 22 September 2023.

7   Myriam Robin, 'Falinski channels his inner NIMBY', *Australian Financial Review*, 1 March 2022, <www.afr.com/rear-window/falinski-channels-his-inner-nimby-20220228-p5a0bj>, accessed 22 September 2023.

8   Liam Walsh and Mark Ludlow, 'Developer hired ALP's Soorley for "advice" on sensitive project', *Australian Financial Review*, 22 October 2020, <www.afr.com/policy/economy/developer-hired-alp-s-soorley-for-advice-on-sensitive-project-20201022-p567i1>, accessed 22 September 203.

9   Chris Herde, 'A proposal for a six-storey retirement facility in New Farm has sparked anger from locals citing over development',

Courier Mail, 12 July 2020, <www.couriermail.com.au/business/prime-site/a-proposal-for-a-sixstorey-retirement-facility-in-new-farm-has-sparked-anger-from-locals-citing-over-development/news-story/642dcc7c2dcf60f23accd9d6c0083bec?amp>, accessed 22 September 2023.

10 Ethan Te Ora, '"The oldest Yimby in town": The woman raising the flag for Wellington's growing housing movement', *Stuff*, 3 July 2021, <www.stuff.co.nz/life-style/homed/housing-affordability/125619493/the-oldest-yimby-in-town-the-woman-raising-the-flag-for-wellingtons-growing-housing-movement>, accessed 22 September 2023.

11 Marta Pascual Juanola, 'Developer warns of planning "civil wars" on the horizon if communities stripped of voice', *WA Today*, 11 March 2021, <www.watoday.com.au/national/western-australia/developer-warns-of-planning-civil-wars-on-the-horizon-if-communities-stripped-of-voice-20210309-p57965.html>, accessed 22 September 2023.

Chapter 12: Mismeasuring manors

1 John Lewis and Fergus Cumming, 'Houses are assets not goods: What the difference between bulbs and flowers tells us about the housing market', *Bank Underground*, 5 September 2019, <https://bankunderground.co.uk/2019/09/05/houses-are-assets-not-goods-what-the-difference-between-bulbs-and-flowers-tells-us-about-the-housing-market/>, accessed 22 September 2023.

2 'QuickFacts: Arlington County, Virginia', *United States Census Bureau*, various dates, <www.census.gov/quickfacts/arlingtoncounty virginia> , accessed 22 September 2023; 'QuickFacts: Houston city, Texas', *United States Census Bureau*, various dates, <www.census.gov/quickfacts/houstoncitytexas>, accessed 22 September 2023.

Chapter 13: Skipping the cycle

1 Fred Harrison, *The Chaos Makers*, quoted in Catherine Cashmore, 'Predicting a crash: The ones who got it right', *LCI*, 29 March 2023, <https://landcycleinvestor.fattail.com.au/predicting-a-crash-the-ones-who-got-it-right/>, accessed 22 September 2023.

2 Tim Fuller, 'Australian housing market: Bear vs bull debate, with Cameron Murray', Nucleus Wealth, 21 May 2020, <https://nucleuswealth.com/webinars/australian-housing-market-bear-vs-

bull-debate-with-cameron-murray-nucleus-investment-insights/>, accessed 22 September 2023.

3   Michael Janda, 'CBA warns Australia risks 32 per cent house price crash in a "prolonged downturn", flags $1.5 billion coronavirus-hit to bank', 13 May 2020, <www.abc.net.au/news/2020-05-13/coronavirus-commonwealth-bank-house-prices-economy-unemploy ment/12241338>, accessed 22 September 2023.

4   Samuel Benner, an Ohio farmer, *Benner's Prophecies of Future Ups and Downs in Prices: What years to make money on pig-iron, hogs, corn, and provisions*, 3rd edn, Robert Clarke & Co., Cincinnati, OH, 1884, <http://ia600904.us.archive.org/14/items/benners prophecie00bennrich/bennersprophecie00bennrich.pdf>, accessed 22 September 2023.

5   Reliable information on the historical record is hard to obtain, but an examination of the available data suggests that even in the 1880s boom in Victoria the peak of the cycle occurred when interest rates were around 6 per cent, and gross yields on housing were a touch under 3 per cent, giving a Speculative Index of a little over two. More detail can be found in my article 'Does Victoria's rollicking 1880s land boom have lessons for today?', *Fresh Economic Thinking*, 18 June 2023, <https://www.fresheconomicthinking.com/p/does-victorias-rollicking-1880s-land?utm_source=profile&utm_medium=reader2>, accessed October 2023.

6   Michael Cannon, *The Land Boomers: The complete illustrated history*, Melbourne, Lloyd O'Neill, 1986, p. 24.

Chapter 14: Proper planning

1   Matthew Townsend, 'Restrictive covenants in Victoria—theory and practice', *Restrictive Covenants and Easements in Victoria*, blog post, 26 May 2023, <https://restrictive-covenants-victoria.com/2022/12/10/restrictive-covenants-in-victoria-theory-and-practice/>, accessed 23 September 2023.

2   John M. Quigley and Larry A. Rosenthal, 'The effects of land use regulation on the price of housing: What do we know? What can we learn?', special issue of *Cityscape* on the theme 'Regulatory Barriers to Affordable Housing', vol. 8, no. 1, 2005, pp. 69–137, <www.jstor.org/stable/20868572>, accessed 23 September 2023.

3   Kathy Mac Dermott, 'Brisbane running out of land for housing', *Australian Financial Review*, 8 May 2003, <https://www.afr.com/

property/brisbane-running-out-of-land-for-housing-20030508-juqt6>, accessed October 2023.

4   Queensland Government Statistician's Office, 'Residential land development activity spreadsheets (table)', <https://www.qgso.qld.gov.au/statistics/theme/industry-development/residential-land-supply-development/residential-development#current-release-residential-land-development-activity-spreadsheet>, accessed October 2023.

5   Custom data supplied by NSW Department of Planning and Environment for the 33 local council areas. Data for FY2023 up to 21 April is 114 days average approval time, 94.5 per cent approval rate, and 55,500 annualised number of dwellings with new planning approvals.

6   Auckland Plan 2050, 'Auckland's capacity for growth', <https://www.aucklandcouncil.govt.nz/plans-projects-policies-reports-bylaws/our-plans-strategies/auckland-plan/development-strategy/Pages/aucklands-capacity-for-growth.aspx>, accessed October 2023.

7   Lewis and Cuming, 'Houses are assets not goods', *Bank Underground*, 5 September 2019, <https://bankunderground.co.uk/2019/09/05/houses-are-assets-not-goods-what-the-difference-between-bulbs-and-flowers-tells-us-about-the-housing-market/>, accessed October 2023.

8   Queensland Government Statistician's Office, 'Residential land development activity spreadsheets (table)', <https://www.qgso.qld.gov.au/statistics/theme/industry-development/residential-land-supply-development/residential-development#current-release-residential-land-development-activity-spreadsheet>, accessed October 2023.

9   SQM Research comparing Caloundra's 4551 postcode and Noosa's 4567 postcode: <https://sqmresearch.com.au/asking-property-prices.php?region=nsw-Sydney&type=c&t=1>, accesssed 24 November 2023.

Chapter 15: Immigration inspection

1   Australian Bureau of Statistics, 'Overseas migration', *ABS*, 2021–22 financial year, <www.abs.gov.au/statistics/people/population/overseas-migration/2021–22-financial-year>, accessed 25 September 2023.

2   Cameron Murray and Leith van Onselen, *Three Economic Myths about Ageing: Participation, Immigration and Infrastructure*, 2020, policy research report prepared for Sustainable Australia, <https://doi.org/10.31219/osf.io/s3grd>, accessed 25 September 2023.

3   Hannah Leal et al., 'Housing market turnover', *Bulletin*, Reserve Bank of Australia, 16 March 2017, <www.rba.gov.au/publications/bulletin/2017/mar/3.html>, accessed 25 September 2023.

4   Australian Bureau of Statistics, 'New insights into the rental market', information paper, *ABS*, 24 April 2023, <www.abs.gov.au/statistics/detailed-methodology-information/information-papers/new-insights-rental-market>, accessed 25 September 2023. Figure 5 turnover rate of 2.5 per cent of three million rental homes.

5   Murray and van Onselen, *Three Economic Myths about Ageing*.

6   Lionel Frost et al., *Water, history and the Australian city: Urbanism, suburbanism and watering a dry continent, 1788–2015*, Cooperative Research Centre for Water Sensitive Cities, Melbourne, July 2016, p. 46, <https://watersensitivecities.org.au/wp-content/uploads/2016/12/A2.1_2_2016_R5-19-12-2016-V2.pdf>, accessed 25 September 2023.

Chapter 16: Vacant villages

1   'Solved: Why no one was home on Census night', *SGS Economics and Planning*, 24 July 2017, <https://sgsep.com.au/publications/insights/why-was-no-one-home-on-census-night>, accessed 25 September 2023.

2   Luci Ellis, 'Housing in the endemic phase', speech to the UDIA 2022 National Congress, Sydney, 25 May 2022, *Reserve Bank of Australia*, <www.rba.gov.au/speeches/2022/pdf/sp-ag-2022-05-25.pdf>, accessed 25 September 2023 and Nalini Agarwal, James Bishop and Iris Day, 'A new measure of average household size', *Bulletin*, Reserve Bank of Australia, 16 March 2023, <www.rba.gov.au/publications/bulletin/2023/mar/a-new-measure-of-average-household-size.html>, accessed 25 September 2023.

3   Australian Bureau of Statistics, 'Building activity, Australia', *ABS*, March 2023, <www.abs.gov.au/statistics/industry/building-and-construction/building-activity-australia/latest-release>, accessed 25 September 2023.

4   Shelley Shan, 'Majority backs vacant house tax, poll finds', *Taipei Times*, 7 June 2023, <www.taipeitimes.com/News/taiwan/archives/2023/06/07/2003801137>, accessed 25 September 2023 and 'A fifth of China's homes are empty. That's 50 million apartments', *Bloomberg*, 9 November 2018, <www.bloomberg.com/news/articles/2018-11-08/a-fifth-of-china-s-homes-are-empty-that-s-50-million-apartments>, accessed 25 September 2023.

5   'Millions of "ghost homes" sit empty in Japan. You can snag one for as little as $550', *National Post*, 1 June 2021, <https://nationalpost. com/news/millions-of-ghost-homes-sit-empty-in-japan-you-can-snag-one-for-as-little-as-550>, accessed 25 September 2023.

6   'Spanish government to make 50,000 foreclosed homes available for rent amid housing crisis', *ABC News*, 19 April 2023, <www. abc.net.au/news/2023-04-19/spain-housing-crisis-foreclosed-homes/102239090>, accessed 25 September 2023.

7   'Perth CBD office market snapshot February 2022', *PVA*, n.d., <https://pvawa.com.au/wp-content/uploads/2022/02/Perth_CBD_Office_Snapshot_Feb_22.pdf>, accessed 25 September 2023.

8   'Vacancy rates: January 2023', *Domain*, 2 February 2023, <www. domain.com.au/research/vacancy-rates-january-2023-1192737/>, accessed 25 September 2023.

9   It is a little more subtle than this because the NAIRU is not about any price change, but accelerating price changes. The natural rate of rental vacancy is probably closer to 2 per cent than 2.5 per cent. Meaning that if rental vacancy is below 2 per cent, then rents are probably rising faster than other goods and services in the consumer price index (CPI), and vice versa.

10 Australian Bureau of Statistics, 'Consumer price index, Australia', [June quarter, 2033], *ABS*, 26 July 2023, <ww.abs.gov.au/ statistics/economy/price-indexes-and-inflation/consumer-price-index-australia/latest-release>, accessed 25 September 2023, Table 9 and 'Weekly rents: City: Sydney', *SQM Research*, n.d., <https:// sqmresearch.com.au/weekly-rents.php?region=nsw-Sydney&type= c&t=1>, accessed 25 September 2023.

11 Final chapter of Cannon, *Land Boomers*.

12 Reserve Bank of Australia, 'Statement on monetary policy—August 2023: 4. Inflation', n.d., *RBA*, <www.rba.gov.au/publications/ smp/2023/aug/inflation.html>, accessed 25 September 2023.

13 Pascal Hansens and Wojciech Ciesla, 'The empty house: A window into Europe's vacant property problem', *Investigate Europe*, 14 December 2022, <www.investigate-europe.eu/en/2022/the-empty-house-a-window-into-europes-vacant-property-problem/>, accessed 25 September 2023.

14 Jen St. Denis, 'The data shows taxing empty homes works', *The Tyee*, 17 June 2022, <https://thetyee.ca/Analysis/2022/06/17/Data-Shows-Taxing-Empty-Homes-Works/>, accessed 25 September 2023.

Chapter 17: Rental rules

1 'Victorian government considering price cap on rental properties', 7NEWS Australia, c. May 2023, <https://youtu.be/rWKcYByw21I>, accessed 25 September 2023.

2 Assar Lindbeck, *The Political Economy of the New Left: An outsider's view*, 1971, p. 39

3 Swiss rent control allows tenants to apply for a reduction if mortgage interest rates fall! 'Rental law/tenancy agreement in Switzerland', *Rental Law*, n.d., <https://rental-law.ch>, accessed 26 September 2023, and 'Specifying the rental tariff', *Rental Law*, n.d., <www.rental-law.ch/specifying-the-rental-tariff>, accessed 26 September 2023.

4 ACAT, Rent Increases: <www.acat.act.gov.au/case-types/rental-disputes/rent-increases>, accessed 26 September 2023.

5 Richard Holden, 'Why rent controls are a zombie idea', *Australian Financial Review*, 14 June 2023, <www.afr.com/property/residential/why-rent-controls-are-a-zombie-idea-20230607-p5dev3>, accessed 26 September 2023.

6 Mathias Dolls, Clemens Fuest, Florian Neumeier and Daniel Stöhlker, 'Ein Jahr Mietendeckel: Wie hat sich der Berliner Immobilienmarkt entwickelt?', *ifo Institut*, 17 March 2021, Forschungsergebnisse [research report], vol. 74, no. 3, <www.ifo.de/publikationen/2021/aufsatz-zeitschrift/ein-jahr-mietendeckel>, accessed 26 September 2023.

7 Andreas Kluth, 'Berlin's rent controls are proving to be a disaster', *Bloomberg*, 2 March 2021, <www.bloomberg.com/opinion/articles/2021-03-02/berlin-s-rent-controls-are-proving-to-be-the-disaster-we-feared>, accessed October 2023.

8 David H. Autor, Christopher J. Palmer and Parag A. Pathak, 'Housing market spillovers: Evidence from the end of rent control in Cambridge, Massachusetts', *Journal of Political Economy*, vol. 122, no. 3, 2014, pp. 661–717, <www.journals.uchicago.edu/doi/abs/10.1086/675536>, accessed 26 September 2023.

9 Robert Albon, 'Rent control, a costly redistributive device? The case of Canberra', December *Economic Record*, vol. 54, issue 3, pp. 303–13, 1978, <https://onlinelibrary.wiley.com/doi/10.1111/j.1475-4932.1978.tb01632.x>, accessed October 2023.

10 Rebecca Diamond, Tim McQuade and Franklin Qian, 'The effects of rent control expansion on tenants, landlords, and inequality: Evidence from San Francisco', *American Economic Review*, vol. 109, no. 19, 2019, pp. 3365–94, <https://pubs.aeaweb.org/doi/pdfplus/10.1257/aer.20181289>, accessed 26 September 2023.

Chapter 18: Supply superstitions

1   <https://www.nytimes.com/2020/02/13/business/economy/housing-crisis-conor-dougherty-golden-gates.html>, accessed 24 November 2023.

2   Nicole Gurran and Peter Phibbs, 'Going bananas over affordable housing', The Conversation, 29 August 2014, <https://theconver sation.com/going-bananas-over-affordable-housing-30029>, accessed 26 September 2023.

3   Real Estate Institute of Australia, *Inquiry into housing affordability and supply in Australia*, September 2021, <www.reia.asn.au/wp-content/uploads/2021/09/REIA-Housing-Affordability-and-Supply-Sub mission-A4-September-2021-HR.pdf>, accessed 26 September 2023, and 'REIA is urging government to improve supply planning around housing development', *The Real Estate Conversation*, 15 July 2021, <https://therealestateconversation.com.au/news/2021/07/15/reia-urging-government-improve-supply-planning-around-housing-development/1626314419>, accessed 26 September 2023.

4   'Inquiry into housing affordability and supply in Australia Submission 154', Property Council of Australia, 25 October 2021, p. 4, <www.aph.gov.au/DocumentStore.ashx?id=234434ba-26f2-478a-82d3-3c2bb7595255&subId= 716744>, accessed October 2023.

5   Australian Taxi Industry Association 2015 State Reports, p. 8, <www.atia.com.au/wp-content/uploads/ATIA-State-Reports-2015-final.pdf>, accessed October 2023.

6   Australian Taxi Industry Association 2014 State Reports, p. 20, <https://www.atia.com.au/wp-content/uploads/atia-state-reports-2014-web.pdf>, accessed 24 November 2023.

7   The Pharmacy Guild of Australia, <https://www.guild.org.au/__data/assets/pdf_file/0022/5386/supermarket-pharmacies.pdf>, accessed October 2023.

8   Matthew Maltman, 'How popular is zoning reform, actually?', *One Final Effort*, blog, 29 September [2022], <https://one finaleffort.com/blog/how-popular-is-zoning-reform-actually->, accessed 26 September 2023, and 'Winton Sustainable Research Survey', *ACT Government*, September 2015, <www.planning.act.gov.au/urban-renewal/public-housing-renewal/about-the-program/winton-sustainable-research-survey>, accessed 26 September 2023.

9   Standing Committee on Tax and Revenue 26 November 2021: Housing affordability and supply in Australia, <https://parlinfo.aph.

gov.au/parlInfo/search/display/display.w3p;db=COMMITTEES;
id=committees%2Fcommrep%2F25325%2F0001;query=Id%3A
%22committees%2Fcommrep%2F25325%2F0000%22>, accessed
October 2023.

10 Cameron Murray, 'Did Germany and Tokyo really get affordable
housing through planning?', *Fresh Economic Thinking*, 12 May 2021,
<https://fresheconomicthinking.substack.com/p/did-germany-and-
tokyo-really-get>, accessed 26 September 2023.

11 'Monthly Property Report', REINZ (Real Estate Institute of New
Zealand), 11 March 2021, p. 3, <https://photos.harcourts.co.nz/
Harcourts.Public.WebTemplates/341/Files/REINZ_Monthly_
Property_Report___February_2021.pdf>, accessed October 2023.

12 'Melbourne's slums', *Murchison Times and Day Dawn Gazette*,
11 September 1897, <https://trove.nla.gov.au/newspaper/article/233236
528?searchTerm=slums%20melbourne>, accessed 26 September 2023.

13 Tim Callanan, 'Most of Melbourne's slum pockets were demolished,
but a few survived,' *ABC News*, 18 January 2021, <www.abc.net.au/
news/2021-01-18/how-f-oswald-barnett-tried-to-rid-melbourne-of-
its-slums/12964604>, accessed 26 September 2023.

14 Ben Phillips, X/Twitter post, 1 June 2023, <https://twitter.com/
BenPhillips_ANU/status/1664060829422190593?s=20>, accessed
26 September 2023.

Chapter 19: Zoning zealots

1 Robin Finn, 'The great air race', *New York Times*, 22 February
2013, <www.nytimes.com/2013/02/24/realestate/the-great-race-for-
manhattan-air-rights.html>, accessed 26 September 2023.

2 In the ACT, the property right system is a leasehold system where
the property rights have a 99-year time limit. Note that this is merely
another legal variation, and subject to political pressures. The first
99-year leasehold property rights to expire have been granted for
another 99 years for a minimal administrative fee (currently less than
$500) rather than requiring owners to repurchase the property rights
from the ACT government for another 99 years.

3 See Section 3.2 in 'Land value capture and social benefits: Toronto
and São Paulo compared' Abigail Friendly, *IMFG Papers on Municipal Finance and Governance*, no. 33, 2017, <https://tspace.library.
utoronto.ca/bitstream/1807/81190/1/imfgpaper_no33_land_value_
capture_abigail_friendly_july_12_2017.pdf>, accessed October 2023.

4   R.W. Archer, 'The Sydney Betterment Levy, 1969–1973: An experiment in functional funding for metropolitan development', *Urban Studies*, 1976, vol. 13, issue 3, pp. 339–42 <https://doi.org/10.1080/00420987620080631>, accessed October 2023.

5   Archer, 'The Sydney Betterment Levy, 1969–1973'.

6   Michael Koziol, 'Minns to turbocharge Sydney's density with affordable housing bonuses for developers', *The Sydney Morning Herald*, 15 June 2023, <www.smh.com.au/politics/nsw/minns-to-turbocharge-sydney-s-density-with-affordable-housing-bonuses-for-developers-20230614-p5dglv.html>, accessed 26 September 2023.

7   T. van Oosten, P. Witte and T. Hartmann, 'Active land policy in small municipalities in the Netherlands: "We don't do it, unless..."' *Land Use Policy*, vol. 77, 2018, pp. 829–36, <https://doi.org/10.1016/j.landusepol.2017.10.029>, accessed October 2023.

8   'The "use it or lose it" policy in the mining sector', *Zimbabwe Independent*, 22 March 2022, <www.pressreader.com/zimbabwe/the-zimbabwe-independent-9fa3/20220325/282522956967452>, accessed 26 September 2022.

Chapter 20: Financial fixes

1   Table 8, <https://www.ato.gov.au/About-ATO/Research-and-statistics/In-detail/Taxation-statistics/Taxation-statistics-2020-21/?anchor=IndividualsStatistics#IndividualsStatistics>; 'Organization / Australian Taxation Office / Taxation Statistics 2019–20 / Individuals – Table 26'; Australian Bureau of Statistics, 'Housing occupancy and costs', 2019–20, *ABS*, 25 May 2022, Table 10, <www.abs.gov.au/statistics/people/housing/housing-occupancy-and-costs/latest-release>, accessed 27 September 2023.

2   John Daley, Danielle Wood and Hugh Parsonage, *Hot Property: Negative gearing and capital gains tax reform*, Grattan Institute, Melbourne, April 2016, <https://grattan.edu.au/wp-content/uploads/2016/04/872-Hot-Property.pdf>, accessed 27 September 2023.

3   C. Evans, 'Taxing capital gains: one step forwards or two steps back?'. *Journal of Australian Taxation*, 2002, vol. 5, no. 1, pp. 114–35, <http://classic.austlii.edu.au/au/journals/JlATax/2002/4.html>, accessed October 2023.

4   Tina Perinotto, 'What Susan Lloyd-Hurwitz said about housing and taxes', *The Fifth Estate*, <https://thefifthestate.com.au/

business/what-susan-lloyd-hurwitz-said-about-housing-and-taxes/>, accessed 24 November 2023.

5   Myriam Robin, 'Susan Lloyd-Hurwitz commits heresy', *Australian Financial Review*, 18 May 2023, <www.afr.com/rear-window/former-property-council-president-susan-lloyd-hurwitz-commits-heresy-20230518-p5d9gv>, accessed 27 September 2023.

6   Sabrina Barr and Sarah Young, 'Stamp duty cut: How might it affect me?', *Independent*, 8 July 2020, <www.independent.co.uk/life-style/stamp-duty-holiday-land-tax-first-time-buyer-rishi-sunak-government-update-a9604106.html>, accessed 27 September 2023.

7   'Additional buyer's stamp duty (ABSD)', Inland Revenue Authority of Singapore, 13 July 2023, <www.iras.gov.sg/taxes/stamp-duty/for-property/buying-or-acquiring-property/additional-buyer's-stamp-duty-(absd)>, accessed 27 September 2023.

8   Cameron Murray, 'A comment on stamp duty', *Fresh Economic Thinking*, 14 June 2022, <https://www.fresheconomicthinking.com/p/a-comment-on-stamp-duty>, accessed October 2023.

9   *Stamp Duty Abolition Act 1999*, 20 May 1999, <www.legislation.govt.nz/act/public/1999/0061/latest/DLM29366.html>, accessed 27 September 2023.

10 Murray, 'A comment on stamp duty'.

11 Property Australia, 'What are the tax settings for build-to-rent across the country?', *Property Council of Australia*, 24 May 2023, <www.propertycouncil.com.au/national/what-are-the-tax-settings-for-build-to-rent-across-the-country>, accessed 27 September 2023.

12 Rhys Jewell et al., 'Build-to-rent sector and "clean building" as reforms announced', *Corrs Chambers Westgarth*, 22 May 2023, <www.corrs.com.au/insights/build-to-rent-sector-and-clean-building-tax-reforms-announced>, accessed 27 September 2023.

13 Michael Janda, 'Home loan crackdown appears imminent as Treasurer, regulators discuss house price surge', 28 September 2021, *ABC News*, <www.abc.net.au/news/2021-09-28/home-loan-crackdown-appears-imminent-amid-house-price-boom/100496824>, accessed 27 September 2023.

14 Cameron Murray, 'Submission to the House of Representatives Standing Committee on Tax and Revenue's inquiry into housing affordability and supply', September 2021, <https://osf.io/download/613841373d2d6a00679febec/>, accessed 27 September 2023.

15   Reserve Bank of Australia, 'Submission to the Inquiry into foreign investment in residential real estate', *RBA*, 9 May 2014, <www.rba. gov.au/publications/submissions/housing-and-housing-finance/pdf/ inquiry-foreign-investment-in-residential-real-estate.pdf>, accessed 27 September 2023.

16   Brendan Coates and Jessie Horder-Geraghty, 'How a rental scheme for poorer Australians became a $1b windfall for developers and investors', *Grattan Institute*, 9 September 2019, <https://grattan.edu. au/news/how-a-rental-scheme-for-poorer-australians-became-a-1b-windfall-for-developers>, accessed 27 September 2023; and Brendan Coates and Jessie Horder-Geraghty, 'Learning from past mistakes: lessons from the National Rental Affordability Scheme', *Grattan Institute*, blog post, 9 September 2019, <https://grattan.edu.au/ news/learning-from-past-mistakes-lessons-from-the-national-rental-affordability-scheme/>, accessed 27 September 2023.

Chapter 21: Favoured first home buyers

1   Saul Eslake, 'Billions in handouts but nothing gained', *The Sydney Morning Herald*, 16 March 2011, <www.smh.com.au/business/ billions-in-handouts-but-nothing-gained-20110315-1bvvs.html>, accessed 27 September 2023.

2   Australian Bureau of Statistics, 'Housing occupancy and costs 2019–20', <https://www.abs.gov.au/statistics/people/housing/housing-occupancy-and-costs/latest-release>, accessed October 2023.

3   'First Home Super Saver Scheme', *Australian Taxation Office*, 1 September 2023, <www.ato.gov.au/Individuals/Super/Withdrawing-and-using-your-super/First-Home-Super-Saver-Scheme/>, accessed 27 September 2023.

4   National Housing Finance and Investment Corporation, 'First home guarantee', *NHFIC*, n.d., <www.nhfic.gov.au/support-buy-home/ first-home-guarantee>, accessed 27 September 2023.

Chapter 22: Managing monopolies

1   Staff writers, 'From the Archives, 1984: Medicare is introduced in Australia', *The Sydney Morning Herald*, 1 February 2019 (originally published in *The Age*, 1 February 1984), <www.smh.com.au/national/ from-the-archives-1984-medicare-is-introduced-in-australia-20190130-p50ui0.html>, accessed 27 September 2023. Also Anne-Marie Boxall and James A. Gillespie, *Making Medicare: The politics*

of universal healthcare in Australia, University of New South Wales Press, Sydney, 2013.

2 Boxall and Gillespie, *Making Medicare*, Chapter 1.

3 Norman Hermant, 'Before Bob Hawke's Medicare, a visit to hospital forced many Australians into bankruptcy', *ABC News*, 18 May 2019, <www.abc.net.au/news/2019-05-18/bob-hawke-what-did-australia-have-before-medicare/11124180>, accessed 27 September 2023.

4 Stephen Duckett, 'Saving Private Health 1: Reining in hospital costs and specialist bills', November 2019, Grattan Institute, <https://grattan.edu.au/wp-content/uploads/2019/11/925-Saving-private-health-1.pdf>, accessed October 2023.

5 Australian Institute of Health and Welfare, 'Income support for older Australians', *AIHW*, 7 September 2023, <www.aihw.gov.au/reports/australias-welfare/age-pension>, accessed 27 September 2023.

6 See Think tank report, Cameron Murray, 'Scrap superannuation', 14 February 2020, <https://osf.io/957kz/>, accessed 27 September 2023.

7 Education NSW, 'Early history', *NSW Government*, 6 March 2023, <https://education.nsw.gov.au/about-us/history-of-nsw-government-schools/government-schools/early-history>, accessed 27 September 2023.

8 National Museum of Australia, 'Aid for non-government schools', *NMA*, 28 September 2022, <www.nma.gov.au/defining-moments/resources/aid-for-non-government-schools>, accessed 27 September 2023.

9 Walter Block, *The Privatization of Roads and Highways: Human and economic factors*, Ludwig von Mises Institute, Auburn, AL, 2009, <https://cdn.mises.org/The%20Privatization%20of%20Roads%20and%20Highways_2.pdf>, accessed 27 September 2023.

10 Even though they are owned privately, these private toll roads always require public power of compulsory acquisition and nearly always involve public financial guarantees to make them viable. See the chapter on transport in Cameron Murray and Paul Frijters, *Rigged: How networks of powerful mates rip off everyday Australians*, Allen & Unwin, Sydney, 2022.

Chapter 23: Perfecting property

1 Winston Churchill, 'The mother of all monopolies', from a speech delivered at King's Theatre, Edinburgh, 17 July 1909, *The School of*

Cooperative Individualism, <www.cooperative-individualism.org/churchill-winston_mother-of-all-monopolies-1909.htm>, accessed 27 September 2023.

2   P. Marcuse, 'A useful installment of socialist work: Housing in Red Vienna in the 1920s', in Rachel Bratt, Chester Hartman and Ann Meyerson (eds), *Critical Perspectives on Housing*, Temple University Press, Philadelphia, 1986, p. 580.

3   City of Vienna, 'The Vienna model', Wien, n.d., <https://social housing.wien/policy/the-vienna-model>, accessed 27 September 2023; and Municipal Housing in Vienna. History, facts & figures. Stadt Wien, <https://www.wienerwohnen.at/dms/workspace/SpacesStore/419fd4ff-eb28-4c25-8e4a-0534c6c71ae1/Municipalhousing.pdf>, accessed October 2023.

4   Francesca Mari, 'Imagine a renters' utopia. It might look like Vienna', *New York Times Magazine*, 23 May 2023, <www.nytimes.com/2023/05/23/magazine/vienna-social-housing.html>, accessed 27 September 2023.

5   R.P. Appelbaum, 'Swedish housing in the postwar period: Some lessons for American housing policy', in Bratt, Hartman and Meyerson, *Critical Perspectives on Housing*, p. 537.

6   'Public housing in Sweden', *Sveriges Allmannytta*, n.d., <www.sverigesallmannytta.se/in-english/public-housing-in-sweden/>, accessed 27 September 2023; and Terner Center for Housing Innovation, *Housing in Sweden: An overview*, Memo, November 2017, <https://ternercenter.berkeley.edu/wp-content/uploads/2020/11/Swedish_Housing_System_Memo.pdf>, accessed 27 September 2023.

7   Arthur Acolin, 'The public sector plays an important role in supporting French renters', Brief, 20 April 2021, *Brookings*, <www.brookings.edu/essay/france-rental-housing-markets/>, accessed 27 September 2023.

8   Marja Salmela and Aleksi Teivainen, 'Study: Helsinki supports its high-income tenants with tens of millions a year', *Helsinki Times*, 17 December 2015, <www.helsinkitimes.fi/finland/finland-news/domestic/13662-study-helsinki-supports-its-high-income-tenants-with-tens-of-millions-a-year.html>, accessed 27 September 2023; and Mika Ronkainen and Elina Eskelä, *Helsinki's housing policy: A historical overview and the current situation*, City of Helsinki, Helsinki, 2022, <hel.fi/static/kanslia/Julkaisut/2022/historical_over view_of_housing_policy.pdf>, accessed 27 September 2023.

9 Christine Whitehead and Kathleen Scanlon (eds), *Social Housing in Europe*, London School of Economics, London, July 2007, <www.lse.ac.uk/geography-and-environment/research/lse-london/documents/Archive/Books-Archived/Social-Housing-in-Europe-I.pdf#page=18>, accessed 27 September 2023.

10 Andy Beckett, 'The right to buy: The housing crisis that Thatcher built', *The Guardian*, 27 August 2015, <www.theguardian.com/society/2015/aug/26/right-to-buy-margaret-thatcher-david-cameron-housing-crisis>, accessed 27 September 2023.

11 Masahiro Kobayashi, *The Housing Market and Housing Policies in Japan*, working paper no. 558, Asian Development Bank Institute, <www.adb.org/sites/default/files/publication/181404/adbi-wp558.pdf>, accessed 27 September 2023.

12 Prime Minister's Office, Singapore, '1965 Flats (Berita Singapura)', *YouTube*, c. 2009, <www.youtube.com/watch?v=-VosvrTlw7c>, accessed 27 September 2023.

13 Ann Wilcox, 'On the land: The Soldier Settlement Scheme', *Old Treasury Building*, n.d., <www.oldtreasurybuilding.org.au/lost-jobs/on-the-land/soldier-settlement-scheme>, accessed 27 September 2023.

14 Museum of Australian Democracy at Old Parliament House, <https://electionspeeches.moadoph.gov.au/speeches/1949-robert-menzies>, accessed 24 November 2023.

15 Museum of Australian Democracy at Old Parliament House, <https://electionspeeches.moadoph.gov.au/speeches/1955-robert-menzies>, accessed 24 November 2023

16 'War Service Homes: Commission's retort', *Maitland Weekly Mercury*, 16 July 1921, p. 9, <https://trove.nla.gov.au/newspaper/article/127134963?searchTerm=1921%20war%20service%20homes%20report>, accessed 27 September 2023.

Chapter 24: HouseMate

1 Charles Siegel, 'Le Plessis-Robinson: A model for smart growth', *Planetizen*, 16 July 2012, <www.planetizen.com/node/57600>, accessed 27 September 2023.

2 Cameron Murray, 'HouseMate: A proposed national institution to build new homes and sell them cheap to any citizen who does not own a home', 9 January 2022, <https://osf.io/nxq2u/>, accessed October 2023.

3 Murray, 'HouseMate'.
4 Murray and Frijters, *Rigged*, p. 26.
5 Rachel G. Bratt, 'Public housing: The controversy and the contribution', in Bratt, Hartman and Meyerson, *Critical Perspectives on Housing*, Temple University Press, Philadelphia, 1986, p. 337.
6 Bratt, 'Public housing'.

Chapter 25: Future foresight

1 Peter Madely, '"A fit country for heroes": 100 years since Lloyd George made legendary speech in Wolverhampton', *Express & Star*, 23 November 2018, <www.expressandstar.com/news/politics/2018/11/23/a-fit-country-for-heroes-100-years-since-lloyd-georges-legendary-wolverhampton-speech>, accessed 27 September 2023.